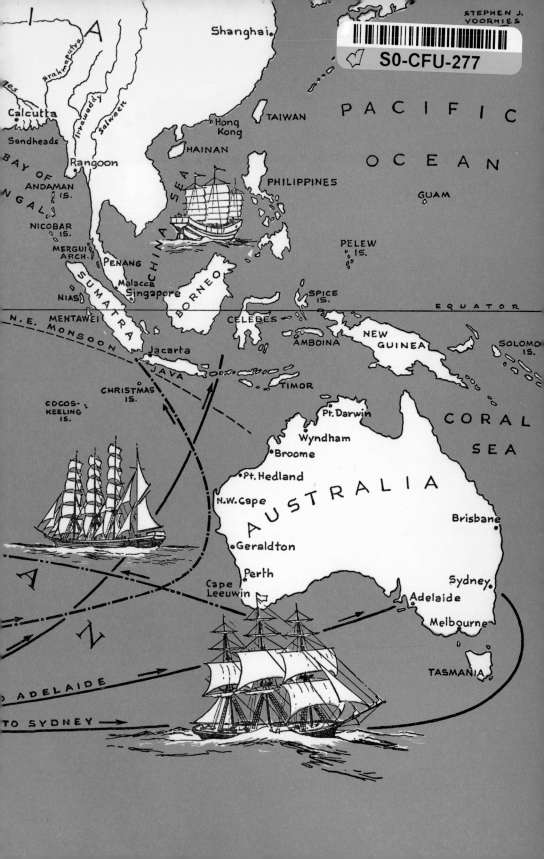

Monsoon Seas

OCEANS OF THE WORLD

The Pacific Ocean *Felix Riesenberg*
The Mediterranean *Emil Ludwig*
The Antarctic Ocean *Russell Owen*
The Coral Sea *Alan Villiers*
Monsoon Seas *Alan Villiers*

BOOKS BY ALAN VILLIERS

Falmouth for Orders
By Way of Cape Horn
Cruise of the *Conrad*
Grain Race
Sons of Sindbad
Whaling in the Frozen South
Last of the Windships
The Making of a Sailor
The Set of the Sails
Quest of the Schooner *Argus*

MONSOON SEAS

The Story of the Indian Ocean

ALAN VILLIERS

McGRAW-HILL BOOK COMPANY, INC.

New York   London   Toronto

MONSOON SEAS

Library of Congress Catalog Card Number: 52-5347

THIRD PRINTING

PUBLISHED BY THE McGRAW-HILL BOOK COMPANY, INC.

Printed in the United States of America

Preface

"Much against my will, I find myself compelled to introduce those preliminary personal observations that are only too common a feature of historical works. I have no intention, however, of enlarging upon my own merits, which would, I am well aware, prove singularly wearisome to my readers, or of attacking my fellow-writers as Anaximenes and Theopompus have done in the prefaces to their histories. My motive is simply to explain the reasons which have induced me personally to embark upon this work, and to give some account of my sources of information."

So wrote the Greek historian Dionysius of Halicarnassus, who died in the latter half of the first century B.C. I find it difficult to improve upon him. The Indian Ocean is a large canvas and, apart from the seafaring directories, such as Findlay's and the Admiralty volumes, the only single book which to my knowledge has attempted to give some picture of that ocean is Mr. Stanley Rogers's work, which was illustrated by himself and published in London in 1932. When I was asked to produce such a book, I was pleased to undertake the duty. I had traveled a good deal in and about the Indian Ocean, in sail and steam. I had taken the ship *Joseph Conrad* from Cape Town to the Dutch East Indies and round the islands, and I had been a sailor in ships both westbound in the trade-wind zone and eastbound in the Roaring Forties. I had spent a year sailing with the Arabs in their dhows, up and down the Persian Gulf, the Red Sea, and along the East Coast of Africa. I had had the experience of visiting the Persian Gulf pearling banks at the height of the season. And, during the war, I had commanded a squadron of lend-lease landing craft in the Bay of Bengal, along the Arakan coast of Burma, at the landing in Rangoon and the rehabilitation of Singapore. I had thus had some opportunity to examine the ships of India, Arabia, and Malaya at first hand.

I had also been interested in the history and the geography of the Indian Ocean for many years, and had the opportunity to read voluminously on the subject, particularly in Lisbon. I must express my thanks especially to Dr. Joaquim Bensaude, of that city, for his help in putting me on the right track among the Portuguese records, and to Dr. Pedro Theotonio Pereira, the former Ambassador of Portugal in the United States of America, who opened many doors.

Some of the information which I gleaned among the Arabs has been drawn upon already in my *Sons of Sindbad,* published by Charles Scribner's Sons in 1940, and I am grateful to them for permission to use some of this material again. Books which I have found useful are listed in the Bibliography.

ALAN VILLIERS

Contents

List of Illustrations

List of Maps

CHAPTER I

The Indian Ocean

The flying fish skimmed away before the curve of the bows where the roll of white water spoke loudly of the ship's fine progress. The sky was a deep and splendid blue and the sea its image, save for that roll of foam and the big barque's wake. Aloft every stitch of the thirty sails was drawing at its best, distended and warmed by the southeast trade wind. The ship rolled gently, for there was little motion in the sea, and the pressure of her 35,000 square feet of canvas held her at an easy angle. The whole ocean seemed at peace. It was days since as much as a fleck of spray had lifted itself over the weather rail. By night the stars shone as if they loved shining and each was trying to light up the sky more brightly than all others. The green and red rays from the running lights sent colored reflections shimmering upon the dark and placid waters, seemingly for miles, and each morning there were flying fish in the scuppers, where they had come over the bulwarks in the night, perhaps attracted by those lights which were the only ones the big barque showed.

It was less than a fortnight since we had rounded stormy Cape Leeuwin, and the four-master was heavily laden with 5,000 tons of Victorian grain. She was bound from Melbourne toward the Channel for orders and the Old Man was taking her the Good Hope way, instead of around the Horn, because the winds had been easterly in the Bight and, once past the Leeuwin, he knew all

1

would be plain sailing. It was the ideal way to go, if you could make it. We were in the tail of the southeast trades between 25 and 28 degrees south of the line, and these steady, balmy winds could be relied upon to take us at least as far as the south of Madagascar. Then we would soon find the Agulhas current, which sets from there toward the southeast and around the Cape. Once around the Cape, the southeast trades of the Atlantic Ocean would waft us on toward the line, for southerly winds predominated at that time of the year, right from Cape Agulhas. It was a flying-fish voyage.

The words of the old shanty

> I'm a flying-fish sailor,
> Just in from Hong-Kong:
> Oh-way-oh, blow the man down!

took for us a new meaning, and the lauded voyages of the shapely clippers in the old tea trade from China became, in retrospect, fine-weather romps. Flying-fish sailors, indeed! Our ship was a big Cape Horner having a rest, and in the southeast trades of the Indian Ocean was a good place to enjoy it.

Later there blew up a bit of a cyclone, somewhere to the southward of Mauritius, and even that big ship had to fight for her life for a day or two, while the seas raged mountainous and the wind screamed. But it was warm, and there was no ice in the footropes. Apart from that touch of cyclone, we had good weather, there, for seventy-five days.

The southeast trade of the Indian Ocean seems designed for the use of big sailing ships. So are the other winds in that great ocean—the wild westerlies of the far south, the dependable monsoons which made possible the sailing commerce of the ancient East and still bring the fleets of Arab, Indian, and Persian dhows upon their voyages between the Persian Gulf, India, and Zanzibar. The west winds could blow a square-rigged ship from Good Hope to Australia in three weeks and less, though the distance is 6,000 miles. How the wind and the sea could play down there! This is their home, this wild reach of the Indian Ocean where wind and sea have almost uninterrupted rule all round the world, where the waters blend south of Good Hope and Australia, and the Horn. Nothing ventured here but the albatross and the sailing ships, bent upon making use of the great west winds and designed as skillfully as men could contrive both to use them and survive in them.

Now no ship sails, upright and graceful, westward upon the breath of the Indian Ocean trades. No ship storms eastward before the wild west winds, under close-reefed sails. The monsoon-using dhows survive, from India and Arabia and—to a less degree —from Persia, and canoes move under sail among the tropic islands. A fleet of Indian brigs maintains communications between the atolls of the Maldives and the Laccadives, and Ceylon; another fleet of brigs, barques, and barquentines survives in the rice trade across the Bay of Bengal, from Palk Straits and from Jaffna. Such ships still understand the way of the Indian Ocean and its winds and weather; but for some years now all European vessels, which carry the bulk of the vast commerce there, have been driven by power.

Of the three great oceans, the Indian was, upon the whole, always the most kindly to sailing ships. It was the flying-fish ocean of the old songs. Though the least of the three oceans—it is less than one-third the area of the great Pacific—it is, in many ways, the most interesting. Upon its vast bosom rest islands and island groups in every way as interesting as any the more "glamorized" Pacific knows. Upon the whole, its weather is better and more reliable. If the Indian Ocean has a hurricane season in the Bay of Bengal and a cyclone season in the area of Mauritius, the Pacific knows only too well the hurricanes of the South Sea Islands, the cyclones of the treacherous Coral Sea, the curving typhoons which reach out from the China Seas. The great calm zones of the Pacific, particularly off the Bay of Panama, were a curse to sailing ships. Both north of 35 north and south of 35 south, Pacific weather can be bad enough. Its litter of coral reefs and islands in so much of the tropic zone is a danger to ships and seamen, even in these days. Too many of its islands are unhealthy and their peoples primitives. The Pacific and the famed South Seas are traditionally regarded as the homes of romance and adventure, the havens of "far-away places with sweet-sounding names," such as Honolulu, Tahiti, Samoa, Tongatabu. But Honolulu has long been virtually a suburb of Los Angeles and Tahiti a French-controlled Chinese settlement. In these days, the Tongans and the Samoans vie for the distinction of being the political Irish of the South Seas. Grass skirts in Hawaii are produced exclusively for tourists, and the lilting melodies of the islands are imported on gramophone records from Hollywood, New York, and Chicago.

It is not so in the Indian Ocean. There, many of the islands remain unspoiled. There, the coconut palms wave gently in the soft trade winds and the silent canoes flit, under sail, upon the waters of the blue lagoons. There, the roar of airplane engines overhead is still almost unknown, for the few long-distance routes pass by upon the fringes—across the Dutch East Indies toward Australia, over Africa itself to the Cape, down the Persian Gulf to India. Away from the great trade routes few European vessels are to be seen; as the years pass they are fewer and fewer. The steamers and the motor ships keep to their own lanes—between Colombo and Fremantle, Aden and the Leeuwin, Aden and Bombay; the Straits of Bab-el-Mandeb, Ceylon, and the Straits of Malacca; down the coast of East Africa and from the Cape toward the ports of West Australia—leaving the rest of the ocean undisturbed, except by the wandering dhow or the Indian brig.

I wonder that more yachtsmen do not set out for the Indian Ocean, instead of making a beaten track toward the so-called romantic South Seas. The real spirit of the South Seas is rather to be found in the Indian Ocean. One could cruise a lifetime there and—choosing the seasons—always have good weather, always have fresh islands and fresh ports of interest to visit.

The Indian Ocean is commonly regarded as including the whole of the area from Cape Agulhas, on 20 degrees east, down to the Antarctic, eastward as far as Australia and Tasmania, and northward to the coast of Asia. Some geographers speak of a so-called Southern Ocean embracing all the waters south of a line joining the Cape of Good Hope, the southern coast of Australia and New Zealand, and Cape Horn. But there is no such ocean. Others speak of an Antarctic and an Arctic Ocean; again, these are seas, and not oceans. The world knows three oceans only—the Pacific, the Atlantic, and the Indian. Of these, the Indian alone is an embayed ocean. The others sweep from ice to ice over the whole length of the watery world; the Indian is checked by Asia. The peninsula of India divides its northern area into two great gulfs, the Arabian Sea and the Bay of Bengal. Off the Arabian Sea are the great arms of the Red Sea and the Persian Gulf, each of which might well form the subject of a book, by itself. From the Bay of Bengal an arm of the Indian Ocean passes down the west coast of the Malay Peninsula between Sumatra and Malaya, to link with the Eastern seas—and again, these are seas, not oceans. Here are the Java Sea, the China Sea, the Sea of Japan. These belong more properly to the Pacific area than to the Indian Ocean and will not be dealt with here. South of Sumatra toward the east, the Indian Ocean washes the lovely chain of Indonesian islands known as the East Indies— Sumatra itself, lovely Java and famed Bali, Lombok, the Lesser Sunda Islands, Timor and Flores, the south coast of New Guinea. Here are the Arafura and the Timor seas.

The total area of the waters of the Indian Ocean is, roughly, 27 million square miles; and the Atlantic's, north and south, total some 31 million. The distances across are enormous. From Colombo to Fremantle, for example, is 3,200 miles. From Colombo to Rangoon, across the mouth of the Bay of Bengal, is 1,250 miles; and to

Aden, 2,100 miles. To Cape Town from Bombay the distance is 4,600 miles, and from Durban to Aden, 3,275. The Red Sea is 1,200 miles long. The Bay of Bengal covers an area equal to half of Europe.

The fact that the Indian Ocean is confined by the continent of Asia upsets the usual system of ocean winds, north of the equator. The southeast trades blow normally, except where they are upset by the hurricane season in the area of Mauritius, from November to March. Hurricane and cyclone are different names for the same sort of violent storm, which elsewhere is also called a typhoon. Hurricanes in the Mauritius area can be very severe and, at times, once having begun, show an extraordinary reluctance to leave the area. There is a record of one which, in February, 1861, remained over the islands of Mauritius and Reunion for *five* days. During this period the axis of the storm passed toward the southwest between the islands, and in its progress each quadrant of the hurricane devastated opposite islands alternately. During the five days, 39.8 inches of rain fell.

North of the equator is the area of the monsoons. The word monsoon means season. It has nothing to do with typhoon or any other kind of storm. On the western side of the Indian Ocean down as far as the Mozambique Channel between Africa and Madagascar, and in the Arabian Sea and the Bay of Bengal and its adjacent waters, there are two monsoons—the southwest and the northeast. The northeast monsoon is really a continuation of the northeast trade wind of the Pacific Ocean, which blows in the Indian when the sun is in the south. But when the sun moves north of the equator and heats the hot lands of southeast Asia, this trade wind cannot blow, and the ocean winds rush in from the southwest across all India, toward Persia and Baluchistan, and over the Bay of Bengal.

The northeast monsoon lasts for approximately half the year, and the southwest for the other half; but there is not always a sharp delineation between them. The southwest monsoon brings the rains to the west coast of India. At Bombay, it is looked for about the end of May. By the end of June it has spread over the whole of the Indian Ocean northward of the equator. It is at its fullest strength everywhere in July and gradually steadies down and lessens then until September, when it usually begins to break up, and during October, it is dispersed. Rain falls heavily during its continuance, and the weather is usually so bad that the exposed ports on the Indian coast are closed and the smaller trading vessels take shelter.

All round the Indian coast and Ceylon, the first signs of the southwest monsoon, taking the form of large clouds which come daily at noon upon the mountains, appear about the end of May. There is much lightning, gradually intensifying, and the days are frequently almost unbearably hot and humid. Then, after perhaps a week of these conditions, suddenly one sunset comes a blast of wind from the clouds in the east, bringing with it heavy rain with thunder and lightning. In an hour or two, the wind has veered to the southwest and there it remains, at first strong but gradually diminishing. The sky is overcast. Frequently, the rains fall for forty or fifty days, with brief intervals of fine weather. It is during this period that the dhows take shelter and the big steamers make the ports of Aden and Colombo, their funnels caked white with salt. Visibility is often very poor, and conditions for navigators can be trying.

The other monsoon—the northeast—is as gracious, as clear, and as balmy as a permanent trade, and it is this wind which wafts the great dhows—the argosies of Araby—on their long voyages from the Persian Gulf to Zanzibar and beyond, and which blows the Indian dhows from the Malabar coast to Mombasa and the Madagascar coast.

There are gales enough elsewhere in the Indian Ocean. The banks off the Cape of Good Hope are notorious for them. The Red Sea, the Mozambique Channel, the Persian Gulf, the Straits of Malacca have more or less their own weather. The Red Sea has an unfavorable reputation for trying sandstorms and great humidity. A troopship northbound in that heated funnel of reefbound water in the summer months can be the most irksome form of transport at sea. Then the southwest monsoon is disturbing the ocean outside and the southerly wind is blowing behind the ship, keeping up with her at her same speed so that not a breath of air blows on board and the smuts from her funnel fall where they emerged. The great heat of the sun warms the whole steel ship and is particularly bad for those whose accommodation is on her port side, for the afternoon sun lingers a long time on this side and is at its hottest. This fact has been well known since the early days of powered transportation in the Red Sea. The knowing traveler always tried to book a cabin on the port side if he found himself outward bound through the Red Sea. The very English word "posh" is said to have originated from this habit. Superior persons, and those who regarded themselves as such, invariably asked the shipping companies to provide them with cabins on the port side for the outward passage, starboard side home. "Port outwards, starboard home," abbreviated, becomes "posh."

Curious phenomena are sometimes encountered in the Indian Ocean. The extraordinary "milk sea," for instance, has frequently been seen. The whole sea seems to boil with light and ships to sail upon liquid fire. Frank Bullen, in his voyage around the world in the New Bedford whaler he immortalized as the *Cachalot,* speaks of this.

It was a lovely night, [he has written] with scarcely any wind, the stars trying to make up for the absence of the moon by shining with intense brightness. The water had been more phosphorescent than usual, so that every little fish left a track of light behind him greatly disproportionate to his size. As the night wore on the sea grew brighter and brighter, until by midnight we seemed to be sailing in a sea of lambent flames. Every little wave that broke against the ship's side sent up a shower of diamondlike spray, wonderfully beautiful to see, while a passing school of porpoises fairly set the sea blazing as they leaped and gamboled in its glowing waters. Looking up from sea to sky, the latter seemed quite black instead of blue. . . . In that shining flood the blackness of the ship stood out in startling contrast, and when we looked over the side our faces were strangely lit up by the brilliant glow. For several hours this beautiful appearance persisted, fading away at last as gradually as it came.*

Other ships have reported this same phenomenon, some speaking of passing through areas of intense light 15 and 20 miles long. On some parts of the Indian coast the same thing sometimes takes the form of brilliantly lit breakers which, when they fall on reefs, give the land the appearance of being assailed by fire. In rough weather the breaking tops of seas seem to be aflame. Phosphorescence at sea is well known elsewhere, but the tiny *Noctiluca* of the Indian Ocean excels itself as an agent for lighting the sea.

In the neighborhood of the Cape of Good Hope oddities of nature are sometimes noted. The presence of the Agulhas Bank off the southeastern tip of Africa, the meeting and intermingling of hot and cold waters brought there by currents from warm areas and from the Antarctic ice, and the disturbed meteorological conditions there, generally, set up extraordinary cloud forms and illusions. One of these may easily have been the origin of the *Flying Dutchman* fable—that phantom ship which is doomed forever to sail in those turbulent waters, to know no peace, and to bring none to any mariners whose unfortunate eyes may fall upon its ghostly shape. The original *Flying Dutchman* was possibly nothing more or less than a curious cloud. It is frequently said, even by sailors, that to sight the *Flying Dutchman* meant doom to a ship and all on board, but this was not the old belief when such superstitions really were important. The Dutchman himself was alleged always to put out a boat and visit ships which were doomed, sometimes sending letters to be mailed at the next port. If these were received, then the fate of the vessel was sealed, and every soul must perish. There are many myths about the *Flying Dutchman,* but there is a basis of truth in some of them. There is at any rate the case of the curious ship seen by H.M. frigate *Leven* while on passage from Algoa Bay

* *The Cruise of the Cachalot,* by Frank T. Bullen, F.R.G.S., London, 1891.

toward the Cape in 1824. The *Leven* had been accompanied by the smaller *Barracouta,* but later this vessel parted company.

In the evening of the 6th of April, [writes Captain Owen of the *Leven*] when off Point Danger, the *Barracouta* was seen about two miles to leeward: struck with the singularity of her being so soon after us, we at first concluded that it could not be she; but the peculiarity of her rigging and other circumstances convinced us that we were not mistaken; nay, so distinctly was she seen, that many well-known faces could be observed on deck, looking towards our ship. After keeping thus for some time, we became surprised that she made no effort to join us, but on the contrary, stood away. . . . At sun-set it was observed that she hove-to, and sent a boat away, apparently for the purpose of picking up a man overboard. During the night we could not distinguish any light or other indication of her. The next morning we anchored in Simon's Bay where, for a whole week, we were in anxious expectation of her arrival; but it afterwards appeared that at this very period the *Barracouta* must have been about three hundred miles from us, and no other vessel of the same class was ever seen about the Cape.

No explanation was ever found of this singular phenomenon.

On the other side of the Indian Ocean, along the Arakan coast of Burma on the Bay of Bengal, volcanic disturbances cause mud islands, which sometimes rise and sometimes sink. Either way, they are a menace to navigation.

Some of the great rivers of the world flow into the Indian Ocean —the ancient Tigris and Euphrates, in whose valleys mankind as we know it may have been nurtured; the Indus, the Ganges, the Irrawaddy, and the Salween, each with its many mouths; in East Africa, the Zambesi, Rufiji, Rovuma, and Limpopo. The products of the lands whose coasts it washes are varied, rich, and infinite. Its Persian Gulf and the waters of Ceylon yield the best pearls in the world. It was the great seaway of the trade in spices, the sea route for China silk. It was the ocean Sindbad roamed. Its waters washed the very cradle of mankind and its blue bosom bore the first seagoing ships. The Indian Ocean was the birthplace of the art of sailing and, by the early 1950s, it looks like being the last home of any kind of ocean-going sailing ship.

The Indian is a fascinating ocean, rich in history, second only to the great Pacific in its wealth of lovely islands, second to none in the story of the great lands by which it is almost, but not quite, embayed.

CHAPTER II

The Fabulous Islands

The islands of the Indian Ocean include some of the most beautiful and interesting in the world. It is outside the scope of this book to treat them all in detail. I can but indicate points of interest of some I personally know, and indicate, besides, something of the background of fascinating islands in an ocean too little known. Madagascar, for example, could well form the subject of a book by itself. It is separated from the African mainland by the 250-mile-wide Mozambique Channel and is considered to be the chief relic of a great archipelago which once connected Asia with Africa. Nearby are the Comoro Islands, where early Portuguese navigators thought they could discern Jewish traits among the natives, to whom names such as Abraham, Lot, Moses, and Gideon were well known though they were unfamiliar with the names of the prophets after Solomon. Farther north are the Seychelles. Beyond them again are the coral Laccadives, which hang upon the map of the blue ocean like pearls from the southern end of India; and then there is the real pearl—Ceylon, which is surely one of the loveliest islands in all the world.

In the Bay of Bengal are the Andaman and the Nicobar Islands, which form a long chain from the southwestern tip of Burma toward the northern end of Sumatra. One of the Andamans is a sort of Devil's Island, with an Indian penal colony of more than 7,000 prisoners, with thousands more on parole. These work in sawmills, as clerks in government offices, as servants, and in the workshops. The islands form an ideal prison. The native Andamanese are a primitive people who still live in the Stone Age. They are small men with kinky black hair, who live by hunting, and their number includes the fierce Jarawas, who shoot on sight. The Jarawas have only the bow and arrow but their shooting is remarkably accurate. Offshore, shark-infested waters make escape by sea impracticable, but the great majority of the convicts are tractable. Most of them are allowed considerable freedom. The penal colony there was first established in 1789, but in those days health conditions were so appalling that the settlement had to be given up. In 1858, it was reformed. This time the malarial swamps were cleared, and nowadays the health record is excellent. Since 1926, freed convicts have been encouraged to settle in the islands with their families.

The Andamans have always been on old Indian Ocean charts used by eastern navigators. The Arabs trading to Malacca and to China knew them well and probably named them. Marco Polo saw them on his voyage home from China. In the early days, the natives had a bad reputation as being savages who ferociously attacked shipwrecked mariners. Early travelers spoke of them as "dog-faced man-eaters," and ships gave them as wide a berth as they could. But there are no records that they were cannibals, and they are in no way "dog-faced."

The Nicobars are to the south of the Andamans and, though they are so close, they are inhabited by a quite different race of people, who look remarkably similar to the Burmese or to Malays. Not nearly so primitive as the Andamanese, they live in houses and understand cultivation. When European ships first moved into the Bay of Bengal the islands were infamous as nests of pirates, who were well placed there for pouncing on shipping as it emerged richly laden from the Straits of Malacca. The Portuguese, Dutch, Danes, and English tried in turn to deal with these, but it was not until fairly recent years that piracy there was brought fully under control.

Almost parallel with the Andamans, and much closer to the

mainland coast, are the islands of the Mergui Archipelago, a picturesque group inhabited largely by a fascinating group of sea gypsies, who live in their *proas* almost the year round, passing from island to island by peaceful inland waterways which offer an abundance of fish and all the turtle shell, trepang, bêche-de-mer, and edible birds' nests they care to collect. These items of trade bring satisfactory prices from the masters of Chinese junks. Bird's-nest soup is counted a great delicacy among the Chinese, who are said to find in it excellent aphrodisiac qualities. Sometimes these sea gypsies set up temporary huts of sticks and leaves on the sandy beaches, but their real homes are their boats.

The life of such simple mariners seems an enviable one. Their islands present a wealth of wild and exceedingly picturesque scenery, the larger ones rising in successive ranges of hills which are often thickly wooded to their tops with trees of rich and varied foliage, and the smaller ones often rocky and precipitous, with rugged, inaccessible sides and irregular, fantastic outlines. The beauty of the whole group is enhanced during the rainy season by the host of cascades and waterfalls interspersed among them. The rocky islands are the abodes of the birds which make the edible nests. All around the group are coral reefs which, as elsewhere in these waters, are littered with the names of long-gone ships which touched upon them and, all too frequently, never came off again.

Farther to the south, but lying to the westward of the great island of Sumatra, are many interesting islands and groups. These include the curiously regular Nias, the largest island of the lot, where pagan slavers and head-hunters carried on their trades with impunity until recent years. The twenty-one islands of the nearby Mentawei group are the homes of natives who show remarkable affinities with the Polynesians of the South Seas. It is considered that they are probably survivors from some early eastward migration of Caucasians toward the Pacific. Nias itself is some 75 miles long, with an average breadth of 20 miles. Its rich valleys are sub-

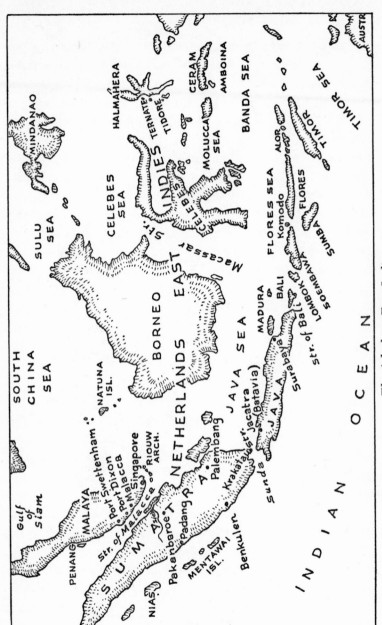

The fabulous East Indies

ject to violent earthquakes, which have been known to dispose of whole villages. Inland, the natives were always more tractable than the warriors of the coast, and the rich land in the interior supported a population of more than 150,000 people, a century ago.

Farther eastward are fabulous Java—that lovely island—and beyond, Bali, Lombok, Soembawa, Flores, Timor, and the rest of the long chain which ends in New Guinea. The story of these belongs properly to the eastern seas, though the waters of the Indian Ocean wash their southern shores, and the straits of Sunda, of Lombok, and of Bali are important highways for ships bound toward the China and other eastern seas. From hot Sumatra, with its remarkable rivers, at least as far as the island of Timor, all these are fascinating islands. At the end of the recent war, I once took a flotilla of LCI(L)—landing-craft infantry, of about 200 tons— more than a hundred miles up the Siak River into the heart of Sumatra. Once the bar at the entrance was crossed, the river was free of dangers throughout that distance, though sometimes my mastheads brushed the jungle foliage and startled the monkeys as I swung around sharp bends.

Some years previously, I had sailed through the straits of Bali by night in a full-rigged ship. In the evening, the peaks of Java towered over me, dwarfing the high masts of the sailing ship, and the night came suddenly. There was no moon. The tide set fast toward the north and, under a press of sail, my ship rushed through. The tide at the narrowest part—only a mile wide—was making 6 knots and the ship was running 16 over the ground, for the wind was fresh and all sail was set. The high land of Java seemed almost upon me and the breaking of the surf was loud and threatening. I could hear the crickets chirping in the forests close by, for my ship made no sound herself except for the rush of water at the bow and along her old iron sides. It was one of those perfect, still tropic nights, when to speak seems sacrilege and all the world is for once at peace, and no discordant voice of man should be heard. There were some eddies and whirlpools in the swift current and, here and there, a backwash from the too-close reefs. My little ship staggered and lurched a little at times, as the movement of the surface waters sought to break her stride. But she ran bravely, with the foam boiling at the prow and the wake phosphorescent as a mile-long line of milk sea, and the stars dipped down to kiss her lightly upon the mastheads. Then she came to the Java Sea, and all the East was spread before her.

In that voyage I had no opportunity to visit other Indian Ocean islands, though I had glimpsed one in the far south. Christmas and Cocos-Keeling, the Chagos, the Maldives, Socotra, the Seychelles and the Amirantes would have to wait. I would see all I wished of Zanzibar and Pemba and the other coastal islands of the East African monsoon belt in the years to come, and Socotra too, with its aloes and its dragon's-blood trees. Socotra was known to the ancients as *Insula Dioscoridis,* and they gave it an ample berth. Its roadsteads are open, and it can be a menace to navigation, particularly when the southwest monsoon obscures the sky. It was first made known to Europe by the Portuguese, like so great a part of the shores and the islands of the Indian Ocean. In 1506, the Portuguese occupied it for a while as a strategic outpost covering the Red Sea, but the trade of those waters is better controlled from Aden and from the sterile rock of Perim in the Straits of Bab-el-Mandeb.

As for the Chagos Archipelago, all I knew of that remote area was its alleged unhealthiness for sailing ships, for its reefs were tormented by strong currents which set always toward them. Heavy rollers and a short, confused sea were caused by the frequent rapid veering of the wind, and swells rising as high as 15 feet had been observed. All the islands offered in the way of sustenance were poultry, coconuts, and an abundance of wild pigs. A valuable breed of pointers originated in the Chagos, and at one time the islands were used for beekeeping on a large scale. Colonies of bees were brought from Mauritius, and they did very well without attention. The gigantic rose tree, which grows rapidly to a height of 200 feet and decays with almost as great speed, was another feature of the islands. But those wild currents and reefs and that dangerous high swell, to say nothing of the hordes of bees, kept me away. Nor could I visit the Seychelles, where the curious double coconut grows. Looking rather like the petrified testicles of some long-dead giant, these strange nuts used to drift ashore on the Malabar coast, where they were highly prized for their alleged medicinal worth. High prices were paid for them until their source was discovered. When they were rare, they used to be pounded up and dissolved into all sorts of mixtures for the "treatment" of ills, ranging from elephantiasis to impotence. The sailing Arabs and Indians had forgotten the Seychelles if they had ever known them, for the islands do not lie upon the usual Africa-to-India sailing route and are too far out in the open sea ever to have been sighted by the big Arab dhows, which used to coast for the greater part of their African voyages. But when the Portuguese stumbled upon the islands and found the double coconut there, they could scarcely sell it at all. It used to be known as the coco de mer, the coconut of the sea.

The tree which gives this nut also yields a beautiful straw, from which the local girls make fancy articles. Turtles abound in the Seychelles, and extensive guano deposits were worked there until recent years. Even toward the end of the sailing-ship era, large sailing ships used to go there from Europe to load guano, which generally was taken to New Zealand.

There has been an important cable station on the Seychelles for many years. It used to be well known among the cable operators for the skill of its staff in originating smoking-room stories. Apparently, the pastime of the staffmen keeping watch in the long nights was to pass on limericks, couplets, and bawdy stories, thinking up new ones when the supply ran out. An operator in the Seychelles would thus pass the time with a colleague in Mauritius or the Cocos-Keeling islands or Zanzibar. A new couplet thought out in the still, midnight hours of the Seychelles might be making the rounds of the saloons in Perth, West Australia, and Cape Town

by the morning, and be in New York, London, and San Francisco
by the next evening. To the man with the Morse key in his hand
the world was a small place, even before the days of radio.

The Seychelles and the Comoro Islands were well known to
the old-time Yankee whalers, as also were the islands of the Chagos
Archipelago. Sperms could be taken in all these waters. The *Cachalot,* with Frank Bullen aboard, was for two months in sight of the
Comoro islands, and during all that time her decks were never clear
of oil.

Of all the islands in the Indian Ocean, or any other ocean, Ceylon
and Madagascar are perhaps the most interesting. Almost the size
of Ireland, Ceylon hangs pendant from the Indian peninsula like a
priceless pearl, and a necklace of reefs and islands all but connects
it to India's southeastern extremity. This is called Adam's Bridge,
and the Moslems believe this was the route of Adam when he was
banished from Paradise and retired to Ceylon. The railway from
Madras to Colombo crosses much of Adam's Bridge, though the last
section of the journey must be made by ferry. In late 1944 and
early 1945, British ocean-going landing craft, released from the
campaign on the Normandy beaches, hurried here to build up the
offensive against the Japanese, then in Malaya. Hundreds of these
shallow vessels, built to carry troops and tanks and to storm upon
beachheads across hundreds of miles of sea, were secured to buoys
at a place called Mandapam. In the southwest season they lay upon
the northern side. In the other season they had only to shift to the
other side. There was a narrow channel connecting the two, with a
hand-operated bridge to carry the railroad. The great pagoda at
Rameswaram overlooked the scene.

On the beach at Mandapam were a half dozen wooden barques,
hauled up there to be out of harm's way until the Bay of Bengal
might be clear again. Most of these square-rigged ships were from
Jaffna, in Ceylon. They were lovely vessels with lofty rigging. One
was a skysail-yarder, perhaps the last of her type. Such vessels were
used—and are still used—in the rice trade to Burma, sailing in the

northeast season and bringing rice to India from Akyab. They had no steps in the rigging, as European sailing ships always had. Their sailors were accustomed to swarm aloft barefoot, and they were experts at it.

One such barque was hove down in a natural dock cut into the sand, not far from the railway bridge. She was a 300-tonner, a graceful vessel very like the old wooden barques which the Nova Scotians built, and the shipwrights of old Maine. There was almost nothing of the East about her from outward view, but her accommodation was primitive. Aft, the poop was one large space, which served, apparently, as sail loft, carpenter's shop, and general accommodation for all hands when the weather was bad. She carried a master but no mates, as we know them, trusted quartermasters taking their place. No chronometer was carried, and her few charts were rather old, but the master had a modern sextant. Her wheel, bell, and sidelights, as well as many of the blocks and much of the equipment, had come from ancient European sailing ships and were acquired, I was told, from a junk yard in Bombay. The bell forward bore the name of some old Sunderland barque, and the wheel was from a Nova Scotian which had come to grief in the Rangoon River fifty years before. She had an enormous name, at least twenty letters long. All these Indian square-rigged ships had long names, which were generally drawn from the Hindu religion.

While my landing craft were at Mandapam, it was not at all unusual to see a single-tops'l brig, under a press of sail, shoot the railway bridge, which the coolies always managed to lift just in time. It was a narrow pass, even for a small landing ship, and the current was strong. Rushing a pretty brig at it must have been an exhilarating experience. I had little time to appreciate such things just then. I had to prepare my ships for the landings at Rangoon, and afterward, for a proposed great blow at the Malay Peninsula, somewhere about Port Dickson and Port Swettenham, for the relief of Singapore.

I had some opportunities to visit Ceylon and had been in Colombo before. The whole island is lovely, from the fringe of coconut palms upon the coast to the great mountains inland. These include Adam's Peak, with the curious hollow in the rocks on its summit which is venerated by most of the religions in India. It is claimed by the Brahmans to be the footstep of Siva, by Buddhists to be that of Buddha, and by the Moslems to be Adam's. It is a place of pilgrimage for all, and the quarantine station at Mandapam was always full of pilgrims going there and to the other shrines in Ceylon.

The Greeks and Romans knew Ceylon as Taprobane. In the island itself there are many ancient records from its past, but fable and fact are so inextricably interwoven that no true story can now emerge. The riches of Ceylon attracted all the wanderers who sailed the Indian Ocean in quest of trade. Its beautiful pearls from the fisheries in Palk Straits; its lavish stores of jewels—rubies, sapphires, amethysts, moonstones, garnets; its forests rich with rare woods, such as ebony and flowered satinwood; its ivory; its spices and, above all, its cinnamon; its sagacious and docile elephants, which still are the bulldozers, tractors, and general haulers of the East; its fragrant coffee (now replaced by tea); its rubber, rice, and cardamoms—all these meant wealth. Tea was introduced when disease wiped out the coffee plants. Indians maintain that the practice of brewing tea began in that land, ascribing its introduction to the saintly Darma. Darma once, they say, decided to remain awake for seven years, in order that he could devote that time to uninterrupted contemplation and reflection upon spiritual matters. He managed four years without great difficulty, but an understandable drowsiness early in the fifth year might have defeated him. However, being hungry, he chanced to pluck some leaves from a bush and chewed them. These were from the tea plant, and they so revived him that all trace of sleep departed. Thus, Darma finished his seven years' vigil as fresh as he began.

But the Chinese declare that their Emperor Shen-Nung was the real discoverer of brewed tea. A man before his time in the matter of personal hygiene, the Emperor always boiled water before drinking it. One day some leaves fell in, and their remarkable fragrance caused him to try the brew. This, we are told, was in the year 2737 B.C.

The Chinese occupied Ceylon for thirty years in the fifteenth century. The Portuguese came after them and left a firm imprint. The sonorous Portuguese names are still proudly borne by many a native of Ceylon, where St. Francis Xavier converted so many to Christianity. Francisco de Almeida landed in Ceylon in 1505, when the island contained seven separate kingdoms. The Portuguese were there for the next century and a half. After them came the Hollanders, for approximately the same period. A corrupted form of the Portuguese language is still used in parts of Ceylon, despite the intervening Dutch sovereignty and the coming of the East India Company from Madras in 1795, as the forerunners of a century and a half of British dominance. Now Ceylon is independent again, a free dominion, with a High Commissioner in London.

Representatives of more than seventy races live upon the 26,000 square miles of Ceylon, and these include descendants of the original inhabitants, a small tribe of primitives who still inhabited the eastern jungles at the turn of the century. Paleolithic implements have been found in their ancient caves. Ceylon is especially rich in wading and water birds, and the ibis, the egret, the heron and the stork abound there. In remoter parts, boas grow to a length of thirty feet. Deer, monkeys, and panther thrive, and the rich insect life includes many varieties of so-called leaf and stick insects, perfect examples of nature's wonderful skill at camouflage.

As for Madagascar, it is probable that something like the giant birds which Sindbad the Sailor spoke of might once have existed there. Sindbad spoke of a bird so huge that it fed grown elephants to its young. Skeletons of extinct wingless birds which must have stood about 12 feet high have been discovered. One species laid an egg more than a foot long. Bones of a gigantic tortoise are also found.

The fauna generally presents an obvious greater affinity with Asia than with Africa. Madagascar is sometimes considered to be the third largest island in the world, but this rating can take no account of Greenland. New Guinea and Borneo are also larger. Madagascar is almost 1,000 miles in its north-south length and its average breadth is about 250 miles. Most of the island consists of an elevated mountainous region, with coastal plains. The east coast is curiously regular, consisting of a long line of sandbanks, inside which are pestilential swamps and turgid lagoons which for years made much of the island a nightmare to Europeans, for the so-called Madagascar fever was notorious. Sandbanks blocked the mouths of the rivers, which, in the dry season, lacked force enough to break out against the surf beating almost constantly along that coast, driven there by the southeast trade wind.

Behind these banks a line of lagoons was formed, looking sometimes almost like a strange river flowing parallel with the coast and frequently blocked by mazelike swamps and pestilential marshes. The miasmata produced by these stagnant marshes, which encircle a considerable part of the island, were believed to have caused the Madagascar fever which carried off so many of the earlier colonists.

The people of Madagascar, called Malagasy, came from the East. Tradition has it that some of them are related to the Nairs of India. The natives are of many tribes, each with its own customs. Many are light in color and of obvious Malayo-Polynesian type. Others look more like Melanesians of the dark islands of the western Pacific. There is considerable similarity between them and many Pacific islanders in appearance, habits, customs, and even language. Some tribes have an undoubted African strain, others have mingled with the Arabs. The dwarfish Vazimba are regarded as the original inhabitants, but not many of these survive.

The great forests of Madagascar include casuarina, palms, bamboos, the baobab, the tamarind, and the mango, as well as the useful traveler's tree (*urania speciosa*). This extraordinary and beautiful

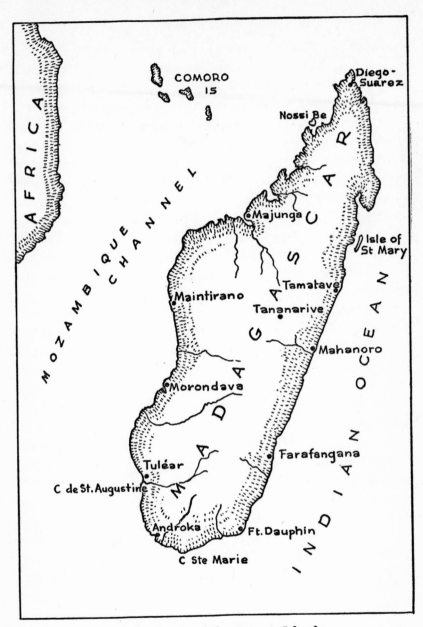

Madagascar and the Comoro Islands

tree provides cool drinking water from its fanlike tuft of leaves, and every part of the tree is of service in building.

Madagascar was known to the Arabs from ancient times. The northeast monsoon blows ships to its shores, and the Arabs could well have been sailing there since first they mastered the science of ocean voyaging, thousands of years ago. Indians and Chinese were also early visitors. The Arab, the Indian, and the Chinese have been ubiquitous merchants and fearless wanderers far longer than it is possible to say. Thousands of years ago, ancient Sindbads were calling at the ports of Madagascar and credulous merchants were carrying stories back to their homelands, which there became embellished and magnified into the fables we now know.

The Arabs traded for beeswax, timber, rice, and gums. They also took slaves, for slavery of all kinds was rife throughout the island until less than a century ago. In later years Americans came, on the eternal quest for trade. On many parts of the great island cattle do well, and it was not long before American ships were putting in to jerk the beef and preserve the hides. When His Majesty's frigate *Leven*, for example, was upon the coast in the 1820s, she spoke several American vessels engaged in filling themselves with beef, tallow, and hides. At a place called Bambatooka, she met three of them, all doing well and hurrying to complete their cargoes before the wet season began. They had combined to erect a slaughter-house ashore and had set up shops to trade with the natives, in regular Yankee fashion. The bullocks were wild, great beasts which were dangerous to handle. The custom was to corral them, hamstringing them as they passed into the corral, and then to slaughter them as required. The meat was boned, jagged, well salted, and then dried in the sun, always being carefully carried in from the heavy night dews.

When H.M.S. *Leven* was on the coast, Madagascar was ruled by the extraordinary monarch known as King Radama I, under whom the rich island might have prospered. King Radama, who spoke and wrote fluently both English and French, was outstanding even as a boy. In Madagascar then, it was customary for royalty and chieftainship to descend only by the female line. When a king died, he was succeeded by his sister's eldest son. The reason for this was the extreme license allowed to women. Not even the chastity of the queen was considered sufficient guarantee for the royal blood, and her children were usually taken away and conveniently "lost" immediately after their birth. The king knew he was the son of his mother, but who his father was he could not be sure. He was also confident that his mother's daughters were his sisters. Therefore their children *must* have royal blood. Hence the descent through the female line.

Radama, however, succeeded his father by his own determination, and he tried to put a stop to the dreadful practice of royal infanticide. He was doing his best to get rid of other superstitious and useless customs which had been handed down among his people for countless centuries. Among these was their filthy habit of wearing their hair long, unwashed, and heavily greased. This habit, which was universal among the Malagasy, was productive of much dirt and disease among the soldiers. Radama tried to set an example by clipping his own hair short, but the women were against the innovation and complained bitterly. It was their pride to dress their husbands' hair and to compete with one another in neatness and design, but never in cleanliness. They raised such a clamor that Radama had to quell them by ordering his guards to seize the noisiest of them, and to "remove their hair in such a fashion that it would never grow again." This the guards succeeded in doing by cutting off the women's heads. The reform was then accepted.

The captain of the *Leven* met King Radama and has left an excellent description of this extraordinary monarch.

Though upwards of thirty, [the captain wrote] he appeared many years younger. His stature did not exceed five feet five inches, and his figure was slight, elegant, and graceful; his demeanour was diffident in the extreme, not at all according with the idea that we are apt to form of one accustomed to a military life and its fatigues, much less to a successful warrior and the terror of surrounding foes. His appearance was altogether that of one better adapted for the courtier than the hero. . . . His features, which were well formed, remained tranquil and collected until some part of the conversation of greater interest engaged his attention. Then a tremulous, half-suppressed movement of the lip and a hasty glance from the dark, expressive eyes, betrayed for an instant a subdued emotion, which almost immediately subsided into the same calm but keenly observant position.*

Radama had an army of well-disciplined troops, who drilled in the European manner to British orders, for the drill sergeant was an Englishman. The soldiers used gold and silver chains as currency, and many of the officers possessed garments which were beautifully woven.

King Radama was determined to abolish slavery and had a fine program for the progress of his country. He introduced missionaries and teachers and was well on his way to uniting Madagascar when, unfortunately, he died at the early age of thirty-one. His successors reversed his policy and the missionaries and all other Europeans were banished from the island. The custom of greasing unshorn and unwashed locks came into use again, and once more inheritance passed to the unchaste female line. It was a pity. Within a few years, English and French frigates were bombarding Tamatave and burned the town. There were no more kings like Radama. Madagascar, which was first made known in Europe by the hearsay report of Marco Polo and was first sighted by the Portuguese navigator Lourenco Almeida in 1506, is, even in the 1950s, a comparatively backward land, where much remains to be done.

Mauritius, Reunion, and Rodriguez are islands in the approximate vicinity of Madagascar, though they have little if any real connection with that island. Reunion, which was discovered by

---

* *Voyages to Africa, Arabia and Madagascar, Performed in H.M. Ships Leven and Barracouta,* by Captain W. F. W. Owen, R.N., London, Richard Bentley, 1833 (2 vols.).

the Portuguese in 1545 and then named Mascarenhas, is inhabited by a mixture of French settlers, Negroes, Indians, Malagasy, and the descendants of slaves. These speak a patois based on Malagasy, Malabar, and Creole French, which is alleged to be easily learned. Reunion is a mass of volcanic mountains, which rise from a narrow cultivated plain to a great, snowy peak, more than 10,000 feet above sea level. The island abounds in mineral springs.

Mauritius was first called Cerne by its Portuguese discoverers, who took it for Pliny's *Cern Ethiopia*. The island has since been Spanish, Dutch, French, and British since 1810, though there is still a strong French influence there. The general appearance of Mauritius seen from the sea is rugged and inhospitable, and a great surf beats upon the coral reefs which almost surround the island. Sugar is extensively cultivated, and in the days before federation in Australia (and the policy of protection for Queensland sugar) its ports were much visited by small clippers from the island of Tasmania, loading sugar to supply that lovely state three thousand miles away. Port Louis, the port of the island, is in the cyclone area, and vessels lying there used to be given terse instructions on how to survive. These instructions included such seaworthy remarks as:

"Keep your vessel ready for sea.

"As soon as you anchor, make the necessary arrangements for slipping.

"On the first appearance of bad weather, strike your topgallant masts and double-reef topsails.

"When the signal is made to put to sea, do so without loss of time as the wind frequently shifts much sooner than anticipated.

"Never attempt to ride the gale out.

"Never lay your vessel's head towards the land during bad weather; the currents run with great force and in most uncertain and improbable directions at such times. Many vessels have been lost by heaving-to head inshore, after making what was considered a sufficient offing. . . ."

The master of a vessel at Port Louis during the cyclone season could not have known much rest.

Rodriguez, sometimes called Diego Rais, is 300 miles to the eastward of Mauritius. It is noteworthy for the dreadful coral reef which surrounds it, for the extraordinary basaltic columns nearly 200 feet high in one of the valleys, and for its limestone caves.

The southern waters of the Indian Ocean contain islands of a different sort. The Crozets and Prince Edward Island, Kerguelen, the craterlike St. Paul, bleak Amsterdam, and Heard Island, all lie in the storm-ridden latitudes which sailors used to call the Roaring Forties and the Shrieking Fifties, for these parallels were notorious for their storms. Sailing ships bound from Europe and America toward Australia used to go that way to run before the hard westerly winds. Most of these islands were discovered from such passing ships. The first sighting of Heard Island, for example, was directly attributable to the introduction of great-circle sailing into the Australian trade. Previously, ships had made easting between the latitudes of 30 and 35 south, where the winds were more variable and of much less strength. In 1849 Captain Godfrey, in the ship *Constance,* sailed down to 51 south and, finding strong westerly winds there, ran to Australia from Europe in the then extraordinary time of seventy-seven days. Captain Forbes of the ship *Marco Polo,* and other prominent masters, followed his example with success.

Among these was Captain Heard of the United States Ship *Oriental,* of Boston, who came upon the islands which now bear his name when racing before a hard westerly wind in 1853. Shortly after him came Captain McDonald in the ship *Samarang,* on the same parallel, and he also "discovered" the islands; within a matter of months, their further "discovery" had been claimed by Captain Hutton of the ship *Earl of Eglinton,* by Captain Attway of the beautifully named *Herald of the Morning,* and by Captain Rees of the *Lincluden Castle.* Despite all these "discoverers," the islands did not amount to much. There were seals and sea elephants, which were soon hunted and destroyed. Then the islands were left again to the sea birds which abound there.

The isolated Crozets, lying in about 46 degrees south and 50 east longitude, have wrecked many a good ship, survivors from which frequently lived for months on sea-elephant meat and boiled Kerguelen cabbage, an unpalatable antiscorbutic which requires an appetite sharpened by shipwreck to appreciate it. A little cutter called the *Princess of Wales,* of less than 100 tons, was cast up there in 1821, and the crew managed to survive for almost two years. One of the crew was Charles Medyett Goodridge, a man of Devon, who later wrote an account of his life in the islands in the Robinson Crusoe manner. The ship *Strathmore* was wrecked on the same islands in 1875 and, though 40 of her people drowned when she struck, the remaining 44 lived there for six months until they were rescued. They used sea birds' feathers for fuel and eggs for sustenance and, in addition to the cabbage, found a sort of turnip top which was almost as unpalatable. The weather was invariably bleak, boisterous, and foggy, but the *Strathmore's* survivors were Scots who were well enough accustomed to that sort of thing.

There is a mystery concerning a more recent wreck on the Crozets. One day, some twenty years ago, an albatross which appeared to be flying with difficulty was noticed to land on a beach near Fremantle, in West Australia. The albatross was easily caught. Round its neck, roughly secured, was a band of metal on which a message had been painfully punched, probably with nails. It was in French. "Thirteen men cast away on the Crozet Islands," it said, adding, "Send help, for the love of God." In due course, a ship visited the Crozets but found none of the Frenchmen. There were signs that some castaways had been there, and it was generally thought that they must have put to sea on a raft. Nothing of them has ever been found. In the wild waters of the southern Indian Ocean, they would stand little chance of survival.

Amsterdam and St. Paul are an interesting pair of islands. Amsterdam Island was supposed to have been discovered by the famous Dutch governor of the Dutch East Indies, Anthony van Diemen, when making a voyage to Batavia in the ship *Nieuw Amsterdam* in the winter of 1633. But later investigation credits its first sighting to the Portuguese with Magellan, on the first circumnavigation of the world. Magellan's ship *Victoria*, returning from the Spice Islands on this famous voyage in 1522, certainly sighted an island in the same latitude, which must have been Amsterdam. The Portuguese position differs by only a few miles from the true one. The pilot, Francisco Alvaro, recorded in his log that "whilst taking the sun we saw a very high island, and we went towards it to anchor, and we could not fetch it, and we struck the sails and lay to until next day."

St. Paul Island is one of the world's natural wonders, though no cruising liner has yet added the place to its itinerary nor is any likely to. It lies in the abode of gales and there is no harbor, though the greater part of the island's area is a lovely crater lake. This is connected to the sea across a dangerous bar; inside, the depths are up to thirty fathoms. With a good entrance the place would make a perfect harbor but, since the sealers destroyed the island's only asset, most visitors have been involuntary ones, who left as soon as they could. The island shows abundant signs of its latent volcanic energy. Hot springs boil on the tongues of land protruding into the waters where crayfish of unusual size and flavor may be easily taken. There are also springs of waters which are said to be an infallible cure for rheumatism.

The waters round the island are full of splendid fish, and a small settlement used to be maintained there to catch and salt them. In 1853 there was a Frenchman named Frédéric Roure who had then been on the island for six years. Goats, pigs, escaped cats and mice from the wrecks of ships, penguins, petrels of all kinds, and the great albatross all thrive there. With these for company and food and only the occasional sight of a passing sailing ship to disturb

him, M. Roure was reported to be well content with his lot and
not in the least interested in a return to civilization. He found the
island wonderfully healthy, with the westerly winds there crisp
and invigorating, and he said there were mineral waters which
could rapidly cure any ill the flesh was heir to. But M. Roure at
length departed from St. Paul and died of a rheumatic fever at
Mauritius.

Kerguelen used to be called the Isle of Desolation. The island
was first sighted by Lieutenant Yves Kerguelen-Tremarec in 1772
when he was in quest of the lost continent of *Terra Australis*. James
Cook, Sir James Clark Ross, and Captain G. S. Nares of the famous
Challenger all visited the island, and the German cruiser *Gazelle*
spent three months there while on a voyage to observe the transit
of Venus, in 1874. Kerguelen is very mountainous, rising to more
than 6,000 feet, and the coasts are rugged and unprepossessing.
The lee side is much broken up by a labyrinth of bays and inlets,
many of which are useful harbors. A depot for castaways was maintained here for many years, but since the sealers and the hunters
of sea-elephant oil worked themselves off the island by destroying
the source of their cargoes, few ships ever go there. In the 1950s,
when steamers hurry more quickly than ever over well-defined
lanes and deepwater sailing ships have disappeared from the long-
voyage routes, all such places are lonelier than they have ever been
since first becoming known to Europeans. For many years, Kerguelen was a great resort of sealers, particularly from America and
from Tasmania. They were accustomed to venture into those dangerous waters in small and decrepit vessels.

Both at Kerguelen and at Heard Island, the *Challenger* expedition reports meeting sealers. It was the custom to leave parties of
men ashore to hunt seals and sea elephants while the schooner
which brought them sailed off to cruise elsewhere. The men ashore
set up rough huts, half buried in the ground for better protection
against the violent gales.

It appeared [says Nares of a party met at Heard Island] that there were some forty or fifty men distributed about the island in small detachments, each party having a defined beat, where they watch for the sea elephants coming ashore. A sealer's life must evidently be a miserable one, living in those desolate regions, completely isolated from the rest of mankind. The parties met with had no boat and were entirely dependent on the return of the sealing schooners for any further supplies or relief. They usually sign an agreement to remain for three years, at the expiration of which, if they have had a lucky season, probably they are the possessors of $250 or $300 to return home with. This is frequently spent in a couple of months, and they again return to their voluntary exile, and live on penguins, young albatross, and sea-birds' eggs for another period.

Captain Nares speaks of a chain of magnificent, well-sheltered harbors on Kerguelen, especially praising that known as Christmas Harbor. Here the insect life included the wingless fly and the wingless mosquito. The few gnats and beetles found were in the same condition, which was explained as being nature's manner of preventing the insects from being blown off the island and out to sea, where they would be lost.

From these islands in the far south, where the wind blows so hard that the very insects do not dare to fly, to the lush tropic islands and the spice-scented lands of the fabulous East is perhaps a long way, but the waters of the Indian Ocean wash them all, and they have all played their part in that great ocean's story.

CHAPTER III

The Arms of the Ocean

As with the islands, so also with the great arms of the Indian Ocean known to us as the Red Sea, the Persian Gulf, the Straits of Malacca; and the huge gulfs of the Arabian Sea and the Bay of Bengal. It is 4,500 miles from Kerguelen to the entrance of the Persian Gulf and almost the same distance to the Straits of Bab-el-Mandeb, which separate Africa from Arabia at the southern end of the Red Sea. To the Arafura Sea, between New Guinea and the northern coast of Australia, the approximate distance is also 4,000 miles. No arms of any sea can be of greater interest, or of more historical importance, than the Red Sea and the Persian Gulf. As the two principal highways—indeed, for thousands of years the only highways—between East and West, each has been the scene of great events. It is highly probable that the Gulf at any rate felt the embrace of seagoing ships long before even the Mediterranean was plowed by the keels of vessels, for in this area was the cradle of our civilization.

The Gulf has long been of importance in world politics, rarely more so than today. On both sides, its hinterland is rich almost beyond belief in all-important oil. In Persia—now called Iran—the fields which were exploited by the Anglo-Iranian Oil Company have yielded oil by the trillion gallons. In King Ibn Saud's Arabia across the Gulf, from an area long regarded as a sterile desert and abandoned until recently to the wandering Beduin, from the

Typical Kuwait *boom*

A Mombasa dhow

A primitive reed boat, of the type still used for fishing, on the beach by
Ras al Ardh, Kuwait Bay

Sewn boat of Shir

Incredibly small vessels sail to Africa in the favorable monsoon

sheikhdom of Kuwait at the head of the Gulf upon the Arab side, and from the island of Bahrein, come a great part of Europe's oil supplies. In Iraq, in the peninsula of Qatar, and in Trucial Oman, there is also oil. Huge tank ships, designed and built expressly for the carriage of oil and for no other cargoes, some of them as large as 32,000 tons, are engaged in the transportation of Persian Gulf oil to the refineries and the markets of Europe and America. Such vessels pass through the Suez Canal in an astonishing stream, until the layman might well wonder whether the world's supply of oil is not being used up too rapidly so that soon there may be none left. But the sources of oil in the Gulf are enormous and the supply apparently unlimited. The exploitation of these oil supplies, at least on a small scale, goes back for several thousand years. Eratosthenes of Cyrene (276–194 B.C.), an Alexandrine geographer who knew Ceylon and the Persian Gulf, seems to be the first to mention the existence of petroleum there.

The liquid asphaltus, which is called naphtha, [he has written] is found in Susiana [part of Babylonia]. It is of a singular nature. When it is brought near a fire, the fire catches it; and if a body smeared over with it is brought near the fire, it burns with a flame which it is impossible to extinguish. . . .

Strabo quotes the later writer Posidonius, who speaks also of "springs of naphtha in Babylonia, some of which produce white, others black, naphtha. . . . The second is liquid asphaltus, and is burned in lamps instead of oil." The great geographer Pliny speaks of an abundance of naphtha in several regions of the Gulf, where its vapors burned by night. In one place, he says "the plain of Babylon throws up flame from a place like a fish-pond, an acre in extent." But apparently use was made of the oil only locally.

The Persian Gulf, which is almost an inland sea, covers an area of 90,000 square miles between Arabia, Iraq at its northern end, and Iran. The deep waters of the Gulf of Oman connect it with the Arabian Sea. Its width is 180 miles at its widest, and less than

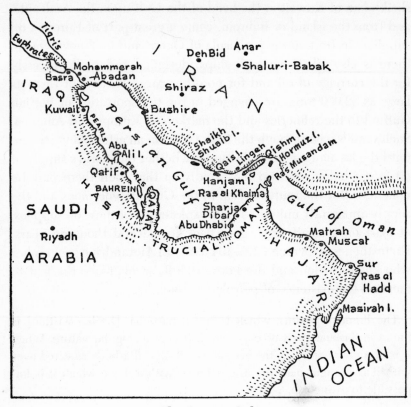

The Persian Gulf

30 at its narrowest. Its length is about 450 miles, from the coast of
Oman to the Basra River, which is the confluence of the Tigris
and Euphrates. It is a shallow sea studded with reefs, especially
on the Arabian side. The Persian coast is generally mountainous
and steep-to, with many islands lying close to it. The Arabian side
is protected by an excessive number of dangers. It is low, fronted
by shoals and reefs. Here the heated water in the summer months
seems to irritate the oysters into the production of vast quantities
of pearls, which are sometimes of unusual size and luster. The
reefs between Bahrein and Kuwait form one of the great pearl
fisheries of the world, if not the greatest.

The mountains on the Persian side, running in a rugged and often precipitous series parallel with the coast, are sometimes beautifully colored, but between them and the sea the belt of low land is regarded as the hottest place in the world. The whole Gulf has a reputation of being exceedingly trying because of the heat in summer, the intense humidity, and the frequency of sandstorms. Yet it is a question whether this reputation is deserved. I spent a summer in the Persian Gulf, living for much of the time in the walled city of Kuwait, or just outside it. The weather was certainly exceedingly trying and a sandstorm once blew almost continuously for twenty days. But I have found some weeks in a summer in New York more trying and would prefer the Gulf climate to Chicago any day. Even in London, during a rare hot and sticky summer's heat wave, I have felt more uncomfortable than I ever did in the Persian Gulf. The secret, I suppose, was that since I was then with the Arabs, I had to live as they did, and they knew how to accept such conditions and suffer least from them. The loose robes, the habit of beginning the day at dawn, the light breakfasts, the midday siesta, the early nights, the absence of hard liquor, frequent bathing in the sea, the habit of sleeping always in the open underneath the stars—these things made the most trying weather acceptable and usable. The only occasion on which I was overcome by the weather was upon a visit to the oil establishment at Bahrein, when I had to live for a while in an air-conditioned bungalow, the temperature of which must have been too low.

Islands in the Gulf include Hormuz, which is formed by the top of a cylinder of salt forced through a crack in the buckling earth millions of years ago, when great pressures threw up the Persian mountains and depressed the area of the Gulf. Qishm, Hanjam, Qais, Shaikh Shuaib, and Larak are other islands of importance on the Persian side. Hormuz was for many years a Portuguese stronghold, chosen for its strategic position at the entrance of the Gulf, and the remains of the fort built there in 1515 still stand. The small island is practically covered by hills, which are low, of confused form, and of various colors. Several of them have white peaks and, under that burning sun, present a curious picture of snow-covered and delightful coolness. But it is only a picture. The hills are almost solid salt. On nearby Qishm there are also the remains of a Portuguese fort.

Here, by one of the strange quirks of fate, are buried the remains of William Baffin, the famous ice-pilot who gave his name to Baffin's Bay and other places in the Arctic seas. Baffin was in the Persian Gulf as master of H.M.S. *London,* which was assisting in an English attack on the Portuguese strongholds there. His death is described by a contemporary, who witnessed it, as follows:

Master Baffin went on shoare with his Geometricall Instruments, for the taking of the height and distance of the Castle wall, for the better levelling of his peece to make his shot; but, as he was about the same, he received a small shot from the Castle into his belly, wherewith he gave three leapes, and died immediately.

Hormuz was visited by Marco Polo. He called it Hormos and described it as a port of the first importance in the Indian trade. He was there twice, in 1272 and in 1293, but at that time there was also a port of the same name on the mainland close by. It was a "great and noble city on the sea," said Marco Polo, adding that it was notable among other things for the excellent breeds of horses and asses there. There was a big trade in these animals to India, going by dhows, which were built of planks sewn together. He had a poor opinion of those dhows—but Marco Polo was no sailor.

Their ships are wretched affairs, and many of them get lost [he reported], for they have no iron fastenings and are only stitched together with twine made from the husk of the Indian nut. . . . The ships are not pitched, but are rubbed with fish-oil. They have one mast, one sail, and one rudder, and no deck. . . .

Such sewn vessels survived until quite recent times, and big dhows "with one mast, one sail, and one rudder" are still employed profitably in the trade between the Persian Gulf and India. In truth, the Italian wanderer must have known little about the ships. Their one sail is for normal use, but in a locker below the poop there are always at least two more, of various sizes, for use in bad weather. The one mast can be increased when necessary and prudent by the simple means of stepping another on the poop, or at the break of the poop. The sewn planks stood up to the sea very well, as they still do in the sewn boats at Shihr in the Hadhramaut, in South Arabia. " 'Tis a perilous business to go a voyage in one of those ships, and many of them are lost," says the unmaritime Polo, "for in that Sea of India the storms are often terrible."

Doubtless it was something of a perilous business to go on a voyage in such ships either then or at most other times, but not for the reasons given. A good dhowmaster knew how to avoid the storms of the Indian Ocean, and it was always the custom to lay the ships up during the greater part of the southwest season. The nearby ports of Kung (sometimes called Kunk) and Lingeh were still, in the 1940s, famous for the excellence of their big deep-sea dhows. I saw a beauty from Lingeh lying in the harbor at Muscat in 1939 which must have been nearly 400 tons. She had just come in with a cargo of teak and coir from the Malabar coast.

The whole area of the Persian Gulf is full of interest, geological, maritime, and historical. In ancient times, an important route to Europe was by some port on the Tigris or the Euphrates (they did not always share the same mouth) and thence by land caravan through Iraq and Syria to the Mediterranean. It was possible to sail ships in the more sheltered waters of the Gulf when the southwest monsoon made the open waters of the Arabian Sea impracticable. The trek across Iraq and the Syrian desert was difficult and expensive, and tribute had to be paid to many on the way.

The Red Sea had the advantage of offering fresh southerly winds to blow ships northward, at any rate as far as the old port of Suakin, which was not far from a bend in the Nile. Strong northerly winds blew—and still blow—down the Red Sea from the Gulf of Suez almost the year round, making it impracticable to beat against them. From Suez to Suakin is 750 miles, and to beat north that distance in the teeth of a fresh and unchanging wind, funneled down between the great mountains, with reefs on either side and the current also adverse, was a sore trial to any mariner. It was easier to land cargoes at Suakin or some nearby place and carry them by ass and camel across to the Nile.

Another porterage port on the Red Sea, in former days, was Kosair (sometimes spelled Cosseir or Qoseir), which is four days by caravan journey from the Nile. This place was much used in the days of the so-called overland route to India during the nineteenth century, before the Suez Canal was constructed, when the early steamships from European ports were able to land passengers at Alexandria for other steamships to embark at Suez or at Kosair for the passage on to India. Kosair is about 250 miles from Suez. It was its nearness to the Nile which made it favored, more particularly on the homeward voyage. The ruins of Luxor were not very far inland, and this was an added inducement to travelers. The Indian steamers used to embark their passengers sometimes at Suez itself for the outward journey, because the passage up the Nile against the stream was tedious and difficult and, in any event, the northerlies of the Gulf of Suez and the northern Red Sea were a help to them when the ships were bound south. They could not avoid the southerlies farther down. Steamers in those early days were far from economic, and the southerly winds of the Red Sea caused a vast consumption of coal. A regular fleet of sailing ships had to be employed for taking out coal from England to ports along the way, especially to Aden and Perim.

This "overland" journey was a considerable test of passengers' endurance, for the donkey or camel ride from Kosair to the Nile could be most trying. From there, the journey by felucca was also something of a hardship, but at least the water was smooth. Camels made the passengers more "seasick" than even the early steamers did. It was necessary to take sufficient boiled water and provisions for the whole journey, which could last a week. Boats hired at Luxor had to be sunk for several days, to drown their vermin, before any European dared embark in them. Even then, many of the vermin refused to die and the boats were washed down twice a day afterward with chloride of lime. There was a little steamer with a passenger capacity of ten, but this spent as much time on the sandbanks as under way. Accommodation ashore was literally lousy. If the luckless traveler arrived at Alexandria by night, the city gates were shut and there was then no alternative but to spend the night under the stars or in one of the villainous cafés beyond the city walls. It was not until the great Peninsula and Oriental Company took the service in hand, in the middle of the century, that there was any marked improvement but, even then, none but the really determined or necessitous traveler went as a passenger to sea, or at any rate on the overland route, to India.

The Red Sea was once part of the ocean we know now as the Mediterranean and had then no connection with the Indian Ocean, but that is countless ages ago. In the days of the Roman Empire it was the principal route by which Eastern produce came to Europe. Egypt then was a Roman province. Throughout most of the Middle Ages, the Red Sea was closed to foreign commerce and Arabs controlled the trade. Because of its long and narrow shape— its greatest breadth is 180 miles and its least less than 15—the Red Sea lent itself well to strategic control at either end. In the Straits of Bab-el-Mandeb—the "Gate of Affliction"—the rocky island of Perim mounts guard. The multitudinous reefs off either shore make navigation there impractical except to skilled pilots with years of local knowledge. Other ships keep to the central waters. The winds blow fiercely up and down, up from the south as far as the latitude of Jiddah (the port for pilgrims bound to Mecca) and down from the north, even more fiercely, as far as the same latitude, with a narrow belt of baffling airs and calms between. In the days of sailing ships, the Red Sea was no place to venture. To this day,

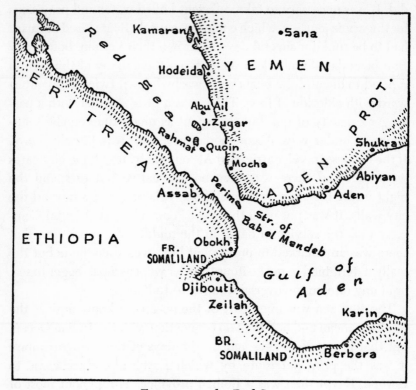

Entrance to the Red Sea

reefs, unpredictable crosscurrents, refraction, sandstorms, and the great humidity make it a trial even to the fastest and best equipped steamships and motor vessels. Arab and Somali dhows still carry on much of its coastal trade and, until quite recent years, still slipped ghostlike and with great speed across by night, running cargoes of arms or Nubian slaves.

The waters of the Red Sea wash the shores of all western Arabia, from Transjordania (which reaches to the Gulf of Aqaba) down all the Hejaz to the productive Yemen, where the old coffee port of Mocha is important still. The protectorate of Aden reaches to its southern fringe. On the other shore are Egypt, the Sudan, the Ethiopian province called Eritrea (an Italian colony, these many years), and French Somaliland. In parts of the Red Sea there are found good pearls, though the banks are not so extensive nor the pearls so lustrous as those in the Persian Gulf. Oil has been found on some of its islands. The Red Sea climate is considered even worse than that of the Gulf, with some reason. A hot day of sandstorms there can be almost suffocating.

I was once a fortnight in a little double-ended dhow of the type known as *zarooks*, sailing from Aden to the port of Gizan in the Red Sea, just north of the Yemen border. She sailed the inside way, between the reefs, and the pilotage was by her Yemenite captain's eye. She stopped at night and we slept on cays among the reefs. She was my first Arab dhow. Whether I was not then sufficiently acclimatized or whether the fast of Ramadhan and the insanitary drinking water did not agree with me I do not know, but at any rate that passage was an exhausting experience. The little dhow would have alarmed Marco Polo, for her one rudder hung precariously from a single pintle and her one sail was fragile indeed. Her planks were iron-fastened, and not sewn together. Had they been sewn, they might have been stronger and the *zarook* a better ship. But she had been trading profitably in the Red Sea, then, for fifty years, and when last I was in Aden in 1944, she was still sailing there.

Just why the Red Sea is known by that name is the subject of controversy. Some geographers have said that the waters are sometimes red because of the profusion of confervae growth. Some of the neighboring mountains are red enough, at times, and their redness is reflected for miles in the sea. But indeed the Red Sea is generally no redder than any other stretch of waters. There was once a time when the ancients knew the Persian Gulf also as the Red Sea; to them, the Mediterranean was the White Sea. The Greeks and Romans knew the whole Indian Ocean as the Erythraean Sea, in so far as they knew it at all. The word *erythra* means red. The term Red Sea may signify that these were the waters of King Erythras, a Persian monarch who dominated these waters.

Another mystery of the Red Sea waters is the Biblical account
of the parting of the sea, with which every schoolboy is familiar.
The origin of this story may well be some abnormally low tide in
the Gulf of Aqaba or possibly in the Gulf of Suez, where the ordinary tidal range is up to 7 feet. The combination of such a tide
together with the hard north-northwest wind blowing the water
out, and the loss by summer evaporation—the Red Sea can lose
up to a foot in level through that cause—may well have exposed a
spit across some arm of the sea which, ordinarily hidden from
view, appeared providential to any group of unfortunates who were
fleeing that way. Such an incident might easily have occurred in
either area. A drop in the wind, in such circumstances, would be
enough to bring the tide back with an abnormal and sudden increase.

The opening of the Suez Canal in 1869 made the Red Sea one of
the great sea highways of the modern world. Meanwhile, the Persian Gulf has become of steadily increasing importance as a route
for air lines and for oil tankers. It is the regular air highway between
Europe and India, the Far East, and Australia. At Basra, Bahrein,
and in Trucial Oman there are important airports.

Both the Red Sea and the Persian Gulf could form the subjects
of books by themselves. So could the astonishing pageant of the
peoples of the Indian Ocean, which may be seen at almost any
port around that great ocean, from Cape Town to Colombo, and
from Aden to Rangoon. The streets of Zanzibar, the bazaars at
Mombasa and at Mogadishu, the Crater at Aden, the *suq* of Kuwait
and the island of Bahrein, Bombay, and Calcutta—each presents
a diversity of races, colors, and creeds. Look for a moment at colorful Zanzibar, where the scent of cloves and perhaps also of ancient
salted shark is heavy on the air. Arabs from Oman, from Sur, and
from Kuwait—each differing from all other Arabs as much as an
Irishman differs from a Yorkshireman or a Finlander from a Dane—
mingle with Indian traders and wanderers from the Hadhramaut,

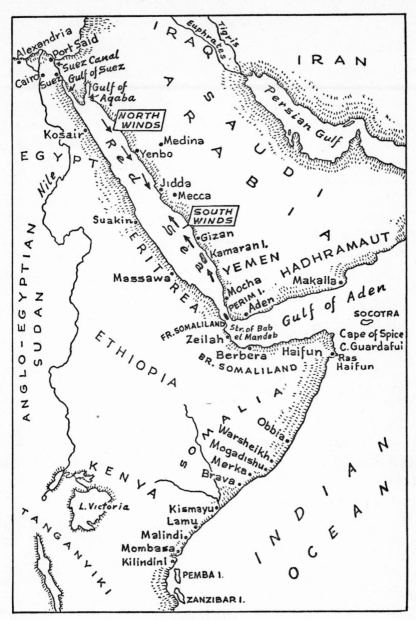

The Red Sea

landed from some recently arrived big dhow. These may include Beduin whose idea of protection against the night air is to anoint their bodies with indigo, and whose eyes are protected from the strong sun's glare by an etching of mascara at their corners. Africans of all kinds, loosely called "Swahili," do much of the labor. These include descendants of slaves, immigrants from the mainland, and relics of the original tribes of Zanzibar and nearby Pemba. In the narrow streets Omani sheikhs rub shoulders with rich Hindu shopkeepers, and the sailors from the fleet of dhows, themselves as cosmopolitan as the Zanzibar crowds, roll along with their seaman's gait. Arab women hooded to the eyes hurry by, as if anxious to reach the seclusion of the *harim* again. An Indian child wife follows her husband demurely.

As for the Negroes, no one can say with certainty whence they came. Today's Swahili of the East African coast are not the original inhabitants. Those may have been a race of dwarfs, whose present-day descendants are limited to the pygmies of the Semliki forest, a few odd tribes among the Somali, and the bushmen of the Kalahari desert. But speculation about the story of any race is only speculation—absorbingly interesting, but leading nowhere. There is a tradition that the first Negro people reached Africa from somewhere in southern Asia. Later came migrations of Hamitic peoples. The so-called Swahili of today are Bantus with an admixture of Arab blood, for the Arab has been sailing and trading on that coast for many centuries.

The peninsula of Arabia is the home of the Semitic peoples, who included the Phoenicians, famed as navigators alike in the Mediterranean and the Indian Ocean. Arabs, Hebrews, and Syrians are alike Semites. So were the Babylonians and the Moabites. All these were wanderers and traders. The Assyrians—another early Semitic race—had conquered the Sumerians and developed their civilization: both Assyrians and Sumerians probably sailed the waters of the Indian Ocean. So did the Chinese and the Indians, and Persians, wandering in their sailing ships wherever the monsoons would take them and wherever profitable trade was offering. Gold, slaves, and ivory were to be had from East Africa, and there were plenty of seekers. It is odd that a good deal of the magic still practiced among the Swahili peoples is similar to magic known to have been used by the Sumerians and the Assyrians, thousands of years ago. The early Hindu mariners knew the "Country of the Moon," which was inland near Lake Victoria, where the Wanjamwezi (people of the moon) lived. These people of the moon were very useful to the Hindus as guides and porters.

There remain many evidences of the remarkable wanderings of the earlier Indian Ocean navigators, particularly along the East Coast of Africa—the mysterious ruins on Zanzibar Island, on some of which inscriptions have been found in Cufic characters; other ruins on the nearby small island of Tumbatu, which are so extensive that this must once have been the site of a great town; the obvious Persian blood in many of the present inhabitants of the Lamu Archipelago, on the coast of Kenya; the discovery of Chinese coins from the early eighth century at several places on the coast, as well as fragments of pottery identified as belonging to the Sung and the Ming dynasties.

The ancient Arabs and Persians divided the known world into the three sections of Hind, Sind, and Zinj, and the Zinjis were black. The name of Zanzibar derives from this—Zanghibar, the coast of the black people. The Portuguese called it Zanghibar. The earlier Japanese referred to the place as "Tsengu, in the Southwest Ocean," and described a great bird which lived there, called the *pheng*, which could swallow camels whole, and whose quills were so big they were used aboard dhows as water casks.

There were, apparently, Sindbads not only in the ports of the Persian Gulf.

CHAPTER IV

The Dawn of Sailing

A good deal has been written about the origin of sailing and about early seafaring man. Some of it is nonsense, most of it is pure conjecture, and a great part of it makes queer reading to a sailor. It is, for instance, difficult to believe that the unwieldy vessels held up as examples of Egyptian shipbuilding art ever braved the open sea, or that the Egyptians themselves were real seafaring pioneers. The ships might have done well on the River Nile where they were intended to operate, but they had neither the stanchness nor the sea-keeping qualities even to run before the fresh northerly winds of the Gulf of Suez. If they had ventured into the open waters in such parts they would have foundered. Moreover, the very constancy of these winds was a menace—for how could a weak ship hope to beat back against them? In the days before steamships, the government of India used to send the mails by fast schooner to Suez, and thence overland. The schooners were designed for the voyage, which always included a dour beat in the Red Sea. It was a common experience that the last three or four hundred miles, beating north from the Brothers' rock to Suez, took as long to make as the other two and a half thousand.

A light galley could, perhaps, be rowed inshore by slaves; but it would not be able to get very far down the Red Sea. The difficulty of carrying water sufficient to keep a crew of oarsmen going would be enough to curtail any such expeditions. There is little water to be

had at most places along the shores of the Red Sea. Nor could a
galley carry much cargo. A vessel propelled by sweeps or oars of
any size, must be finely built, or she could not be moved in a seaway. If she was finely built, she could not carry much. Moreover,
the use of big sweeps was a laborious business, wasteful of man
power. Even in the small dhows which go pearling in the Persian
Gulf, the number of oarsmen is astonishing. It requires four men to
move one sweep, and these men, who must be in magnificent physi-
cal condition if they are to be of any use at such work, need quite
an area of deck to work on. The idea of oarsmen sitting calmly on
some sort of thwart and pulling at a long oar is quite mistaken.
Sweeps had to be *marched* along by men with room to tramp a solid
deck, if ships—as apart from boats—were to be moved through the
water by their power.

I know there are excellent pictures and carvings of Egyptian vessels dating from as early as 1500 B.C. There is an account of Queen
Hatshepsut's alleged expedition by sea to Punt, dating from this
time. The publicity given to this voyage surely indicates its unusual-
ness. Her ships are said to have passed down the delta of the Nile
and through the Wadi Tumilat to the Red Sea. They coasted down
the Egyptian side of the Red Sea to the Straits of Bab-el-Mandeb
and safely reached the harbor of Zeilah. Here an enormous cargo
was embarked. Huge piles of resins, whole myrrh trees complete
with their roots (thirty-one trees in all), whole tusks of ivory, ebony, cassia, gold, cinnamon wood, and a collection of animals which
would have crowded the Bronx Zoo, were taken aboard. These included baboons, leopards, dogs, giraffes, and more than three thousand cattle—and all of these were loaded into five small vessels!
There is something wrong with this story. Even if the dogs and the
leopards fed on the cattle, they would not have sailed far. Water
shortage would have been enough to stop them. To water such a
menagerie would have kept a fleet of water dhows employed. For
five smallish vessels, it was impossible.

Yet again and again one reads of the alleged development of

deep-sea sailing among the ancient Egyptians. It seems likely that some of their vessels did go down the Red Sea, which they could perhaps manage by keeping carefully inside the reefs and choosing their weather. It is true that they did establish trade between lower Red Sea ports, and Kosair. But rowing a boat along the coasts of the Red Sea, though arduous for the oarsmen, is scarcely ocean voyaging, and craft developed for this sort of coastwise passage-making would never progress into real ocean-going ships. It is, I think, probable that real ships originated elsewhere, along the shores of the western Indian Ocean. Rivers rarely produce good ocean seamen or good ocean-going ships. There is a monotonous similarity, and almost an equal degree of unseaworthiness, between many of the river boats of the Ganges, Irrawaddy, Euphrates, and the Nile. The theory that such vessels ever developed into seagoing ships is, I think, erroneous. They were sufficient for their purpose, and their efficiency for that is demonstrated by their survival. So is their lack of development. In a seaway any of them would drown all hands as soon as it came on to blow and a bit of a slop got up on the surface of the water. Many of these early boats are still in use round the rivers which flow into the Indian Ocean, boats made of reeds, of skins, of wickerwork, from hollowed logs. They have not developed any further, for they still carry on quite satisfactorily the sheltered work for which they were designed. The same thing applies to the *proas* and canoes, which were satisfactory craft in the East Indies.

It is a fact unfortunate for the historian that early man, wherever he was, had found out how to look after himself quite well long before it occurred to him to invent a means of writing about it. He could till the land, broil his beef, clothe himself, and make rough tools before he thought of leaving any record of his doings. And he could, if he lived upon inland waterways or in a sheltered bay, get himself about on a tree-trunk canoe or a bundle of reeds or a boat of inflated skins. It is easy to concoct an apparently connected narrative pointing out how such early watermen and their vessels developed into the ships and seamen of today, the sail developing from a piece of bark or of woven cloth held up to catch the wind, the paddle from the first feeble attempts to pole a canoe along, the ship from the canoe. Maybe they did. But such narratives are largely conjecture. We just do not know and are very unlikely to find out. One of the few certainties is that, long before the period when any reconstruction can be based on written or sculptured records, there *were* seagoing ships, and some of them at least were plying for passengers and cargo in the monsoonal waters of the western Indian Ocean. Scholars of renown have established that there was direct commerce between Babylon, at the head of the Persian Gulf, and India, more than three thousand years before the birth of Christ. Such a commerce would have been impossible without hundreds of years of prior exploration by sea and of slowly nurtured attempts at trading. And the conditions there were ideal —there and nowhere else.

Of course, we have a record that the Egyptian King Snefru sent a fleet of forty ships to Phoenicia, about 3000 B.C., to bring back logs cut in the forests of Lebanon. This was coasting, and short-voyage coasting at that. It is probable that the sailors were Phoenicians and not Egyptians, for the Phoenicians early understood the art of managing ships. The ancient Egyptians had a firm belief that to travel by sea was to cause defilement. We have the evidence of Plutarch that the Egyptian priesthood, at any rate, held themselves aloof from the sea. They were of the expressed opinion that "to sail from Egypt was one of the most unholy of things." This is admittedly no proof in itself that Egyptians did not follow the profession of seafaring. Mohammed declared that "he who twice embarks on the sea is truly an infidel," a sentiment which has been echoed down the ages, not only by Moslems. But Mohammed was a landsman, and so were the Egyptian priests. Among Mohammed's countrymen there had long been skilled seamen who did not share his view.

Before the Phoenicians of the land we now know as Syria were extending their coastwise voyages along the north coast of Africa until they passed the "Pillars of Hercules" (Gibraltar) and set up their farthest outpost at Gades, which is now Cadiz, the ancient peoples of the Persian Gulf—the Sumerians, Elamites, Assyrians, Chaldeans, and Babylonians—must have been proficient at the art of navigation. Ptolemy, Strabo, Pliny, and others make references to their voyages, both military and commercial. Definite proof of a commerce with ports in India is perhaps lacking, but there is a very strong probability, amounting I think to certainty, that such a trade had long been established. The Indian records themselves are so mixed with religious fable that, though great antiquity is claimed—and probably rightly—for Indian navigators, no written proof of their voyages is now forthcoming.

The waters of the Persian Gulf, the waters of Arabia, and the seas which washed the coasts of India were, in the northeast monsoon, the ideal place to develop sailing. Fish were essential foodstuff in all these countries, and fish were plentiful. Open-sea fishermen are good sailors, for they must be if they are to survive. River craft will not do for them, for they must contend with the open sea. It is, I think, most probable that the art of sailing was developed by fishermen working in the waters of the Indian Ocean. Along the coasts of southern Arabia and elsewhere, there were no rivers available to them. They were well aware of the nature of the seasons. There were men who understood something of the regular movements of the stars. Anyone who has spent a northeast monsoon along the southern coasts of Arabia will know how brightly the stars shine there, almost compelling the dullest nonastronomer to take an interest in them. An interest once aroused would lead in time to knowledge, and that knowledge could be used to guide both desert caravans (as it was) and ships at sea, as it was also. The assured good weather, the continuance for weeks and months of a pleasant sailing breeze, and the necessity to go to sea in quest of goods and materials not available in Arabia or along the coasts of Persia encouraged the art of ocean voyaging. Later on, so did the valuable trade in spices.

Consider the sailing conditions of the northwestern Indian Ocean again, for a moment. To state that voyages were made one way with the northeast monsoon, and the other with the southwest, is a little too sweeping a generality. Indeed it is not correct, for the southwest is a season of much bad weather and, when it has set in properly, conditions are often quite unfit for sailing. Sailing traders in the Indian Ocean had to use the good season—the northeast —for their passages *both* ways, taking care to get back to port before the full force of the southwest monsoon broke on them.

This is exactly what the Arab, Persian, and Indian seagoing dhows have done from time immemorial. To sail like this, they had to have a type of vessel which Egyptian conditions—and conditions generally in the Mediterranean—did not produce. The ships had to be good weatherly sailers, fast, good carriers, deep-drafted, and able to go to windward well. In short, they had to be *real* sailing ships. To a vessel setting out from, say, Aden, bound for some emporium in India, the northeast monsoon was not a fair wind. She could not run. The direction in which the ship had to steer was practically due east to reach the rich Malabar coast, a little south of east to reach Ceylon, and north of east toward Cutch and Kathiawar.

To make all such courses, the ship must go to windward. The northeast wind would be upon her port beam and she could not run before it. If she were a good ship, well designed, she would not have to beat. The so-called dhows of all Arabia, of India, and of Persia *are* such ships and must have been so since sailing there began. The big lateen sail is the ideal means of converting wind power into favorable forward motion for a good hull. A dhow with its lateen rig can lie up 4½ points, and even better, to the direction of the wind, which is to say that with the wind at a constant northeast, the navigator in a dhow had the choice of sailing in *any* direc-

tion away from the eyes of the wind, between east-half-north and
north-half-east, or better, right around the compass. To some
degree the precise direction he could steer, close to the wind,
depended upon the minor fluctuations of the monsoon which are
always to be found in the direction of the wind upon the open sea.
So he could quite well sail from Aden to Cochin on one long reach,
with his vessel on the port tack—that is to say, with the wind upon
his port side, and the sail trimmed to keep the ship pointing as near
into the direction of the wind as possible—and then coast upon
all the western side of India, with the wind upon his other beam,
as he willed. When his cargo was completed, he could run home
again, now bounding away like a bird, with the wind filling his
great lateen sail and the yard swung free. The long lateen yard,
cumbersome as it may appear to European eyes, is indeed the ideal
means of setting a big running or a reaching sail, and the dhows of
the Indian Ocean had the qualities of yachts for centuries before
yachts were ever thought of. What they had to avoid was being
caught out in really bad weather, when in any event most of the
ports in India were closed.

Early vessels of the Mediterranean have been the subject of
much learned study, with great thoroughness; but the upshot of
all this—to my mind, at least—is to demonstrate the superiority
of the Indian Ocean ships, at any rate for sailing on long voyages.
The sailing qualities of most Mediterranean craft were poor by
comparison. It is doubtful if they would go to windward at all.
Many of them were primarily craft which were propelled by
sweeps or oars. They could not enjoy a really settled sailing wind.
Many were designed to be hauled up on the beaches, when the
sea was rough, or carried over the land, as they were at Corinth,
for example, where special facilities were provided for such an
operation. The galleys were fast under oars, slim, shallow, narrow-
gutted, and they made good fighting craft. But it is significant that
when that great pioneer, Prince Henry the Navigator, required
seagoing ships of real endurance for his exploratory voyages in the

North Atlantic and toward the Cape of Good Hope in the fifteenth century, he had to develop a satisfactory type himself before his sailors could get very far. Yet he surely had the whole store of seafaring knowledge of the Mediterranean behind him. Prince Henry developed the caravel, in which there is more than a trace of the Indian Ocean dhow.

Be these things as they may, there are written records of great voyages quite early in the story of the Eastern seas, long centuries before any mariner in Europe ever dreamed of getting beyond the sight of land. There are references in the Bible to these early ships and shipping. Isaiah indicates the pride of the Chaldeans and Babylonians in their ships: "Thus saith the Lord, your redeemer, the Holy One of Israel; For your sake I have sent to Babylon, and I will bring down all of them as fugitives, even the Chaldeans, in the ships of their rejoicing." Nebuchadnezzar II (604–561 B.C.) developed the harbor of Teredon for the Indian trade, in the swamps to the west of the Euphrates. Agatharchides, Herodotus, Theophrastus, and Pliny all indicate something of the extent of this Indian Ocean seafaring. Theophrastus, for instance, knew the good qualities of Indian teak for building ships and speaks of teak planks lasting two hundred years.

The military genius of Alexander the Great was attracted by this rich Indian Ocean trade. Babylon was the capital of his eastern empire, and he sought to extend its trade with India. Alexander advanced into India but turned about when his forces reached the river Jhelum, one of the tributaries of the Indus. Here he prepared to march overland back to Persia, but he also planned to send a considerable part of his force by sea, in a great fleet of more than a thousand vessels under the command of his admiral, Nearchus. Some account of Nearchus's voyage has come down to us. Many of the vessels were built by the riverside, but all were designed for use on the open sea. It took the huge fleet almost a year to reach the mouth of the Indus, Alexander with his army marching along with

them as they sailed slowly down toward the sea. The king intended
to march near the coast in order to be near his fleet, but this proved
impossible. Leaving a harbor which must have been very near the
modern Karachi, Nearchus sailed in November in the year 326 B.C.
The northeast monsoon was already with him and he could sail
along pleasantly by the coast, with the wind upon his beam. His
vessels were assembled largely by Indian craftsmen, many of whom
had been brought from the river mouth and other ports for the
purpose.

The places which Nearchus mentions in his narrative have in
general been located, though now known by other names. He made
his voyage by easy stages, calling in from time to time to replenish
stores and food. One to two thousand vessels, all under sail, moving
up the Gulf of Oman, with the picturesque mountains of Baluchistan in the background, the sea a lovely indigo blue and the sky
cobalt, the ships with pennants flying and the noise of martial
trumpets in the air, must have been a grand sight. But Nearchus
paints no pen pictures, except of various natives here and there who
opposed his landings. These "barbarians" he does not praise, though
he mentions that they "were not without courage." Some of them
were covered with "shaggy hair all over their bodies," with nails
long and sharpened like claws, which they used for splitting fire-
wood and such tasks. At a place called Karbine the fleet had to
accept mutton which tasted strongly of fish, for there were no
pastures and the sheep were fed on fish.

The fleet passed Hormuz and Ras Musandam, at the entrance
of the Persian Gulf, and at length came safely to the mouth of the
Euphrates at the head of the Gulf—truly a remarkable voyage.
Other ships, very naturally, kept well out of Nearchus's way. Alexander considered this achievement of Nearchus so good that he
made plans at once for a circumnavigation of the peninsula of
Arabia and the subjugation of all that land. He thereupon set about
the construction of another great fleet, which was to be assembled
at Babylon. Because of the shortage of local woods, many of the

vessels were prefabricated at places as far away as Phoenicia and
Cyprus. Strabo records that "some were in separate pieces, others
in parts fastened together by bolts. These, after being conveyed
to Thapsacus in seven distances of a day's march, were then to be
transported down the river to Babylon. He constructed other
boats in Babylonia from cypress trees in the groves and parks. . . ."
But before Nearchus could take this wonderful fleet of prefabricated vessels to sea, Alexander died.

The subjugation of Arabia at that time would have put great
riches in his grasp, for even then the Sabaeans of southern Arabia
were so affluent, from their control of the Indian Ocean trade and
the aromatics business, that their houses had "doors, walls and roofs
variegated with inlaid ivory, gold, silver, and precious stones," and
they possessed in great quantities "wrought articles in gold and
silver, as couches, tripods, basins, and drinking vessels." *

The next insight we get into the ancient commerce of the Indian
Ocean is from the famous *Periplus of the Erythraean Sea.* This is
a sort of mariners' Directory of the Indian Ocean, compiled by a
Greek master mariner or merchant adventurer, of unknown name,
during the first century of the Christian Era. Mariners' directories
of this sort have long been in use in that ocean, among the Persians,
Arabs, Indians, and Chinese. I have before me as I write just such
a directory, in Arabic, for the masters of Arab dhows in the trade to
East Africa. It is weather-stained, ancient, much used, and not
verbose. It describes landmarks and gives silhouette pictures of
the more important of them, and it gives distances, courses, and
directions for entering such places as Berbera, Haifun, Mogadishu,
Kismayu, Lamu, Malindi, Mombasa, Zanzibar, and the delta of
the Rufiji River. It is prepared by shipmasters for shipmasters' use

The *Periplus of the Erythraean Sea* is a much more human document. Nothing is known of its compiler other than the surmise that
he was a Roman subject, a Greek domiciled in Egypt, who seized

* Strabo.

the opportunity given by Roman expansion to probe the sailing and the commercial mysteries of the Indian Ocean. He had been preceded there by at least one Roman, who was drifted away in a small boat in bad weather from a point somewhere beyond the Straits of Bab-el-Mandeb and in fifteen days—we are told—found himself in Ceylon. The famous Hippalus, who gave his name to the monsoon winds, must have followed soon afterward. Hippalus is generally hailed as the "discoverer" of the monsoons, but he did not discover them. He merely observed their use and introduced them to early European navigators. They were already well known to Eastern seamen.

The *Periplus* gives interesting descriptions of the various ports of call on a voyage from the Red Sea toward the Persian Gulf, to India, and down the east coast of Africa. The publicity given by Hippalus to the good conditions for sailing in the Indian Ocean had led to a sudden increase in the demand for Eastern goods in Rome. For the time being, the Red Sea route was dominated by Rome, which gave ready access to an apparently insatiable market. "Gold, and silver, and precious stones, and pearls, and fine linen, and purple, and silk, and scarlet, and all sweet wood, and all manner vessels of ivory, and all manner vessels of most precious wood, and of brass and iron and marble, and cinnamon, and odours, and ointments, and frankincense, and wine, and oil, and fine flour, and wheat, and beasts, and sheep, and horses, and chariots, and slaves," as the writer in The Revelation describes the great Eastern trade of Rome when bewailing the burning of that city, "wherein were made rich all that had ships in the sea." The burning of Rome and the later plague put an end, in time, to this great trade, which had indeed caused a considerable drainage of Roman treasure to pay for it. It was almost all an import trade, with very little export. The Roman ladies had a great liking for fine raiment from India, and for cosmetics and all such things.

The writer of the *Periplus* had obviously not heard of the burning of Rome and was quite happy describing the sources of its

Eastern commerce. To him, Cape Guardafui was the "Cape of Spices," and like all the other shipmasters who sailed in this brief Roman trade, he had obviously only the haziest idea where the rich spices originated. The Arabs carefully hid the source of the richest trade from the Romans, doing this so successfully that, though Roman ships were then frequently upon the Malabar coast and they knew Ceylon, they never learned, apparently, that cinnamon was produced there and always obtained their supplies through Arab middlemen. This was despite the fact that Greek merchants settled, for the time being, in Indian ports, and sought to eliminate other middlemen. Arab dominance in the Indian Ocean trade was strong and subtle, and they preserved many secrets until the final coming of the European round the Cape of Good Hope, fourteen centuries later.

The shipmaster-writer of the *Periplus* knew the Berber coast well, but he thought it was the source of cinnamon and of frankincense. Frankincense, a resin exuded from a certain kind of tree, was a valuable item in ancient trade. It was much used for religious ceremonies. At the place now known as Haifun, not far to the south of Cape Guardafui—and still an important port of call for dhows in the Arabian–East African trade—he found "slaves of the better sort," and tortoise shell and, again, cinnamon. He goes on:

The voyage to all these far-side market-towns [the towns of the Somali coast] is made from Egypt about the month of July. And ships are customarily fitted out from places across this sea [the Indian Ocean] bringing to these far-side market-towns the products of their own places—wheat, rice, clarified butter, sesame oil, cotton cloth, girdles, and honey from the reed called sacchari. Some make the journey especially to these market-towns, and others exchange their cargoes while sailing along the coast.

He mentions two ports in northwestern India as sending ships in this trade. The cargo he describes is almost precisely that which I saw being exchanged by Arab dhows at Haifun and along the coast of Somaliland in 1939. The honey then was found from Hadhramaut, and so was the clarified butter, called ghee. Ghee is made by heating butter for some hours and then removing the oil, which is then put into skins or earthen pots. The chronicler goes on to recount the trade of the ports of Mogadishu (which he calls Serapion), Brava, Lamu, and so to Pemba and Zanzibar, to which he gives the name of Menouthias. Here he found "sewed boats and canoes hollowed from single logs," and the inhabitants caught fish in wicker baskets, a method which is still practiced there.

Along this coast live men of piratical habits, very great of stature, and under separate chiefs for each place [the *Periplus* continues]. The Mapharitic chief governs it by some ancient right, that subjects it to the sovereignty of the state which has become the first in Arabia. And the people of Muza [Mocha, the coffee port in the Yemen] now hold it under his authority, and send thither many large ships using Arab captains and agents, who are familiar with them, and know the whole coast and understand the language.

This tribute to the antiquity of Arab seafaring in the Indian Ocean is most interesting. A right which was "ancient" in the first century must have been old indeed. The Maphiritic chief was the sheikh of the Ma'afir tribe in southern Arabia, and Mocha was then the tribe's chief port.

The Romans secured ivory in large quantities, palm oil, and tortoise shell from these distant ports and landed in them "hatchets and daggers and awls, and various kinds of glass; and at some places, a little wine and wheat, not for trade but to get the good will of the savages." This is a description of the trade goods which were used in Africa and, later, in the South Seas, and which in some remote parts are still used.

Beyond Zanzibar and the "markets of Azania" the chronicler did not go, for "the unexplored ocean curves round toward the west . . . and mingles with the western sea." He must have known at least the tradition of a sea route connecting the Indian and Atlantic Oceans. But who had gone that way? There is a persistent legend that at least one group of Phoenicians had circumnavigated Africa, and the Greek geographers were convinced that there was open ocean to the south of that continent. Herodotus gives an account of an alleged Phoenician expedition which took two years to sail around Africa, from the Red Sea to the Mediterranean, about six hundred years before the birth of Christ. The Guinea coast on the western side of Africa was slightly known to the Greeks and the Romans.

A fortunate Phoenician ship *may* have sailed around Africa, but I very much doubt it. Herodotus, though always interesting, is sometimes not a reliable informant. It is true that, from the point of view of the actual sailing involved, the passage around Africa from east to west is simpler than the other way, and it could have been made, if not by the Phoenicians in their weaker Mediterranean ships, at any rate in a well-built Indian dhow, or in an Arab one, if she had good fortune. The winds at the time of the northeast monsoon are favorable almost the whole way, and, once clear of the Mozambique Channel, the ship would be helped by the Agulhas current to weather the Cape of Good Hope. But she would have to be inordinately fortunate to get around that long headland, where no sheltered harbors were available and the seas were enough to cause even large and well-found steamers to go missing, more than a thousand years later. Again, it would hardly have been possible to coast back around all Africa: once blown off the coast and out into the zone of the northeast trade winds of the Atlantic Ocean, what chance would a vessel have of reaching port again, without a greater knowledge of methods of ocean navigation than then was possible?

The author of the *Periplus*, here at any rate, was doubtless passing on some hearsay. But his Directory is nonetheless interesting for that, and most of his facts stand. Indeed, the modern world still gets its small supply of frankincense by means of Arab dhows which carry it to Aden, and both Arab and Indian sailing ships and merchants are still to be found carrying on almost precisely the trades which the inquisitive Greco-Roman first reported, nineteen hundred years ago.

CHAPTER V

The Argosies from Incense Land

A sort of "frankincense trust" in South Arabia is probably as old as trade itself, for the products of "Incense Land" were the source of great riches. The Dhofar mountains in the neighborhood of the Kuria Muria Islands, the Hadhramaut Valley, and part of the Red Sea coast of Somaliland in Africa were the main sources of the valuable incense. To the ancient world this territory was a true Eldorado, "sought by the great empires and fought for by every Arab tribe that managed to enrich itself by trading incense for temple-service on the Nile or Euphrates, on Mount Zion, or in Persia, India, or China."

It is difficult today to appreciate just how important and valuable the trade in incense was, or to understand why anyone should become excited over the odoriferous qualities of a gum exuded by a tree growing in what are nowadays considered such remote places. Frankincense was regarded as holy. The Bible has many references to it and to its uses. The sacred incense used among the Hebrews was formed of "sweet spices . . . with pure frankincense; of each a like weight" and the result was regarded as "pure and holy." * Frankincense was stored in special rooms in the temple at

* Exodus 30:34–35.

Jerusalem, where it was kept under priestly guard. The Song of
Solomon speaks of "myrrh and frankincense": "Who is it that
cometh out of the wilderness like pillars of smoke, perfumed with
myrrh and frankincense, with all powders of the merchant?"

The Queen of Sheba gave King Solomon a "very great store" of
spices and precious stones, as she well could do, for, at the time, she
controlled the frankincense trust. The three wise men from the
east brought gifts of gold, frankincense, and myrrh to the infant
Saviour at Bethlehem, and these things signified the kingship, the
divinity, and the healing powers of the Child.

The use of frankincense and other spices, balms, and incense
originated along the shores of the Indian Ocean and spread at
least as far as ancient Rome. Pliny observed with disapproval the
vast quantity of perfumes burned by the Emperor Nero at the bier
of his wife Poppaea.

Then let us only take into account the vast number of funerals that
are celebrated throughout the whole world each year, [Pliny pointed
out] and the heaps of odors that are piled up in honor of the bodies of
the dead; the vast quantities, too, that are offered to the gods in single
grains. . . . How large a portion, I should like to know, of all these
perfumes really comes to the gods of heaven?

Herodotus, the Father of History, has a lot to say about the use
of spices and incense among the Egyptians, particularly for embalming. He described something of the methods used when they
deal with a body of the "better sort."

[They] make a cut along the flank with a sharp Ethiopian stone, and
take out the contents of the abdomen, which they then cleanse, washing it thoroughly with palm wine, and again frequently with an in-
fusion of powdered aromatics. After this they fill the cavity with the
purest bruised myrrh, with cassia, and every other sort of spicery except frankincense, and sew up the opening. Then the body is placed
in natrum for seventy days, and covered entirely over. After the expiration of that space of time, which must not be exceeded, the body
is washed and wrapped round, from head to foot, with bandages of

fine linen cloth smeared over with gum, and in this state it is given back to the relations, who enclose it in a wooden case which they have made for the purpose, shaped into the figure of a man. . . . Such is the most costly way of embalming the dead.

The frankincense was kept for burning at the bier, in offering to the gods. The Egyptians, Persians, and other early civilizations, and the Greeks and Romans, when they learned about these customs, made great use of fragrant ointments. The Persians (according to Pliny) particularly delighted in soaking themselves in such things, to "counteract the bad odors which are produced by dirt." The ladies of Egypt knew more about cosmetics than any make-up artist in Hollywood today. The formula for one "cream" which has been unearthed demanded an extensive array of ingredients, including "myrobalanus, costus, amomum, cinnamon, comacum, cardamom, spikenard, marum, myrrh, cassia, storax, ladanum, opobalsamum, Syrian sweet-rush and Syrian calamus, oenanthe, malabathrum, serichatum, cypress, aspralathus, panax, saffron, cypirus, sweet marjoram, lotus, honey, and wine." The whole East had to be scoured to secure such products and obviously there were fortunes to be made in a trade so artificial, then as now. Myrrh came from trees, just as frankincense does, but it was much more freely available. The modern practice of bulk selling, if not of bulk buying, was known in this trade in aromatics in remote times. Generally the local ruler demanded that all myrrh, or all frankincense, or whatever other product could be marketed in his area, should be brought to him and sold at a fixed price, always very low. Then he sold to the merchants at a very high price. By the time any of these things reached their wealthy consumers, the prices were fantastic. Rigid rules were enforced in the gathering of frankincense. Various ports were appointed as receiving centers where, for instance, all frankincense had to be taken. Anyone found taking any elsewhere was summarily put to death.

The spices and aromatics, important as they were, were one branch only of the great and flourishing trade of the Indian Ocean,

from time immemorial. Cargoes changed hands along the open
roadsteads of the Malabar coast (which were usable only during
the period of the northeast monsoon), at Aden and at Hormuz, at
Makalla, and at Mocha, and along the ports of the Gulf of Aden and
Somaliland. The Arabs were the leaders in this trade and in the
slave and ivory trades from East African ports. They established
colonies and trading centers in India and all down the African coast
as far as the monsoon blows. They knew Madagascar and Malaya.
They had a great emporium as far distant as Canton, in China. They
knew the sources of the gold of Sofala and profited greatly from
this trade.

All these pursuits and the migrations of people related to them
required ships, and the monsoonal waters of the Indian Ocean were
crisscrossed by great fleets of sail-blown argosies, long centuries—
probably thousands of years—before Vasco da Gama sailed around
the Cape of Good Hope. So great was the Arab share in all this
trade and seafaring that for many centuries the legend persisted
in Europe that Arabia itself was the fabulous source of many of the
costly goods involved—a legend which the Arabs themselves fostered. If possible competitors were misled into believing in a wondrous *Arabia Felix*, they would be less likely to find the real sources
of Semitic wealth.

Despite its obvious fables, *The Arabian Nights* gives a fair idea
of the kind of fantastic voyages the early Arab mariners must have
made. Most of Sindbad's stories have at least a foundation of truth,
and the voyages he describes were real voyages. The original Sindbad might have been a member of one of the great Arab trading
families, such as still exist, which send sons and brothers far and
wide over the Indian Ocean and its lands, in quest of trade. Arab
trade is far more personal than much of the trade we know in other
lands, and the family is a more self-contained unit. For example,
immediately prior to the war of 1939 to 1945, when I was in Kuwait,
there were prominent families there which sent younger sons as

Pearl merchant at work, Persian Gulf

Sudanese slave, a first-rate
sailor

Arab dhow captain

Turkish mate of a Red Sea
dhow

A merchant from Sur

Method of using the sweep

Sailing up the horrible Rufiji, in Tanganyika

far as Berbera, Jiddah, Bombay, and even to New York and Manchester on occasion, and thought nothing of it. The custom then was, and had been from ancient times, that a member of the family should look after the family interests wherever those interests were important—at Berbera in the caravan season; at Bombay, Aden, Basra, and Kuwait, the year round; at Makalla in the Hadhramaut when the big date-carrying dhows were calling there; or anywhere else that prospects for trade appeared sufficient to warrant the expense. One son of the well-known al-Hamad family, before he was twenty-five years old, knew all these places, and the caravan route across Arabia to Mecca and Jiddah, which he had traveled both by camel and by automobile. He could sell pearls in Bombay or in Paris and control the family's trade interests in Jiddah, Damascus, Cairo, or Liverpool. He spoke excellent English and French, for he had received some education in a college in Iraq and further at a university in Syria, and he was master of several Indian languages, as well as his own Arabic, and Persian. He had had many adventures; indeed, he might well have been a Sindbad. I should have said, he *was* one.

The Arabs then did not use banking. There were no banks in Kuwait before the oilmen came, and no banks in King Ibn Saud's Arabia. The ruling sheiks and emirs acted as bankers, and so did the leading members of the great trading families themselves. Indian rupees, Austrian thalers (minted in San Francisco and in London for the purpose) and Arabian silver reals were the coinage, and gold was welcome anywhere. Neither was insurance in general use, or charter parties, or any other of the manifold written paraphernalia of shipping which generally accompany the movement of trade and ships in other waters. Hence there is a scarcity of written records. But down the centuries there are records enough. A bill of lading has been found, dating from three thousand years ago, showing the cargo carried by a large Arab ship which had been absent on a voyage to Dilmun for two years, on charter to the temple of Nin-Gal of Ur. This vessel discharged on the quayside at Ur, among other things, "gold, copper, ore, ivory, precious woods, and fine stone for making statues and vases."

Whenever ancient travelers reached the Indian Ocean, they noted its great sailing commerce. When the Greek invaders reached India, they found an ancient and highly organized society, with a great trade, and the teak of Malabar was already going into the hulls of seagoing ships by the thousand. This teak was the only good shipbuilding timber to be had for the building of large ships round the whole littoral, from the southern tip of India on the east, round the western coast of India, the coast of Baluchistan, the Persian Gulf and all Arabia, and down the coast of Africa as far as the Zambesi River. There were good forests in Africa, but not near the coasts; or the trade to Arabia and the Gulf in mangrove poles from the deltas of the great rivers and from Lamu would not have been so important. The ships required for the carriage of Malabar teak and cordage and the other needs of the shipbuilding centers of the Persian Gulf and of south Arabia must have formed a considerable fleet by themselves. They still do.

Ibn Batuta, the greatest of the Moslem wanderers, Marco Polo, Idrisi the map maker, and Masudi the encyclopedist, all give their evidence of the extent of Indian Ocean commerce. So do several classical Chinese writers. Ibn Batuta, who left his native Tangier as a young man and traveled fearlessly almost throughout the known world, was for a time a royal official in the Maldive Islands, when shipwreck temporarily marooned him there. The wanderer, who was no stranger to shipwreck and other forms of adversity, had been stranded on the coast when a junk with all his goods and slave girls sailed off and left him there. This sort of thing was commonplace and he soon consoled himself by marrying the daughter of the vizier and three other comely young women.

"It is easy to get married in these islands," he wrote. He used his power to try to induce the women in the islands to wear clothes and attend the mosque more regularly. But he failed and, the visier becoming suspicious of him, he thought it expedient to move on. The Maldives exported a great quantity of coconuts and coir for making rope to the ports of southern India, and this is their trade until this day.

Ibn Batuta visited Ceylon, was wrecked on the Coromandel coast, almost died of fever, sailed back to the Malabar coast, sailed to Chittagong and then to Java. This last was a passage of forty days. After visiting ports in the Malay Peninsula, he went on to China. Later he wandered through much of West Africa, the Sudan, and Arabia, and into Spain. It is obvious that in the Indian Ocean he was able to take ship freely for a host of places, populous and wealthy, which were to remain closed to European commerce for almost another two hundred years. He wrote interesting accounts of his journeys. In these he mentions casually that, when the ship sailed off and left him at the Maldives, he heard later from two of his slaves who got back to Calicut that "the ruler of Java the Less had taken my slave girls, my goods had been seized by various hands, and my companions were scattered to China, Sumatra, and Bengal."

Ibn Batuta also sailed down the African coast with the annual passage of the trading dhows, visiting Mogadishu, Mombasa, and ports as far south as Kilwa, where he heard of the gold-trade port, Sofala, said to be two weeks' sail to the south.

Marco Polo once made a most interesting voyage from China to the Persian Gulf, with long stopovers in Java, Sumatra, and Ceylon. The passage from China to Java occupied three months and the whole progress was extremely leisurely. Marco Polo had sailed in a Chinese ship so large that it carried 600 passengers, and he records that all but 18 of these died from the hardships of the passage and from fevers on the way. It would be unfair to ascribe all these deaths to the ship, though she must have been woefully overcrowded. A stay of almost a half year was made somewhere in Sumatra, where a fortress had to be constructed to keep the hostile natives at bay. Some of the six hundred might have died there. The ship was a special one carrying a princess of the blood, by name Cocachin—said to have been seventeen and very beautiful—who was to be betrothed in Persia. But while she was at sea, her proposed husband died. However, she promptly married his son and, very probably, lived happily ever afterward. After that voyage, a jaunt from Hormuz back to Venice was nothing in the lives of the Polo family.

The Portuguese found the Arabs in undisputed control of the Indian Ocean trade, when at last the European burst into that great sea at the end of the fifteenth century. Not the Portuguese, nor the Dutch, the British, or the French after them, not the opening of the Suez Canal nor the coming of great ocean liners, speeding across the ocean in days, nor the air age, nor wars—not any of these things put an end to the great sailing commerce of the Indian Ocean. In the East, much of so-called progress is known as a brash and destructive substitute for unnecessary and, in the end, wasteful change. The argosies of Incense Land still sail and they still make ocean voyages, though they carry no spices and little myrrh and frankincense now, and precious little gold. They remain important in their own trade, as they always did, and the great steel vessels from Europe and America hurry by upon their rigorous schedules, in a new world of their own. To the Indian Ocean mariner, it may well be a passing world. After all, it is very new, and obviously already out of gear. The world and the way of life the sailing Arabs and the Indians know has endured for some time. While a teak tree grows in Malabar and cotton can be woven into sails and a compass needle swings, they can sail.

As for the great liners, any blow at the complex economic and political structure from which they spring, and only under which they may survive, can put an end to them. The sailor in the wandering argosy knows that quite well.

CHAPTER VI

In an Indian Ocean Dhow

When I first heard of the survival of this interesting sailing commerce in the Indian Ocean, I decided that, when I could, I would go there and look into it, for this was an obvious and most interesting manner of actually living with much of the history of that absorbing ocean. In the middle of 1938 this was possible, and I went to Aden in South Arabia, as a good place to begin. A French liner landed me at Steamer Point, and Aden there was no different from any other modern port in Eastern waters. But farther up the harbor was Ma'alla, where the ships had probably changed little in the preceding thousand years. So long as one kept one's face toward the sea, the modern age was not begun. Ashore, the bitumin roads and the fuel tanks, the blaring of the taxicabs taking passengers on a run to the reservoir and the village of Sheikh Othman, and the rattle of winches aboard the steamships off Steamer Point were reminders enough that this was mid-twentieth century. But at Ma'alla there were fifty dhows jostling by the waterfront, and more hauled up on the smelly beach for repair, and their commerce was still much as it had been in Biblical times.

These were the dhows engaged in the distributing trade from Aden, taking the goods landed from the ocean steamers to the smaller outports of the Yemen and the Hadhramaut, across the Red Sea to Djibouti and Zeilah, and to Berbera in British Somaliland, and bringing the cargoes of these ports for transshipment.

They traded also well into the Red Sea, as far as the south wind
blew there. But they were not ocean-going dhows. The largest was
perhaps of 70 tons. They were almost all undecked, with one large
lateen sail. Though many showed two masts, the second mast was
little used. Many of the dhows were double-ended and all looked to
be fast vessels, but they did not, at first sight, strike me as being particularly seaworthy. I noticed that their crews always rigged up a
sort of extra bulwark of matting as they pulled away from the little
quay to go to sea, and I thought that they must have an assurance
of good weather if they considered these mats stout enough to keep
out the sea.

I learned later that indeed they did have good weather, for this
was the early northeast season. When the weather was bad, they
did not sail. Cargo damage was rare.

My purpose was to ship in one of the large Arab vessels in the
trade down the east coast of Africa, or to India, but I soon learned
that Aden itself no longer had a fleet of these. Only a few Indian
dhows still traded directly across the Indian Ocean from the Malabar coast and from Cutch, and none was then in port. It was the first
week of November, and too early. In a month or so, the annual
visit from the fleet of the big Kuwait *booms* was expected. These
were the large sailing vessels which brought dates from the Basra
River to hawk round the Hadhramaut coast and to Somaliland, and
they called at Aden, when the dates were sold, to embark salt and
trade goods for the ancient trading run down Africa. They were
accustomed to empty their date cargoes and to beach at Ma'alla, to
have their undersides looked after there. When they came, they
would be in port for several weeks.

So I went first for a sort of trial run in the Red Sea with a little
double-ended dhow which was very fast and very beautiful, and
which nearly killed me. Like all true Arab dhows, she was without
accommodation of any kind. There was a tiny deck aft by the tiller,
and there I slept on a piece of ancient carpet beneath the stars. Her
crew of seven slept on top of the cargo. She sailed by day inside

the reefs, for the way was dangerous in the coastal waters of the
Red Sea. She had no lights, no charts, no log and no log line, no
anchor save a grapnel and a handy piece of stone. Her fresh water
was stored in an ancient drum, which was kept in the sun, and the
marine creatures living in this were interesting but not palatable.
There was no place to cook but a small firebox, which was kept
forward, and there was little fuel and almost nothing to cook. It
was the fasting season of Ramadhan. The sun roasted us by day
and the nights were cold, but it was, I think, the drinking water
which got me down.

The captain was a nice young man from the Yemen, the mate was
a former Turk, and the crew included a slave from the Sudan and
several boys. The little dhow—she was 55 feet long—sailed like
a bird and the lateen sail pulled beautifully. But she leaked a lot
and she smelled abominably, for she had recently been smothered
in fish oil. She had no pumps, but the water was baled out of her
with an old leather bucket and a kerosene can, and poured over the
side through a trough. The reek of this bilge water was almost visible, and I could not become used to it. I had stupidly taken it for
granted that I was a person inured to maritime hardship, merely
because I had been a whaler in the Antarctic and had been a few
times around Cape Horn. But that little double-ended dhow found
me out.

We went to Kamaran and to a port called Gizan, which was full
of lovely dhows; and later I visited Jiddah, and Port Sudan, and
returned to Aden via Mocha in the Yemen. I was still rather weak
from the aftereffects of dysentery and a few fevers when I reached
Aden again, but it was December then and the Kuwait fleet was in.
These big ocean-goers were obviously in a very different class from
the pretty little *sambuks* and double-enders of the Red Sea. There
were more than two dozen in the harbor, most of them large
double-enders with built-up stemposts, carried up from a raking
bow, and two enormous masts, of which the main was a whole tree.
These were the *booms*, a distinctive Persian Gulf type, said to have

come down in true descent from the Indian Ocean traders of thousands of years ago. The Persians and the Arabs of old liked the double-ended hull for its greater safety in the sea and its economy in timber, and the sea had not changed its habits. The big fellows were well-kept vessels, and the smallest was about 100 tons. The largest in port then was perhaps 250, but there was one 300-tonner still in the trade. Several of these *booms* had part cargoes of Basra dates, which they carried in large round baskets, made of matting. Times were bad, and they had not been able to sell as much as they had expected at Berbera and along the Hadhramaut. These date cargoes were of such importance and had been for so long, that the size of all the deep-sea dhows was invariably spoken of in terms of their capacity to stow round baskets of Iraqi dates. No other measurement was used, or known, among the Arabs.

In addition to the *booms,* there were several large vessels of different type. These had sterns which were beautifully carved in oiled teak, and rows of square ports across their shapely counters, and small quarter galleries. They looked like the galleons of hundreds of years ago, except for their rig. These vessels were without the long stempost of the *boom* (which they told me was a phallic symbol, or had been). Instead, they had rounded cutwaters finishing in a graceful stemhead, which was carved like the beak of a medieval galley. The vessels with the ornate sterns were called *baggalas. Booms* and *baggalas* were rigged the same. The difference between them was one of hull form. They were about the same size.

I wished to ship in one of the *baggalas* as soon as I saw these stately vessels, but my friends the al-Hamads had no interest in any of these. They operated a fleet of *booms,* and so it was arranged that I should take passage in one of these. She was loading salt and general goods—rice and flour in sacks, cotton stuffs, sugar, ghee in used kerosene cans—for the passage toward Zanzibar, and she would trade on the way. She was to load further cargo and embark passengers along the Hadhramaut and the Mahra coasts before heading south. Zanzibar was to be the final port of discharge in

Africa. From there, she would load mangrove poles somewhere along the mouths of the great rivers of Tanganyika, for the return passage to Arabia.

So I joined this ship. I did not know her name and it had not been mentioned, but her captain was a fine young man, a hawk-nosed Arab of Nejd who had been at sea since he was eight years old and obviously was a first-rate sailor, merchant, and disciplinarian. I went aboard on December 9, 1938, at anchorage off Ma'alla in Aden, and the same night we went to sea. Her captain did not come with her then but handed her over to the mate for the run to Makalla, main port of the Hadhramaut. He was going there by airplane the next day, to steal a march on his rival dhowmasters and round up all the migrants bound for Zanzibar. This migrant trade between the Hadhramaut and Zanzibar and the ports along the Kenya coast was a very ancient one, but there were restrictions nowadays—some nonsense about passenger lists, vaccinations, identity papers, and that sort of thing—and the two dozen *booms* and *baggalas* had difficulty in finding passengers enough to fill them. Since none of the dhows had any accommodation except a bit of an airless cabin beneath the poop, I thought the passenger trade could hardly concern them much. I was wrong.

The *boom* I sailed in was a most interesting vessel, and there I remained for the next half year and more, learning all I could. The conditions I was able to observe were, roughly, those which had existed through the preceding thousand years, at least. She was manned by some thirty stalwart fellows, many of them freed slaves, others Persians, but all acknowledging the Persian Gulf port of Kuwait as their home. Kuwait was obviously the twentieth-century home of the ocean-going dhow, and I determined to visit there. Each sailor in the *boom* kept a large sea chest on the poop, which was arranged with chests two, and even four, deep along both sides and across the break. These chests held the men's own trade goods for sale in the African bazaars, for from time immemorial they had been accustomed to bring their own ventures. This was part of their

reward for the voyage, but many of them could not afford to fill
their chests and traded on credit, which allowed them little reward.

In addition to the crew, several passengers were already aboard.
These were traders in their own right, regular Sindbads, who dealt
in haberdashery, perfumes, and the cheaper kinds of cigarettes.
All these things they had obtained, probably on credit, at the
Crater, in Aden. They were Arabs from the port of Sur, not Kuwait
Arabs. There were no Kuwait passengers. The Suri passengers were
armed with daggers, and one had a sword and a shield. He looked
rather fierce. No one else was armed and there were no arms on
board, apart from these few personal weapons.

These Suri merchants and I occupied a piece of the poop near
the wheel. There was a bench here, shaped roughly round the
counter, and there was room on this for four men to sleep, head to
feet. The captain gave me 6 feet of this bench for myself, before
he went off to board his airplane. The mate had another 6 feet.
Some of the Suri slept on the deck nearby. They had chests, which
were kept apart from those of the sailors, and they also had goods
stored somewhere in the mysterious great cabin underneath the
poop. I looked in there only once. It stank, and very large cock-
roaches scampered there. What else might be down there I did
not know, but the place was not inviting.

Fresh water was carried in two large wooden tanks. The sea
was used for all toilet purposes. Sanitary arrangements were primitive but efficient. They consisted merely of four or five boxes slung
outboard and secured to the bulwarks, and the bottom of each box
had planks enough only to keep the squatting occupant from falling
through. When nature called, the mariners climbed into a box and
squatted there, facing outboard. Afterward, they hauled up water
from the sea in a tin kept by the box for the purpose, washed themselves methodically with their left hands, and climbed back inboard
again. When a crowd of passengers came aboard, more boxes were
hung over the side. It was all very simple.

Cooking was done at a firebox, and there was a proper cook.

The *boom* had a capstan, a steering wheel, a ship's bell, and an Indian spirit compass. Most of these things were from a junk yard at Bombay which, apparently, specializes in such items of sailing-ship equipment, securing them from broken-up and wrecked old ships.

In addition to the cook and the carpenter, the crew included a boatswain and a boatswain's mate, four quartermasters (who did all the steering), and a captain's steward. There was also a second mate, who was the captain's younger brother, under training to become a captain himself. The mate was not from the captain's family and would never enjoy a permanent command in the big dhows unless by some freak he made money enough to induce a merchant to put up the rest of the finance, so that he could buy one.

I did not know all these things as the dark mariners, chanting and stamping their enormous, horny feet, manhandled the longboat aboard and hoisted the tremendous lateen yard. This yard was 105 feet long, and the over-all length of the *boom* was the same. The lateen yards were pieces of some pliable Indian tree, fished and lashed together so that they were tremendously strong. Pieces could be removed from each yard to shorten it, in bad weather, and there were sails of different sizes. Neither mast was supported by any sort of permanent rigging. The main leaned forward, the better to swing the lateen yard when going about. The few stays used to support the mast when the sail was set were lengths of coir rope set up with tackles, and these were shifted every time the sail was trimmed. If the masts would not stand by themselves, so much the worse for them, but the main was a solid tree.

We sailed from Aden quietly on the night of December 9, and were at Makalla ten days later. The northeast monsoon blew right into the Gulf of Aden, but the big vessel lay up to the wind beautifully and ghosted along in the quiet water by the land. Once she was forced a little too close inshore and the mate tacked her, to get out of it. This was the only time I saw her tacked at sea. On all other occasions she wore round, which is to say that she ran off before the wind and the big lateen yard was swung laboriously by the sailors as the ship was before the wind. To tack her meant to throw the lateen flat aback, which set up a serious pressure on both the yard and the mast. But she spun round like a top, and the actual maneuver was no more trouble than wearing. She was round without losing her way, but I could see the mate was relieved that nothing had parted.

All the coast of Arabia in those parts was grim and mountainous, the mountains looking very old and fierce and distorted as if they had been flung there by a Creator in a hurry. Far inland, there was a hazy vista of table-topped giants massed one behind the other as if daring the traveler to proceed against them, and there was nowhere any water but the sea, and there was never rain. Every day there blew a pleasant sailing breeze and the ship slipped along delightfully under ideal conditions, apart from the smell of her fish-oiled sides and the appalling stench of bilge water when she was baled out. We ate unleavened bread at the crack of dawn, with a little oversweet tea, always served in very small glasses, to wash it down. Then at midmorning was the main meal, which was usually of rice and fish. The fish was caught as we went along. The evening meal was taken just after sundown. On the poop we all ate at a large mat spread between the sea chests, each man crouching as best he might and eating carefully with the fingers of the right hand only. After we had eaten, the sailors ate there, too.

All ate the same sort of food. There was water to drink. Several times a day we had the very sweet tea, or bitter coffee in even tinier cups, and the coffee was flavored with cardamoms. We showed no lights and needed none, for no shipping came there except small fishing craft, equally unlighted, and other dhows. All big dhows were bound in the same direction, as this was the time for moving along the Gulf to get to windward of Cape Guardafui, the ancient Cape of Spices. Even if there were no cargoes or passengers to pick up at places like Makalla and as-Shihr, the ship would still have to get out of the Gulf of Aden, and the route would be the same.

Like the Red Sea dhow, she was piloted by eye. No charts were
used at that stage of the voyage. Her safety was in the mate's well-
trained eyes, and he knew those waters. The visibility was always
good, and he was well aware of the dangers.

At Makalla she took in further cargo in the shape of ghee, Hadhramaut honey, and cooking stones—flat stones used for pounding
grains and suchlike culinary jobs, the Arab counterpart of an American electric mixing machine—and the sailors filled their chests
with fans and the local basketware. The captain's steward laid in
a good supply of these things. He also had a venture in aviators'
caps for children. These were made in Japan, from artificial leather.
His other goods included a gross of minute bottles of rosewater,
some dozens of gay turbans, Japanese cotton vests, printed sarongs,
and packaged cigarettes bearing the brands of famous companies,
which had never been nearer any of the companies' warehouses
than the stern of an Aden camel. He amused himself by removing
the rosewater from the tiny bottles, adding more water and no
roses, and putting the mixture back into four times the number of
bottles which were even more minute. He was a nice fellow from
somewhere in the interior of Persia. He suffered from trachoma and
looked forward to the time when we would have some women passengers aboard, for he declared that no medicine half so much
benefited his poor eyes as good human milk.

Few passengers offered at picturesque Makalla and we moved
on without delay to as-Shihr, our Nejdi captain going there by
bus and camel, for no airplane flew as far as that. As-Shihr was
an open roadstead with a surf running on the beach, and the surf-
boats were sewn. The *boom* herself was iron-fastened, like all the
other twentieth-century Arab dhows. I had not seen a sewn boat
before, but the Arabs said this type was good in the surf and more
resilient than an iron-fastened vessel. There were ten *booms* at
anchor off as-Shihr, one of them a Persian. All were in the East
African trade.

Here we embarked 200 passengers, a feat I would have believed impossible if I had not seen it done. The passengers came at the ship in the sewn boats from all directions, and, when close by, each endeavored to heave something over the rail—preferably a piece of his belongings, if he had any belongings. Then he leaped over the rail himself as quickly as he could and, lighting on the place where his gear had fallen, immediately claimed that piece of the deck as his for the passage down to Mogadishu, or to Mombasa, or Zanzibar, or wherever else he thought he was going. One party of forty Bedu had their belongings in one communal bundle, but this they did not heave over the rail. They were dignified men, lithe and gaunt, clad in black rags, with smears of indigo over their chests. They were armed with curved daggers in silver scabbards. If they had nothing else, they had a belt and a dagger. They had recently come in from some stricken valley and were new to the very idea of the sea. They looked around at first with astonishment, but quickly settled down. I saw them stuffing old paper in their ears, to prevent seasickness.

Other passengers included young businessmen, some tradesmen, a few old beggars, and a *seyyid* (descendant of the Prophet, a sort of holy man, whose holiness was mainly shown by his disdain for work). He was bound for Mombasa to collect dues. There were also some boys, several whole families, including their goats, and a whole *harim* which was bound to Zanzibar. The members of the *harim* came aboard when it was dark. They were at once bundled into the noisome great cabin down below, and the scuttle was locked on them. Women were kept in their place aboard the Kuwait *boom,* and that was the last I saw of them until they landed in Africa, many weary weeks afterward. There were several blind men, almost every one of whom had a small boy or two to lead him and to do his begging. All the passengers except the distinguished merchants living on the poop provided their own food. The fare from anywhere along the Hadhramaut coast to anywhere in East Africa was about $3, and an extra $1 if they consumed the ship's food.

We had a feast on the poop to celebrate the arrival of the passengers whom the captain had rounded up. It was a good feast. We had a small sheep roasted whole and stuffed with ghee-soaked rice, hard-boiled eggs, and plums, and the hors d'oeuvres were a chicken and a plaice apiece; afterward, we had bananas and sweetmeats, coffee and tea. No spirituous liquor was ever used or allowed aboard, for this is forbidden by the Koran. Religious ritual and rules were alike observed punctiliously throughout the voyage. All hands and all passengers offered their prayers five times a day, in the proper manner, and no precept of the Prophet was willingly broken.

This descent upon the *boom* of a couple of hundred passengers made the ship a bedlam, and there was scarcely room to move. I had to struggle to keep my 6 feet of the officers' bench, but the captain came back aboard, his wanderings by airplane and camel being over for the time being, and brought some order with him. He controlled the passengers with martial discipline and, as far as they were concerned, there was one rule of the ship only. This was the same rule which applied aboard troopships in time of war—the passenger is never right. Since the only way the crew could work the ship was by rushing about the deck with various bits and pieces of gear—runners, sheets, and the like—and the lateen sail itself, whenever necessary; and since when they rushed they did so in a headlong manner like a score-odd noisy human bulldozers; and since the only place the unfortunate passengers could go was on that same deck, naturally there were collisions and rows and incidents of all kinds. The passengers had to get out of the way. Their $3 fare entitled them to come along with the ship as far as Zanzibar, but they could have nothing to say while they were on board; and if they could not all fit inboard, then they could hang on along the rails. This many of them did, and they hung their gear outboard because there was not room enough for it inside the bulwarks. Indeed, the *boom* could have taken 50 more. The captain, disconsolate over the poor state of trade in general, said she

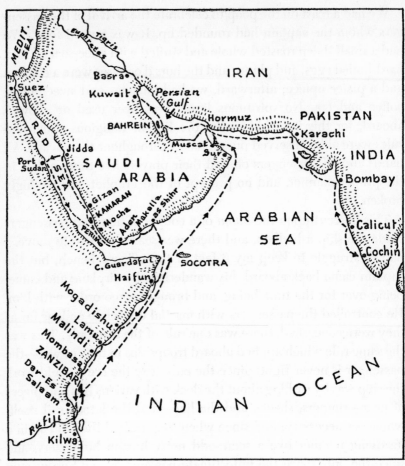

Arab dhow voyages

could have taken another hundred. If she had, she would not have
taken me.

After this experience, I read the stories about the crowding of
hundreds of persons aboard ancient ships—not only in the East—
with an informed eye. Marco Polo's junks with crews of 300 and
600 passengers became quite credible, and the junks need not have
been so large. Our *boom*, I suppose, was of about 150 tons, and
she was very full of cargo.

It was dawn on the third of January, 1939, when we got under way from the anchorage off as-Shihr (which is also called al-Shihr, and just plain Shihr). We continued to beat out of the Gulf of Aden for the following few days. Then we could square away and run down to clear Cape Guardafui, sailing inside the island of Socotra, where we made no call. The captain said that nothing offered in the way of trade there now. Socotra was under the control of the Hadhramaut. We carried no frankincense and no myrrh, and round our decks was no pungent odor of spices. We had, apparently, no merchants in dragon's blood, which was formerly an important product of Socotra.

Our first call was at a place called Haifun. Here a girl in the *harim*—still virtually imprisoned aft—died, and was buried ashore. A Somali dresser nonchalantly vaccinated all hands, and the Italian port officials looked depressed. Our captain tried to sell some goods, failed, and the crew and passengers caught fish and dried them in the sun. We waited at Haifun about eight days, finally selling a little rice. Then we had to wait to collect the money due for it, but finally sailed without this. A relation of the captain was left behind to collect, and we moved on down the coast toward Mogadishu. The northeast monsoon was now a fine, fair wind and day after day the sea was azure, dimpling in the sun, and the great lateen sail pulled the sharp *boom* along at the rate of knots. There was scarcely a roll in her and never a bit of pitching. The African coast was in sight throughout, and the captain knew the landmarks. So did the merchants, some of whom had been captains in their time. Life would have been pleasant enough if it hadn't been for our infernal crowd of passengers, who cluttered up the decks and made life a little hell, all day long. I could scarcely raise an elbow to wield a pen. They were good-mannered folk and they tried to be quiet. There were just too many of them.

So the big *boom* passed along the East African coast, always with her kind, and the ships of Europe and America belonged to another world. We saw them sometimes, going into Haifun to load salt or

to Mogadishu to disembark Italian soldiers and settlers, or toward
Mombasa or Dar-es Salaam. But they were like steel beasts slinking
on the horizon, enormous, foreign, remote. In all the ports we visited we were moored among tiers of other Arab vessels, from the
Persian Gulf, from the Hadhramaut, from Trucial Oman, and from
Muscat and Sur. At Mombasa there were Indians, and sometimes
we met Persian dhows. The big dhows carried on their own trade
as if steamships had no existence and as if—superficially, at any
rate—Vasco da Gama had never rounded the Cape of Good Hope.
The Italian flag flying over Haifun, Merka, Brava, and Mogadishu
was an odd note, but the red flag of Oman flew at the fortress at
Lamu and at Mombasa, and an Arab Sultan still ruled in Zanzibar.

We landed most of our passengers at Mombasa and sold parcels
from our cargo wherever a chance offered. The carpenter had
finished his small dhow by the time Lamu was reached, and it was
sold there for a thousand East African shillings. There were no
sewn boats left at Lamu in February, 1939, but there was a large
fleet of very fast small dhows sailing from there in the trade to
Malindi, Mombasa, and other ports on the coast. These little dhows
were stylish vessels, which always departed with music and song,
and their lateen sails were beautifully cut. Mombasa, too, was a
picturesque port, with the sweet smell of copra by the customs
steps in the native harbor and the singing of the sailors at their work
—always singing, and working like Trojans—and the picturesque
and so varied ships, all sailing vessels, all sweet of line and graceful
as a crowd of costly yachts at some anchorage in the Mediterranean, and the white lateen sails always seemed piratical and picturesque.

It was the custom for the Arabs to drum themselves into their
ancient stronghold of Mombasa, and our boatswain excelled himself with the resonance of his goatskin drums. Some of the dhows
which came in there from Arabia were astonishingly small. I saw

several which were not much more than 30 feet long. They all had passengers—crowds of them—and they were all engaged in trade. Some of the passengers from the more remote coastal areas looked like wild men. Our captain said they would cut our throats cheerfully, if they dared, for they were still pirates at heart, and he told a story of a big Kuwait *boom* which had been cut out in a bay near the Kuria Muria islands, a year or two earlier, by just such fellows.

After Mombasa came Zanzibar, and another crowded dhow anchorage. The extent of the sailing trade in these ports was astonishing. I saw some official figures * at Mombasa, showing that in 1937—the latest year for which statistics were then available— more than 1,400 dhows had touched at the port, and their gross tonnage was 36,840 tons. This number included the Lamu boats and Swahilis from Zanzibar and covered several visits, probably, by the same dhow. Many were Arabs, Persians, or Indians. The largest dhow in the trade was of nearly 400 tons. On the whole Kenya coast—covering the ports of Mombasa, Vanga, Malindi, Kipini, Lamu, and one or two other small places—the total number of dhows entered inward and outward in 1937 was 6,894, with a total of almost 150,000 registered tons. At Zanzibar, one day in early March, I counted more than 50 dhows at the anchorage, 34 of them Arabs. There was a small dhow in from the Comoro Islands, flying the flag of France, and there were several large Indians. A Somali from Mogadishu was flying the Italian flag.

The statistics kept in His Highness the Sultan's customs house showed that 104 big dhows had entered Zanzibar in the first six weeks of the northeast monsoon. Most were from the Persian Gulf. They brought salt, dried fish, a few carpets, a great many passengers, particularly from Oman. At the height of the season the big dhows frequently arrived at the rate of five or six a day. Many of the Arabs came without papers, for their voyages originated in the

* "Report on the Administration of the Railways and Harbours (Kenya and Uganda)."

open roadsteads of minor sheikdoms. Those who brought papers sometimes had false or incomplete documents. The Indian dhows were properly registered and documented, but the Arabs had a confirmed prejudice against being too easily identified. To them, port dues and charges, customs fees, and so on had always been someone's "racket," and they were opposed to the idea of further enriching the European or anyone else by paying anything which could possibly be avoided.

While at Zanzibar, I went aboard a very large *boom*, built at Kuwait but then under a Persian flag, and measured her. She was 120 feet between perpendiculars, 137 feet over all, had a 32½-foot beam, and her hold was nearly 16 feet deep. The girth of her mainmast was over 6 feet at the deck, and she had a crew of 45 strong men. She was said to be twenty-seven years old. She had a longboat aboard which was 36 feet long. This was built on the voyage and was for sale. She had two capstans, and there were more than 50 sea chests on her poop. When empty of her cargo, she looked like a large weatherboard warehouse.

The *boom* completed all the business of her outward passage at Zanzibar, and this was ordinarily as far as the Arabs continued in these days, though some went on to Lindi, Mikindani, and Kilwa. I heard of some which went as far as Portuguese East Africa, but I saw none of these. Our own *boom* continued to the south but this was really part of the homeward voyage, for she went down to the Rufiji Delta only to load for the Persian Gulf. She took no cargo there for trade and no passengers. Many of the Arabs beached on the flats at Zanzibar to clean, when they had completed, and then sailed to Lamu to load mangrove poles for home. All these cargoes were paid for with cash, and one of the Arab difficulties was to collect cash for the goods sold on the outward passage. We left merchants and representatives at every port we came to, and later, the captain's brother was left behind to make yet a further round of the ports, to stir the laggard debtors. As for the merchants from Oman who were with us on their own account, we very soon dropped them. The mysterious young man who went well armed was missing at the first port.

Our captain remained at Zanzibar, ostensibly to look after the ship's business there but, in truth, Zanzibar was a pleasant place to dally in, and the Rufiji River was not. So the mate took the ship to the delta. When I last saw our captain, he was seated upon a carpeted couch with another young master mariner from a Kuwait *boom*, while a Swahili played upon the violin for them and they cast sheep's eyes at a bevy of maidens behind some iron bars across the court. They had lunched extremely well on rice and fish and young chicken, with fruit to follow, and life was good. But down in the Rufiji Delta, life was not good at all.

The *booms*—and all the dhows—in the East African and the Indian trade have to be hauled out about every three months, when their undersides are cleaned off and covered with a mixture of fat and lime—any kind of fat, usually from camels. This treatment is called "paying," and is meant to preserve the teak from the ravages of the teredo, the borer which, in warm waters, can soon ruin a wooden ship. So the annual voyages were planned with this in mind. We beached on Kwale, which is a good place in the northeast season. The ship was rigged down and then hauled up on a high tide, propped up with mangrove poles, and left there on the sand for a tide or two, to dry out. Alongside were two shapely *baggalas*, one from Sur and the other, fifty years old, one of the last surviving trio from Kuwait. The true *baggala* type was becoming rare, and no more were being built. They were lovely ships, and I conceived the idea of acquiring one, at the end of the *boom*'s voyage, and sailing it to Europe or America, where it might be preserved.

That idea had to wait. Meanwhile, we had to spend six weeks far up an arm of the delta of the accursed Rufiji, where the mosquitoes bit like flying dogs, and hippos skulked in the muddy water. Frankincense and myrrh and the fabulous gold from famed Ophir? No one there had heard of such things. The unfortunate sailors, with a crowd of sad Swahili recruited to assist them, set about cutting a cargo of mangrove poles in the malarial swamps, to fill the ship for the voyage back to the Persian Gulf, more than two and a half thousand miles away. Not a breath of any spice ever sweetened the hot and humid air, and the twentieth century might have been a thousand years away.

CHAPTER VII

Kuwait, Port of Swift *Booms*

Our *boom* carried a musician who was expert with the guitar, but even he was silent throughout the long stay in the dreadful delta. The crew thinned down, and their shins were thick with ulcerated wounds from working so long in the foul mud. The whole ship was wet and sticky with mud which came aboard like glue sticking to the mangrove poles, and the weeks in the Rufiji left their mark on everyone. By the end of March we were loaded, the mangroves were paid for with silver shillings, and off we sailed. The river raised its sticky hands to stop us as we went, and the laden ship took the ground once. But she slid off the mud again and all was well. The way to Zanzibar was reef-strewn and dangerous; but once outside the bar, the sun shone. We had to stop at Kwale Island again to clear the ship outward, for there was only a forester along the Rufiji and he had no authority to pass the papers of seagoing ships.

At Zanzibar again, we found our captain, who had collected three Swahili passengers for Muscat, some coconuts, and a venture in vermicelli, which he thought might sell well in Kuwait. The ship was laden to the top of the bulwarks with mangrove poles and there was not really room, even by her standards, for many passengers. Though we had no further business there, we still tarried at Zanzibar, for there was never any hurry in the dhows. The town and the port were always interesting to me, and I did not mind. Away from the few main streets, the town was a maze of shop-lined narrow alleys through which a ricksha passed with difficulty, and all the perambulators which dusky nursemaids pushed about were fitted with bicycle bells to give warning at the frequent corners, all abrupt, blind, and dangerous. The Zanzibar dhows themselves were small and neither as shapely nor as fast as the Lamu vessels, but fast little lateen-rigged craft came in from the Comoro Islands and from Madagascar, and an Indian dhow drummed in, one day, carrying big lateen topsails.

The captain added to his ventures by buying a chest of new Maria Teresa thalers, dated 1780, but freshly arrived from the San Francisco mint. Our passengers, despairing of the ship's ever sailing, tired of it after a week or so and went ashore. Then we shipped three more and sailed.

It was then April 14, and the wind was already in the southwest, with some rain and squalls, but there was no vice in the squalls and the real weight of the southwest monsoon had not arrived. Our captain had dallied rather long in Zanzibar and boasted of having left about $730 in the place, which was a lot of money. He was a strange fellow, and I wondered how closely he resembled the scores of thousands of Indian Ocean sailing masters who had preceded him down the centuries. Some of them, I think, were better men. Our captain was a magnificent sailor, but he had no knowledge of real ocean navigation. He had no sextant and he could not take sights. It seemed that the twentieth-century sailing Arabs had forgotten the mathematics in which once their forebears had excelled, and our captain showed no eagerness to master the science again. He was well content with such knowledge as he had, and this was considerable.

Both shores of the Persian Gulf, all Baluchistan and the west coast of India, the shores of the Gulf of Oman and south Arabia, Socotra and the Red Sea on both sides as far as Kamaran and Eritrea, and East Africa down as far as Mikindani—for these his local knowledge was thorough and near enough to complete. He used no pilots, no tugs, no shore assistance ever. He cut the sails, and he designed the small dhow which was built aboard. He ruled the passengers. He sold the cargo. He outwitted the port authorities wherever he went, defeating alike the close mesh of the Italians' currency restrictions (which upset trade) and the desire of the British to know who was landing in Kenya, which upset the passenger business. Though not an active smuggler himself, he was an expert in that black art, which was of considerable importance aboard the *boom* and all the dhows. He was a spendthrift and a fornicator on a large scale. He took a curiously long view of things and was remarkably well informed. He spoke of Vasco da Gama as more or less a recent arrival in the Indian Ocean, and was still angry about the Arab who had piloted the explorer from Malindi to Calicut. But he claimed that this Arab was a Kuwaiti, like himself. He could trace his own lineage back a thousand years and regarded those who could not as upstarts. To him a few centuries were as nothing, and the European, he claimed, would soon be gone. God had given him too much money and too many arms, but he had lost control of his women and would destroy himself, in good time—pretty soon, he thought. So long as he did not drag the Arabs down with him, all would be well. He hoped no oil would be found at Kuwait as it had been at Bahrein.

Our captain reclined on the bench abaft the wheel all day and expounded his views to all who would listen. We sailed in company with another *boom*, commanded by the young man who had been his companion in the orgies at Zanzibar. This vessel was slower than ours, which was deliberately kept back to allow the two captains to yarn together. The early threat of the southwest to blow with strength soon faded away, and the weather north of Malindi was glorious. The two captains shared meals together on many days, visiting each other by means of their small gigs, and yarned and argued throughout the long afternoons. Thus the days passed pleasantly. The African coast continued in sight. We had sailed down with the familiar landmarks on our starboard beam. Now they were

on the port beam and we did not have to put in anywhere, and that
was about the only difference.

One night our companion's *boom* was dropped astern, for it
blew fresh for a while and the mate, who was on watch, let our
ship run. We did not go back to look for her and she could not
catch us up. So our captain then spoke every vessel we overhauled
and went aboard whenever possible. He would do anything for an
audience and missed our collection of red-whiskered Sindbads,
some of whom had left without paying their fares. One day we
visited a small *boom* hailing from the roadstead of Dibai, in Trucial
Oman, not far past Ras Musandam. This vessel had a certificate
of measurement from the port authorities at Karachi among her
papers, and this said that she was of 37 tons. She did not look much
more. She had a crew of 15, who included 6 boys, and she was 16
days out from Zanzibar, bound for Makalla, in the first instance,
with a cargo of mangrove poles and one Persian passenger. Her
captain, a quiet man with a very gentle face, had no chart other
than an insurance company's wall map of the world, many years
old, but he had a copy of Isa Kitami's *Periplus,* or directory of the
Indian Ocean, much read. The compass in her ancient binnacle
was marked "C. Hutchinson and Co., Sunderland."

The captain said that he usually traded on the Indian coast and
this was his first African voyage. He generally managed to make
two Indian voyages a year, while the good weather lasted. He had
taken 170 passengers to Zanzibar. Some died and were thrown
overboard.

We frequently saw Arab vessels in this trade which were even
smaller than the Dibai *boom.* Some of the smallest were from minor
ports in the Hadhramaut. Nobody knew the actual number of
dhows engaged in this trade, but our captain said it was over a
thousand. He said there were more than 2,000 dhows trading round
the coasts of Arabia, and half of them would certainly run down
to Africa if there was anything to be gained from the voyage and
they were doing nothing else. After all, it cost them little. The

crews paid for the communal food, and any ship could find some passengers and some trade.

The weather was so good that we stepped the longboat's mast on the after end of the poop and set the longboat's sail on that, so the *boom* became a three-masted vessel, for the moment. There was a permanent place to step the longboat's mast on the poop. A sort of flying jib boom was rigged out along the stempost and a big headsail was carried there, beyond the luff of the lateen main. The wind was still mainly from northeast as we sailed to the north, and we had to beat. This was acceptable, and the passage of over two thousand miles between Zanzibar and our first stop of Muscat was made in a little over three weeks. We coasted up past Cape Guardafui; by the end of April, we had sailed northward inside Socotra and were standing along the South Arabian coast, where the land breeze helped us by night and there was a current in our favor. We were out of sight of land only upon one day. All along the Arab coast and in the Gulf of Oman the weather remained excellent. We were continuing well ahead of the real coming of the southwest monsoon, but there was variety enough in the winds we had to make a reasonable passage without too much beating.

We anchored in Mutrah Bay, just north of Muscat, and once again, European ships and Europeans were as completely absent as if da Gama had never blown into the Indian Ocean. There were Persian, Indian, and all sorts of Arab dhows at anchor in the bay, but trade was bad there, and we soon sailed again toward Bahrein. Our cargo of mangrove poles would bring a good price there, it was hoped, for King Ibn Saud, in funds from the new strike of oil in his nearby territories, was buying all the building material he could put his hands on. In Arabia, mangrove poles are important in house construction, and many a room—many a whole house—owes its dimensions to the height of the mangroves which grow along the steamy Rufiji.

Our cargo was sold at Bahrein to the agents of King Ibn Saud, without difficulty and at a good price. I noticed that we sold a good many more than had been listed in the manifest on which the ship had paid. There were some strange goings on in that delta, and there was a well-organized system for cheating with the poles. The long-voyage dhowmen were expert at that sort of thing. They had to be to live. After her eight-month voyage, the *boom*—which paid by results—offered her hard-worked sailors only $30 or $40 each as their return for the voyage. They had done well if they were able to double that from the profits on their own ventures and a little smuggling. Many of them had no permanent homes. They lived in the bazaar at Kuwait, sleeping wrapped in their cloaks on a bench in a coffee shop or on the beach.

At Muscat and at Bahrein we met dhows in the Indian trade. There was a big beauty at Muscat called the *Samhan,* which was registered as 305 tons, with a capacity of 5,000 packages of Iraqi dates. She was 150 feet on deck, her mainmast was 110 feet high, and her main lateen yard was formed of three large trees. She carried two navigators, each with an ancient quadrant, and she had a small radio receiving set to listen to the news. Her longboat was larger than some of the little Hadhrami dhows we had seen in the trade to Zanzibar. She was commanded by a man named Yusuf bin Isa, son of Isa Kitami who had compiled the Kuwait *Periplus.*

This big *boom* made longer voyages round the Indian Ocean than most dhows did. The majority either sailed between the Persian Gulf and the Indian coast or down to Africa via the Hadhramaut and Aden. The *Samhan,* when we saw her, was completing a voyage begun at Basra the previous September, with dates to Karachi, Bombay, and Mangalore: thence she had sailed with an Indian cargo directly to Mombasa, and after calling also at Malindi, had loaded mangrove poles at Lamu for the homeward journey. The previous season she had gone from India to Aden. The dhows in the Indian trade which we saw had cargoes of teak, coir for rope-making, sea chests, bamboos, and some chairs and other furniture. The bulk of their cargoes was always timber, for which there was an insatiable demand. A good deal of it was imported to keep Kuwait's shipbuilding industry going.

The idea of building Arab ships on the Malabar coast itself had fallen into disfavor for several reasons. First, a ship is a property very easily harassed, and therefore best built at home. Secondly, a magnificent great *boom* of more than five hundred tons, the last Kuwaiti built on the Malabar coast, had foundered on her first voyage. The name of this great ship was the *Light of the Earth and Sea,* but it was a light that failed. She carried a crew of eighty and her main halyards were made from coir rope with nineteen strands. She was built by two famous Kuwait master shipwrights, Mohammed Thwaini and Salim bin Rashid, with more than a hundred Indians to assist them, and she was reputed to have cost 120,000 Indian rupees. She took six months to build. The underlying idea was to save the freight on the timber to Kuwait. While they were about it, they built as large a ship as they could, to save as much freight as possible.

There was no insurance on this vessel. There never is on any of them. That is not part of Arab shipowning practice, which regards insurance premiums as an unwarranted gamble against the will of God. It is no part of the duties of an Arab captain, apparently, to foresee anything. Both for captain and crew, the supreme disposer and judge of the waters is Allah; that granted, preparation for contingencies is both unnecessary and futile.

It was the seventh of June when our *boom* finally arrived back at Kuwait, and I saw at once that the famous walled port was all I had heard of it, and more. In 1939, the place was still truly Arab and quite unspoiled. The oilmen were there, but they had as yet found nothing. Kuwait was still a real Indian Ocean seaport of the old times. I found the city to be composed of some eight thousand houses and—as near as anyone knew, for no vital statistics were kept then—perhaps 70,000 or 80,000 persons. Its roads were unmade (except for a brief mile or so running to the Sheik's town palace, at the eastern end), its narrow streets a windy, sanded maze, threading in and out among the low-walled houses and the roofed bazaars. In the north, it lay open to its wide bay. Its landward sides were walled and the gates guarded. The wall was hurriedly put up, little more than twenty years previously, when the Wahabi Beduin of Nejd were marching on the town. Beduin coming into the town must leave their rifles at the gates, and here any day a weird collection of ancient arms could be seen, some tied together with pieces of wire, more dangerous to whoever dared to fire them than to anyone else.

There probably always was some sort of fishing village on Kuwait Bay, for the waters teem with good fish. There the old reed canoe still survives, one of the most primitive forms of boat. It is nothing but a bundle of reeds shaped roughly like a boat and tied at both ends. In these small raftlike things the fishermen of Kuwait Bay go out in all weathers, for, frail as they are, these small craft are at any rate unsinkable. No one tries to keep out the water, which sweeps through the reeds as it will. The vessel can never break up so long as its few lashings hold together, and, in a place where there is no wood, it is the cheapest kind of fishing craft. It sometimes carries a mast 3 or 4 feet high, on which the fisherman spreads a pocket handkerchief of a sail when he wants to run home. In 1939, these reed boats were to be seen by the dozen round Kuwait Bay.

But it was the waterfront which interested me. Here any day during the summer months, from the first light of predawn until the last glimmer of day, a round of maritime activity went on by those two miles of ships, all standing high and dry when the tide was out, their bows to the sea and shapely sterns inshore. Not one among them was unlovely. The Arab, left to himself, cannot build an unsightly vessel, though he builds always by eye, with an adze and an Indian saw, and without prepared plans. The dhow form is traditional. The great *booms*, double-ended craft with their characteristic long stemposts reaching high before them, their big rudders unshipped and lying on the sand, stood empty and idle, with their deserted decks covered with matting and skirts of coir protecting their carvel sides. The little pearlers were farther up, looking like children beside the deepwater ships. Many of the older vessels were lavishly carved. Here and there the high, carved stern of some great *baggala,* that lovely galleon of the eastern seas, towered above its neighbors. The *baggala's* ornate carving, galleried decorations, and tier of stern windows were explained as being a copy from the Portuguese ships which first came to the Gulf more than four hundred years ago. It is unlikely that Sindbad, that prevaricator from old Basra so near to Kuwait, ever saw a *baggala.*

Even in 1939, Kuwait shipbuilding was affected to some extent by non-Arab ideas. Carving and embellishment had become rare; workmanship was beginning to be hurried; the slow, steady progress and perfection of former days had largely gone. A *baggala* of 200 tons would have taken six months to build. In 1939, a *boom* of like capacity was built from the Malabar logs to the finished job in six weeks. There were a dozen such *booms* being built along the waterfront then. Here and there the oiled stemposts of new *booms* poked high over low mud walls. When the ship was ready to be launched, the wall in front of her was simply knocked down and, with a series of big anchors embedded in the mud and wire tackles led to capstans, she was dragged toward the sea, always at low water. The high water floated her off and she was then taken away to be rigged. The wall was mended and a new keel laid. Persian laborers worked in the saw pits, sawing planks from teak logs while the carpenters still worked with adze and bow drill, as in Biblical times. A master shipwright of Kuwait was a highly respected man. It was honorable to have anything to do with the sea.

Along the sandy waterfront road, where it wound its picturesque way past mosque and business house. Sheik's palace and school, a crowd of white-gowned captains, mates, serangs, quartermasters, sea cooks, and mariners hurried by, the captains always dressed in purest white from headcloth to ankle, with round their heads

the heavy lamb's-wool *aghal,* that picturesque double headrope of
the true Arab dress. Over their shoulders would be camel's-hair
cloaks, in brown or white or black, decorated always with gold
wire and cloth of gold. In each left hand swung an amber rosary,
without which a captain rarely went abroad. In his right hand was
a stick from Zanzibar, a cane from the Calicut coast, or an Indian
umbrella to shield his head from the hot sun. On his feet were
sandals, easily kicked off before entering mosques and homes. The
sailors also dressed in white during the few days they were ashore
not working. White is the proper color for all men of Kuwait. What
few women were to be seen—and it was not considered good
that members of the *harim* should venture in the streets—were
shrouded heavily in black, for the Islamic law is strict in Kuwait
and there were then no newfangled notions about women's freedom and such changes. Poorer women came down to the beach to
wash their household laundry in the sea, but they bent over their
heavy tasks, still shrouded in funereal black.

Along the waterfront I saw a small water *boom,* with a skelter
of braying asses and a welter of hurrying coolies carrying tins and
leaking skins, discharging fresh water from the Basra River above
Fao, for this was the city's water supply. It was hawked through
the port in skins. Near the Sheik's town palace—the old palace
that Sheik Mubarak built, which was famous for its ceilings of
lithographs of actresses and queens—some Persian craft, Iraqi,
and small fry from Kuwait were discharging green stuff for the
household cows, fresh dates from the Basra River, onions from the
Hasa coast, corn from Bushire. Everywhere hereabouts were ships
and boats and the appurtenances of seafaring. The children knew
how to play only with models of *booms,* and their chanting songs
were of the sea. Bower anchors by the score, ship's longboats,
worm-eaten rudders, solid great masts and long, lashed yards,
washboards that had kept out many an Indian sea, capstans,
benches in the shaded places for the shipmasters to sit upon and
watch what went on—all along the waterfront these abounded.

Here a group of sweating mariners struggled with a great teak chest, splendid with its decorations of lavishly embellished brass, hand-beaten and etched, which they were carrying from a merchant's house to some Mombasa-bound *boom:* in the shade of the al-Khalifa mosque a group of sailmakers sat sewing on a lateen main. They worked on their haunches, as the Easterner so often does, squatting to the sail, which was nailed down, cloth by cloth, to the hard earth, its coir roping stretched between large pegs. The sailcloth was cheap Indian cotton stuff, for gossamer sails could stand the northeast monsoon. Sailmaking was simple, consisting mainly of joining the seams with a plain, round stitch. A serang and a captain watched zealously.

Farther on, a marine blacksmith beat out iron spikes for fastenings, each one by hand—frightful work in that torrid place—and the sweat streamed from him and the slave pumping the bellows of his forge. His shop was filled with marine hardware belonging to the ages—stone slabs, spiked with a single piece of iron to hold in coral holes, which are the oldest form of anchor; primitive capstans, brought in for repair, and hand-wrought anchor chains; ancient ship's wheels; and a few old galleon's guns. No Kuwait ship went armed to sea then, not even with small arms to repel the possible marauders of the Mahra coast; but not so long before, every ship had had to be prepared to fight pirates and all had carried muzzle-loading guns. By 1939 the guns, breeches deep in sand, stood along the waterfront as bollards for the pearlers' lines. Some of them looked to be of Portuguese manufacture.

In the shade from a high wall a group of old captains yarned away the prelunch hours of the long morning, discussing the queer behavior of the monsoon, that year, off Zanzibar and the scarcity of fish in Haifun Bay. The voice of an old man was raised in maritime chronicles of long ago; beside him a bearded shipmaster, a handsome giant of a man, studied laboriously in a book entitled "The Book of the Directory of the Oceans, and the Way on the Sea," the product of one Isa ibn Abdul-wahab ibn Abdul-aziz al-Kitami,

wherein were directions for reaching the Seychelles Islands and
the Comoros, and the Yemen and all of India. Now and again men
of the nearby household brought the sitters a round of coffee, which
was served in tiny cups with great ceremony, or they brought small
glasses of sweetened black tea. The captains were important in
Kuwait then, and each had his own servants.

In the street a thorn-laden camel padded past with stately tread,
looking as if the work it was performing was much beneath its
dignity but it was too dignified to desist. A Bedu in desert-stained
rags plodded beside it, upright and dignified as his beast, for all
his rags, and handsome with his gaunt, strong-featured face. Persian
burden bearers, laden with piles of rugs, others with baskets of
fresh fruit, ripe dates from Basra, red and brown, walked with the
quick, nervous step of the coolie of the East. A crowd of merry
schoolboys, just released from the school where their melodic
chanting of some verses from the Koran fell upon my ears as I
passed by, played among the ships, pretending they were launching
a new *boom* with a song and measured stamp. One had a tiny
Indian drum. On the beach were ship's boats and spars and yards
and masts and water tanks, made from rough planks which were
nailed together and caulked with raw cotton, and the shells of
old pearlers past their day, piles of palm fronds from the Basra
River, bundles of coir from the husks of Indian coconuts, Malabar
teak, knees and beams for ships from some twisted Persian wood,
mangrove poles from the Kenya coast and the Rufiji.

Before each captain's house stood his collection of shipbuilding
material. Even if he built no ships, it was his ambition to do so.
Most of the Kuwait shipowning was in the hands of captains'
families. An old man of good character and well-known integrity,
after a long career at sea, would approach the Sheik or one of the
leading merchants for finances to help build his first *boom*. Then
he would take her to sea himself and earn enough to build a second.
Each *boom* big enough for the Indian Ocean trade cost, then, from
9,000 to 12,000 Indian rupees, which was less than $6,000. Grad-

ually the old man would pass command over to his sons and would stay ashore himself, to look after the business there.

The number of big ocean-going dhows in Kuwait, when I was there, was 104. Of these, about thirty usually voyaged to Zanzibar and the others were in the Indian trade. They all began their voyages in the date season by loading dates in the Basra River. The Arab Port Director there told me that usually between 400 and 500 long-voyage dhows loaded in the Shatt-al-Arab each season (and he added, incidentally, that the cleverest rogues were from Kuwait). There were some 300 trading dhows owned in Kuwait, all told, not reckoning vessels used only for pearl diving. There were less than a score of large vessels left in this business, but there were several hundred small decked boats which still went pearling. These statistics were from the Sheik's own books and were accurate, though it was not generally easy to collect reliable statistics at an Arab port.

All this great maritime activity was going on while the oil prospectors bored for oil in the hinterland close by, and Bahrein and the new Saudi-Arabian fields were flourishing and bringing in wealth previously undreamt of. But Kuwait, too, was soon to see all this sailing economy upset, perhaps fatally, by the wealth of oil. No one knew it then, but half the sheikdom swam upon a vast underground lake of oil, which in the past five years has been producing at the rate of more than a million barrels monthly. One result has been a great demand for labor, and this soon upset the traditional recruitment of big dhow crews. By 1950, all the *baggalas* had long gone and less than half a dozen Kuwaiti *booms* still traded to Africa. A small fleet continued in the Indian trade, manned largely with Persian crews, but the indications were that, if the prosperity brought by oil continued much longer, the deepsea dhows of Kuwait were doomed. The shipwrights were building lighters, and the sailors could earn what to them were fantastic sums as unskilled laborers in the plants and on the oil fields.

The outbreak of World War II prevented me from putting my plan for saving a *baggala* into effect, though I had a beauty under offer for 4,000 rupees, and I think a voyage could have been made (via Suez, and not around the Cape of Good Hope).

I think I saw this great Indian Ocean port with its sailing commerce intact, only just in time. It was an astonishingly interesting picture from the illustrious, romantic past. Now, after only a decade, this last of the Indian Ocean sailing ports has changed its character, and much which belonged to the past has already gone.

CHAPTER VIII

The Indians and the Chinese

A glance at the map of the Indian Ocean shows at once the favorable situation of the peninsula of India itself to dominate the monsoonal sailing trade and control the Indian Ocean. It is favored by geography and by nature alike, even more so than the two other peninsulas of that great Ocean—Arabia and Malaya. If the coasts of Arabia were athwart the main highways between East and West, India *was* the East, and many of the rich products sought by western markets originated there. Those which did not had been brought and traded there from time immemorial. For half the year the northeast monsoon was a reliable and pleasant source of power, which simplified sailing voyages up and down the western coast, up the Persian Gulf, and as far as the mouth of the Red Sea. The same monsoon, used properly by mariners who understood the art of sailing (as the Indians at any rate of Cutch, Kathiawar, and the Malabar coast certainly did, thousands of years ago), enabled voyages to be made with large ships to Burma, Malaya, and all the East Indies. Beyond these, other good seasonal winds could be used to go on to Indo-China, the Philippines, and even to China itself. India, moreover, was the source of the best of all shipbuilding timbers, Malabar teak. It was the home of the coconut, which provided cordage. It was the home of flax and cotton, which provided sails. It had metals for fastenings.

Hemmed in by mountain masses in the north, its triangular ex-

tremity washed for 700 miles on each side by the azure waters of
the Indian Ocean, rich in the resources of wooden shipbuilding,
overpopulated by hard-working races, which include some splendid seafaring men, India *should* have dominated eastern trade
and its rulers should have dominated eastern sea power. Yet there
is little evidence that they did so. There is plenty of evidence of
their seafaring, their far-flung trade, and their many successful
colonies which were founded by sea. We know about the Romans,
the Greeks, the Arabs, the Persians, and the Chinese, who sailed
in the Indian trade. The Roman emperor Trajan traveled to the
mouth of the Euphrates to watch the great argosies setting out on
their voyage to India, but these were not Indian ships. The emperor Marcus Aurelius sent a mission to China, after which Chinese
junks appear to have brought goods to the ports of the Malabar
coast for transshipment on to Antioch and Alexandria. But Arabs
sailed most of these goods across the Arabian Sea.

There are plenty of references in Sanskrit and Pali writings to
seafaring matters, and there is no doubt that some states in India
were important maritime powers. But it is probable, I think, that
the Indian coasting trade itself and the trade across the Bay of
Bengal kept by far the largest proportion of the Indian sailing
ships effectively employed, and the deepwater trades were, in some
degree, left to others. After all, deep-sea sailors have always been
recruited from those nations which themselves offered little future
to their boldest sons, and so-called aptitude for the sea has its roots
in that fact. The hard-bitten coasts of sterile Arabia; the rock-bound
coasts of distant, cold, and stormy Norway; the too-often unfertile
and unsmiling shores of much of the grim North Sea—these were
the backgrounds which forced men to take to the deep sea. In
India the main chance was always ashore.

Indian coastal sailing was carried on on a vast scale, as it is to
this day when, in the west coast trade alone, more than five thousand sailing ships of one sort and another are still employed. Indian
sailing ships which I saw trading to Mombasa and Zanzibar in 1938

and 1939 were, on the whole, better built and stancher vessels than their Arab counterparts. The Arabs had to freight their shipbuilding materials 2,000 miles at least; the Indians had an abundance at home. Moreover, there had then been nearly four centuries of close European influence on Indian shipping and, for over a century, some control. The result of this had been to increase the strength of ships and generally to improve shipbuilding methods, which had been sound to begin with.

Some of the Indian *kotias* I saw at Mombasa could have rounded the Cape of Good Hope. They were lateen-rigged, just as the ships of the Arabs and the Persians were, but they had adopted refinements which made the big and rather awkward lateen yard safer, stronger, and easier to handle. They habitually carried much smaller crews than the Arabs did. Their rigging, on the whole, was stouter. They hailed from what was then British India, and they were properly registered and subject to some sort of real control and inspection. Though the control and inspection might have brought about some useful innovations, on the whole the probability is that this superiority of the Indian-built vessels goes back a long time. The whole Malabar, Cutch, and Kathiawar coasts stand open to the full force of the sea during the onslaught of the southwest monsoon, and there was scarcely a usable harbor along the whole length of the shore line until modern refinements, such as breakwaters and expensive dredging programs, made them so. The Indian shipwright *had* to build strong ships, and he had the materials. The Indian mariner knew the strength of his enemy, though he was accustomed to sail under good conditions only and to lay his ship up in the southwest season. He would insist on some reserve of strength in his vessel, lest he be caught out in her and have to survive bad weather.

Much of Indian literature is so deeply religious in motif as not to concern itself with mundane facts. Though references to what must have been very considerable voyages are frequent, it is almost impossible to track them down. Old stories in Ceylon also throw some light on what must have gone on. The Vijayan legends speak of a royal bride being brought to the island in a ship which accommodated her suite without difficulty. A royal suite was a royal suite in those days. Besides eighteen officers of state, seventy-five servants and numbers of slaves, a party of seven hundred virgins traveled in the same vessel. But we don't know where they came from. The sculptures in the Buddhist temple of Boro Budur in Java show ships in full sail, and these have been accepted by competent scholars as probably representing Indian sailing ships of the first century. The Gujarati exodus to Java dates from the beginning of the seventh century, but ship design changed slowly in the Indian Ocean. A mere five hundred years would have brought about little difference.

This migration to Java indicates the ease with which the west-coast Indians of those days could organize mass movements of peoples. In A.D. 603, the King of Gujarat sent his son, with 5,000 followers, in a fleet of more than a hundred ships, to found a new kingdom. After a voyage said to have occupied four months, they reached Java and settled there. They were reinforced by a second fleet bringing another two thousand colonists, and the new colony flourished and continued to trade with the parent land. Voyages between the ports of northwestern India and Java, via Ceylon, were commonplace.

Four months seems a long time to occupy on a voyage from Gujarat to Java, but it must be remembered that on all such voyages the ships had to be self-contained. There were no docking facilities, repair gangs, or anything of the kind, save as the ships provided such things for themselves. Wooden hulls had to be hauled out once a quarter for examination and recoating against the ravages of the teredo, and this could not be done—and still is not done—until the ships had first been completely unloaded and then rigged down, at least of their heavier mast or masts. The Eastern mariner works hard and swiftly but, even so, these were big jobs. Food supplies and water supplies were problems. Food supplies were frequently taken care of by stopping at a convenient spot and growing a crop, and there is evidence that some larger ships could distill water and liquors, but never sufficient for all their people. Pirates had to be fought, for these abounded. The jealousies of princes and their ability to make port charges and customs tolls and the like, had to be met. Delay to a few ships would probably mean delays to them all, at any rate on the first migratory voyage. Early Indian coins give representations of able, two-masted vessels which should have made the passage from Gujarat to Java in one month, if they had gone direct. But they could not go direct.

The legend that Buddha sailed to Cambodia implies the early influence of India in that direction, and there were several migrations from India to Indo-China. Some scholars hold that the famous ruins of Angkor Wat in Cambodia are also of Hindu origin. It may well be so. The author of the *Periplus* obviously regarded the ports of South India and of Ceylon as centers for an important trade with the farther East, in which more and larger ships were customarily employed than ever sailed toward Egypt. The sea route to China was probably through the Straits of Malacca. There, pirates would be a real danger. The narrow straits abound in natural hide-outs for swift *proas,* and the cargoes borne in those ancient argosies were often incredibly valuable. The ships carried companies of archers to defend them.

The coastal peoples of Gujarat and Cutch were good sailors, and still remain so. In addition to their voyages to the farther East, they also knew the coast of East Africa well. There were trading communities of Indians, from these and other communities, settled very early in the ports of East Africa. Along much of the coast there is a persistent legend of some strangers known to the Swahili as the Wadebuli, who came in sailing ships made of palm leaves— which sounds odd. Precisely who the Wadebuli could have been no one now can say, but it is quite probable that they were mariners and merchants from Dabbol, a port on India's west coast which enjoyed some measure of importance. On the other hand, they might have been Malays. As for the palm leaves, these probably were shelters built over the main deck, the length of the ship. This sort of shelter is still seen frequently in Eastern vessels, particularly round the waters of Indonesia. The Arabs, when loading mangrove poles in the delta of the Rufiji, are also accustomed to construct such houses of palm leaves over at least the afterpart of their vessels.

The sailing history of the Indian Ocean must remain in part conjecture, though it is certain that the use of seagoing sailing ships there was extensive and very ancient. Just who sailed where or in what, scholars may argue, but it is very unlikely that anyone can now know with real certainty. The reality of a great sailing commerce is fascinating enough, carried on through the years by means of graceful and able vessels, sailed well by mariners who understood enough about ocean voyages to get on with making them. Some knew the compass. Some used land-seeking birds, and the Indians are said especially to have done this. But they all certainly knew many things of the way of a ship in the midst of the sea which are lost to us now, and they could find their way across the great waters without the paraphernalia and the host of instruments now thought necessary.

Doubly fascinating is the fact that much of this commerce should still survive, at any rate, in India and Arabia. I saw the Arab sailing for myself and intended later to do something the same on the coasts of India and from the Malay Peninsula, and to finish up in the China Seas. Wars and generally upset world conditions spoiled that plan. But a book * published in Bombay a short time ago shows the astonishing extent of the survival of Indian sailing commerce, even after the recent war. The author speaks of Cutch-Kathiawar *kotias*—a type very similar to the Arab *baggala*—trading from their home ports as far afield as Calcutta, Malacca,

* *The Sailing Vessel Traffic on the West Coast of India,* by K. B. Vaidya, The Popular Book Depot, Bombay, 1945.

Basra, Aden, and Zanzibar. The *kotia* is a particularly well-built type, which can make two Persian Gulf voyages a season or three coastal runs between Cutch and the Malabar coast, carrying cargoes both ways. In the war, a few of these vessels were given powerful engines and used for special raiding parties across the Bay of Bengal. They did quite well. At that time, I saw many of these and other Indian types laid up ashore during the southwest monsoons. Their lines were invariably most attractive and they were real little ships.

There were more than 900 seagoing sailing vessels of one sort or another registered in the ports of the Malabar coast alone, immediately after the end of World War II. These vessels were well designed and well built, though almost always following purely traditional lines. Indian shipbuilders and Indian shipbuilding materials were acknowledged by both the Portuguese and the British to be so good that these leading maritime powers made a habit very early of having many of their own vessels built in India. Some of these vessels still survive, notably the old frigate *Don Fernando Y Gloria* at Lisbon and the *Foudroyant* at Portsmouth. If, indeed, the Indian shipwrights and seafaring men had developed the art of naval warfare to the same extent as their European rivals had done, the story of the struggle for the control of the Indian Ocean might be very different. But their ships were trading ships, though they carried some cannon. Fighting at sea, on the whole, was left to the pirates, who did it well but only for themselves.

In present-day Indian sailing ships, as in those of the Arabs, captains and crews work cargo, repair the ships, haul them out for cleaning, do their own towing by means of their own boats, and commission them at the beginning of each season and lay them up at its end, all without any extra pay. The captain is also frequently a merchant, or acts as one. He is invariably his own ship chandler, though he sometimes has to employ a broker ashore to secure his ship a cargo. The usual sailing season on the west coast of India is regarded as lasting from Coconut Day—about the beginning or

middle of August—until mid-May or mid-June, depending upon
the local habits of the southwest monsoon in their own home ports.
These habits are well known. The early start means that trouble-
some voyages may have to be made, but the assumption is that by
that time, the southwest monsoon is well established in the interior
of India and conditions on the coast have settled down. In November there can be sudden spells of bad weather, in which the coasters
are all too frequently caught out, but from then until March the
northeast monsoon brings fair conditions. Ships based on Malabar
and South Indian ports must be home and out of harm's way before mid-May. Karachi ships can take a chance on another month,
but the ships of Kathiawar try to be home at the latest by the first
week in June. As on the Arab coast, ships go to their own home
ports during the bad season. This is essential, to allow the necessary
refit to be carried on under the owner's eye and to give the crews
time to recuperate in their own homes. The Malabar ships do not
usually begin to sail much before November. They allow about
one hundred days for a Persian Gulf voyage and twice that for a
round voyage to East Africa. No Indian leaves his home waters for
Arabian ports before November or after March, but Arabs sail
from India as late as the end of April, as they do not have to return
to lay up their vessels.

It was estimated that, in 1945, about eighty Indian sailing vessels
were still engaged in the annual voyages to East Africa, going as
far as Mozambique. They carried passengers besides, although
there was also in existence then a considerable, and growing, Indian merchant navy, composed wholly of large modern vessels,
steamers and motor ships.

It is obvious that this matter of being able to lay up a vessel conveniently and safely during the bad-weather seasons has been of
the utmost importance in the development of the sailing commerce
of the Indian Ocean. Herein lies the reason for the absence of
Chinese junks from so much of that ocean, where the dhow still

plies. A trading voyage from a port in China down the length of the China Seas and through the labyrinth of reefs which to this day remain in large part unsurveyed between the Philippines and the coast of Indo-China, through the Malacca Straits, across the Bay of Bengal, past Ceylon and the coasts of India and Baluchistan, up the Gulf of Oman and to the head of the Persian Gulf—this was too much for one ship, and one venture. There are many reasons why such voyages would have been difficult. In the first place, consider the matter of navigational dangers. These abounded, particularly in the South China Sea soon after the setting out, and in the Persian Gulf at the end. Then, there were difficulties about fitting a voyage to the seasons. To make a reasonable passage, a junk must have fairly good weather. A fresh wind in the face would deter most junks, weatherly and stout seagoing ships though they are. If one of them began her voyage toward Persia at Canton, she would have to get away as soon as the northeast monsoon there was well set in, in October, but then she would have to chance a stray typhoon. Thence her route would probably have been to skirt the coast of southern Indo-China, slip across the Gulf of Siam, and run down the Malay Peninsula until she could get past the island which was later to become famous as Singapore—and was then a nest for pirates—and begin the passage of the Straits of Malacca. If she stopped nowhere else, she would stop at Malacca.

There is evidence that many junks on long voyages put into Sumatra and remained there a season. The winds in the Straits of Malacca would be variable and the junk could work through without too great difficulty. But the southwest monsoon would begin in the Bay of Bengal some time in May, and no junk would willingly seek battle against that somber, windy, and depressing tumult. So, until the northeast blew again, she would spend the season either trading at Malacca, or hauled out somewhere, empty of cargo, while her people grew a crop or defended themselves against local marauders. With the coming of the northeast monsoon in the Bay of Bengal, she could continue, *if* all was well and she had not been delayed by "Act of God, perils of the sea, fire on board, in hulk, in craft, or on shore, barratry of the master or crew, enemies, pirates, assailing thieves, arrests and restraints of Princes, Rulers, and People" (as the standard form of British charter-party has it to this day). "Restraints of princes" included the taking of a liking to merchants' cargoes, which would have to be landed and stored while the junk was hauled out. A merchant took his ventures in his hands and his life with them, in those days.

By the time the junk had wandered across the southern reaches of the Bay of Bengal and passed Ceylon, she had still more than three thousand miles to go. Why pass all those excellent markets? Perhaps, of course, she would not, but call in to permit her merchants to change their goods over and over again. This they could do, doubtless to their considerable profit, but such transactions must have caused great prolongation of voyages. Yet there was then no other way to trade. Junks and dhows carried no freights as we know them. They carried goods for trading, for sale; and they had to sell one lot before they could buy the next, just as my Kuwait *boom* had to do in 1939. They could carry on a certain amount of trade by barter, but cash had to be collected sometimes. This would cause delays. It always has done so. Hence, very likely, the ancient accounts of voyages that lasted as many years as we know they could be accomplished in months, even under sail. And we know the ancients had a good knowledge of the monsoonal winds and the use of them and that those men were experts at such navigation as they needed. Junks were good ships.

At the very best, a big junk might make the run from Canton direct to Basra, say, in the one season, and then return with the next northeast monsoon. But then she would have to wait somewhere near Singapore or Malacca until the southwest season was established in the South China Sea, and with that, she would run a very real chance of total loss from a typhoon when nearing home. A round voyage would occupy no less than one year or even fifteen months.

Yet, very early in our era, and again in the Middle Ages, Chinese junks did visit the northern ports of the Persian Gulf as a matter of habit, and there is plenty of evidence of voyages made by them to East African ports. Chinese coins dating back to early in the eighth century have been unearthed at various points along the Swahili coast, and there are references in a Chinese history to a visit paid to Mogadishu by a fleet of junks in the year 1430. But the great Chinese monk I-Ching, who voyaged from China to India in the year 671, used a Persian or an Arab ship to transport him. I-Ching has left a record of his voyage.

"Long were we held over the immense abyss," he wrote. "Great waves, high as mountains, lay across the sea, over the whole valley of the vasty deep the waters rose like clouds to heaven." This is poetic stuff, and landsman's poetry. The learned monk could have cared little for his voyage, for the weather could not have been so bad as that. He reached Sumatra in due course and sighted the Nicobars on his way across the Bay of Bengal. As many later travelers were to do, he gave the inhabitants of those islands a bad name. He called the Nicobars the "land of the naked men," and said that if the ship's people refused to barter with them, the islanders immediately opened up with poisoned arrows.

Chinese records of the seventh century speak of the route followed by the junks on their long passage from Canton toward the Euphrates. One such record mentions that they usually occupied about twenty days on the section of the passage between the mouths of the Indus and the island of Hormuz, which even then was marked by an excellent lighthouse. It is significant that the Arabs themselves had a large trading establishment in Canton at that time, for such long voyages could have been made only by a power which dominated the entire length of the sea route or had an abiding alliance with some powerful ally who did. The evidence suggests that it was the Arabs who dominated much of these seas, not the Chinese.

Within a century or so, the big junks were gone from the Gulf.

and they did not return. For a while—perhaps for a long time—
they brought their cargoes to India, and Marco Polo speaks of seeing them there. But before very long they were not sailing beyond
the Straits of Malacca. Except for smaller junks penetrating the
waters of the Bay of Bengal, in search of *bêches-de-mer* and edible
birds' nests, and the coasting junks of the East Indies, big Chinese
sailing ships have not been seen on ordinary voyages in the Indian
Ocean for several centuries.

They were good ships, the best of which could well have made the
long voyage around the Cape of Good Hope to Europe. About a
century ago, when the accomplishment had become, perhaps, more
spectacular than useful, one did so, and the arrival of the beautiful
big junk in the Thames amazed the Victorian English. Her size,
her excellent accommodation, and her ornate decoration astonished
landsmen and seamen alike, but the seamen noted also the massive
strength of the well-constructed hull, the serviceability of the
enormous rigging, and the excellent safety device of subdivid-
ing the hold into many watertight compartments—an innovation
which, thousands of years old in the good ships of China, they had
yet to see introduced on a large scale in their own vessels.

Like Marco Polo, they marveled. Marco Polo wrote of a big
four-masted junk which had sixty separate cabins for merchants,
in the afterpart of the ship, and a hold subdivided into thirteen
watertight compartments.

It would have been odd if the mariners of the civilized East, sailing in such vessels, *had* rounded the Cape of Good Hope and sailed
northward to "discover" western Europe and perhaps America, as
well, centuries before Columbus and Vasco da Gama set out on
their epoch-making voyages. This the big Chinese junk or the
stout forerunner of the Indian *kotia* could indeed have done. The
results would have been most interesting.

CHAPTER IX

The Portuguese Pioneers

The Point of Sagres is a long way from the Indian Ocean. With Cape St. Vincent, it forms the extreme southwestern corner of Europe. Open to the wild Atlantic on three sides, no tree seems able to rise from its flat and rocky surface and, even on the calmest day, the sea beats violently at the base of its high cliffs. It is a place of strong winds and turbulent seas. When the wind is in the west and strong, the spray drives over the cliffs and breaks upon the lighthouse of Cape St. Vincent close by, flying hundreds of feet into the air as if determined to obscure the light. On quiet days, the sea roars through caverns and tunnels deep into the rock, as if the Atlantic Ocean were discontented to find itself confined and was determined to wash away that abrupt corner of Europe. On top of the cliffs the surface is covered with small gray rocks, among which the loveliest flowers grow, out of the wind; the vegetation cannot rise more than a foot or so above the ground. To the east, in the distance, are the hills of the kingdom of Algarve, where here and there the white houses of small villages partly reassure the wanderer, appalled, in the presence of such grandeur, by thoughts of the utter inconsequence of man. The Point of Sagres is the ideal locale for the visionary, the dreamer. Here, under the dome of the Atlantic sky where for thousands of years the ocean roared an exultant defiance at the efforts of seafaring man, great ideals might be born, and nurtured.

117

Here, in the early fifteenth century, came the man who, though he saw nothing of these great things in his own lifetime, was destined to open up the Indian Ocean and all the eastern world to the commerce of Europe, to blaze the seaway around the Cape of Good Hope, to alter the balance of power in the known world, and to pioneer the modern age. He was a Portuguese prince, by name the Infante Henrique, which in English is Prince Henry, the son of an English mother, the brother of the Portuguese king. He was twenty-four years old when, of his own volition, he retired to Sagres. He had already distinguished himself in military action against the "Moors," those virile and capable warriors who, under the spur of Islam, had carried the word and the sword of the Prophet through the Mediterranean and threatened to engulf Europe. In his lifetime, these so-called Moors were a very real threat to Christian civilization, and their arms were powerful. To fight them back, step by step, port by port, beach by beach, through the length and breadth of the Mediterranean, would obviously be a long and immensely costly process, if it were possible at all. But why not turn their flank? Better still, why not attack the source of their wealth at its roots? For the legend of Araby the Blest was then exploded. The wealth of the Islamic world rested not upon the trade and resources of Arabia, but upon control of the rich sea routes of the Indian Ocean. Through their hands came all the costly products of the East—spices and jewels and silks and raiment, ivory and incense. In Arabia there was little wealth upon which to found a world-dominating power. The routes up the Red Sea and the Persian Gulf, the monsoonal traffic to India and on to the Malay Peninsula and the China Sea—these things, and the land caravans, they sat astride and dominated. They were fearless and competent seamen. They were mathematicians, navigators, and shipbuilders without peer. They were merchants, traders, linguists. Their physique and their endurance, bred of the desert, were alike magnificent. Moreover, all sources of rich trade were in their keeping, so long as they could dominate the eastern seas.

The idea which came to Prince Henry was to overwhelm the sea power of the Islamic world at its source, and that he could only do by finding the sea route to India and eliminating altogether the Red Sea and Persian Gulf dhows and the overland caravans. Sea route to India? Who knew there was such a thing? In Prince Henry's day, it was customary to accept what was known as the useful limit of knowledge. It was a brave man who even conceived the idea of sailing where men had not sailed before. But there *was* a myth of a voyage around the length of Africa and into the Erythraean Sea, which had been made by the ships of Necho. There *had* been two Genoese ships which passed the Straits of Gibraltar and set their prows bravely southward "that they might go by sea to the ports of India." True, nothing more was ever heard of them, and they had been missing for almost a century and a half when Prince Henry went to Sagres. But the idea—that was the thing. Sea route to India? There *must* be something in the vague belief of geographer after geographer, from the ancient times, that Africa was not an infinite land, that in the south there was a way around it which would lead brave ships into the Indian seas. And if there were, a vast commerce could arise in which the infidel "Moors" would have no hand at all.

Prince Henry resolved to find that way. Inspired by his faith and his religious zeal, he set himself with lifelong determination and never diminished zeal to find what no man had found before him and what few believed could exist. He went to work slowly, as a scientist and as a statesman, a master navigator, a master shipwright, a prince of cartographers. In fact, he was himself none of these things, and the difficulties against him were immense. His homeland of Portugal was small, poor, and thinly populated. Others dominated the Mediterranean trade. Others provided much of the shipping which then plied between the Middle and the Baltic seas. All along the coasts of Portugal, the Atlantic Ocean roared its defiance at man and his weak ships. Moreover, the merchants of Venice and of Genoa who were already profiting from the absence of any direct link between West and East, would be equally determined that none should come into existence, if they could prevent it. Eastern goods found their eventual market in Europe through the merchants of these ports, and their profit was great.

The Portuguese, at that time, had no particular knowledge of navigation or of deepwater voyages. Their ships were good coastal vessels, as they had to be to survive in the Atlantic seas. But they were not long-voyage ships. No one then made long voyages from Europe. There were no ships fit for such enterprises. Prince Henry had first to foster the science of navigation and to bring into being ships, and seamen, capable of making voyages of twice the number of thousands of miles that vessels were then accustomed to make in hundreds of miles. It was a formidable undertaking. Against him were superstition, established trade and all its vested interests, the strength and power of the bold Moors themselves. Against him also were thousands upon thousands of miles of sea, some stormy, some not, almost all of it equally unknown.

At his lonely hermitage of Sagres the west winds screamed defiance at him. The salt spray drove into his melancholy face, and the rough, tempestuous, and angry sea shouted its derision day and night, ceaselessly. There were times when Sagres was to him a terrifying place. Could man hope to defeat the elements, noisy and implacable, which had dominated him for so long? Who could sail the "sea of darkness" and bring light? Yet, if it were God's will, he knew he would succeed. His country was poor in resources, but it was rich in courage. Its seamen had not as yet made long voyages, but they were bold and hardy men, expert from childhood in the way of a boat in the anger of the surf. The good fisherman makes a good sailor. They had been schooled down the centuries in the hardest school of all—in small ships upon a stormy coast. They had had to find their living and their food in the sea. That way breeds hardiness and skill, endurance and fortitude. Give them the seagoing ships, and they would sail them! And so the caravel was developed, a stout ship and seaworthy, which could sail.

But the ships were useless if no one understood the science of conducting them safely from place to place. Stars and familiar landmarks were all very well for short passages, to which men were accustomed. But to blaze out into the unknown and, finding what was there hidden, bring back account and directions of it good enough for men to follow—these were different skills. To navigate with success required instruments, skill in using them, nautical tables showing the movements of the heavenly bodies, and accurate charts. There were already then early astronomical navigators who knew, having measured the angle of the sun at its midday height, how to compute from that the distance of the ship, measured in degrees from the place where the sun was overhead. But for such methods to be of use, the navigator in his ship must have tables showing where the sun *was* overhead, at all times of the year, for the sun traveled. Indeed, it never stopped. There was nothing easy about these problems, and they had to be overcome.

Prince Henry slowly assembled the best mathematical, astronomical, and navigational brains he could find and, with these, the cartographers and the practical seamen, and he set about creating the science of navigation as it has, very largely, come down to us today. Some of his experts were Semitic persons, skilled with figures, with seafaring ancestry and keen minds, and their efforts flourished under the genius of the Navigator Prince. The compass rose, laid out in rough stones taken from Sagres Point, still stands where they put it upon the earth, the better to comprehend some of their problems. Nothing else they knew now stands on Sagres, but the voyages they made possible reached the ends of the earth.

What sort of man was this Prince Henry, this princeling pioneer of modern seafaring? His likenesses show a somber countenance and a bearing almost melancholy. "Devoid of affability, without any personal charm, reserved, vague in his speech, distrait, almost misanthropic," a Portuguese scholar has described him.[*] But the same historian has pointed out that

[*] *The Sons of King John I*, by J. F. Oliveira Martins.

the sympathetic quality and the greatness of men like the Infante Dom Henrique are not to be discovered in their character or their individuality, but in the tasks they undertook to carry out. The Infante's plan was sound and fruitful. . . . His temperament burned with a feverish feat, but this was because he was possessed by an idea in which he ardently believed. His bearing was reserved, his speech gentle. His genius was constant in adversity and quite void of the vanity of the weak. He was modest as the strong are always, because they know no need to exhibit themselves, to show off, to display their importance. He was modest because he was an ascetic. He was chaste and abstemious, and he fasted half the year. . . . He spent all his days and he spent long, watchful nights, studying, searching, meditating; not lost in the fantastic speculations of the metaphysician but pondering the positive, the practical reality of the world, sketched before him in the crude charts of his day. Like an alchemist, he sought to extract the secrets of the world from those parchments. He was not in search of any chimera. "And it seemed as though his body, thus constrained, put upon itself another nature." He sought the possible. And it was so possible that, within a century, it had become fact.

This then was the man who, from the nearby Lagos Bay, sent ship after ship questing down the west coast of Africa upon the "sea of darkness," who never was perturbed by criticisms and calumnies, who inspired reluctant mariners and sometimes mediocre leaders never to give up hope, to brave the reputed dangers of the torrid zone and the long and seemingly hopeless way over the treacherous sea, toward India. Not all his mariners were reluctant, nor were all his captains mediocre, by any means. But the voyages had to be paid for somehow. The quest of knowledge was slow, and costly. There were never lacking those who, having discovered a little, having for instance lit upon the profitable Guinea trade, were too happy to cry, "Enough! Let us profit from what has now been found, and seek no more!" Caravel after caravel followed one another down the seemingly interminable African coast, many hesitant to pass even a league beyond the point already discovered by their predecessors, some boldly pushing on 20 leagues, 50 leagues, perhaps even 100, but always coming back. Coming back, coming back, and never one near the end of the long brown land, none even hearing rumor of any eastward trend or sound of the Indian Ocean. Naked savages and treachery, queer beasts and strange woods, sometimes slaves and ivory, and a little gold—these things they found. Each expedition had to pay for its own outlay. The Prince could not finance discovery for its own sake. The captains found recompense and reward in the fruits of their own voyages, and it was inevitable that often these things would become the main aim. It took fifteen years to round Cape Bojador, just south of the Canary Islands, and another twenty to pass Cape Verde. There was a great reluctance, first, to pass Cape Bojador at all, for many seamen regarded this headland as encompassing the useful world; having once passed it, a reluctance persisted to go much farther.

Said the mariners, this much is clear, that beyond this Cape of Bojador there is no race of men or place of inhabitants: nor is the land less sandy than the deserts of Libya, where there is no water, no tree, no green herb—and the sea so shallow that a whole league from the land it is only a fathom deep, while the currents are so terrible that a ship, having once passed the Cape, will never be able to return.

So recorded the historian of that time, Azurara, and there was indeed a great deal to be said for the seamen's point of view. So far as they knew, the coast of Africa there *was* most uninviting. It was bounded by shallows; the land was a desert; there appeared no prospects of trade. The new voyage whereof the outcome cannot be known is always long and trying. It is difficult, perhaps, to picture now just what a quietly courageous kind of seafaring was being steadily pursued by the Portuguese at that time. There is no modern analogy, and there can be none. The leaders might reap the reward of honor as well as wealth, but the common seamen would forever know only hardship and danger, without compensatory recompense beyond the good of their own spirits. Why, then, persist in what seemed a futile struggle to blaze a path to nowhere? To seek endlessly what might, after all, not be there?

Yet the mariners were bold enough, or they would not have found the Azores or made out into the broad Atlantic, as they did. They could not coast to the Azores, and there is evidence that they sailed much farther than those Atlantic islands. It was known that the world was round, and the theory had long been put forward that it was possible to reach the East by sailing west. Prince Henry was aware of two ways to the Indian Ocean, and he sent out ships to explore both. The existence of Greenland was known, for it had been discovered by the Norsemen in the tenth century. There was an established commerce with Iceland. There were at least legends of lands far out to the west, far across the great sea which stretched away, a fathomless and angry challenge, from Sagres Point.

But the main hope was to sail around Africa. Year after year, decade after decade, the quest went on—past the coast of Guinea, the Ivory Coast, the Gold Coast; past the great rivers, the Senegal, the Niger, down to the mighty Congo. It was a great disappointment when, the bulge of West Africa being safely passed, navigators returned yet from voyage after voyage to report that the endless land turned south again, and continued to the south, on and on and on. Would it never end? As the equator was crossed and the ships still quested ever to the southward, their sailing and navigational problems increased greatly. It was no longer possible to sail and return on the same winds, even with the most weatherly vessels. It was no longer possible to make real progress by coasting. They had to strike out into the open sea, and to do this they had to master the wind system of the Atlantic Ocean. In these days of powered vessels when the sea route to anywhere is the shortest distance between two points, we are apt to forget how immensely difficult it must have been to strike out into the broad Atlantic in a sailing ship when there was not even knowledge of its trade-wind systems.

In the Indian Ocean the monsoons alternate, first one way and then the other. But in the Atlantic the trade winds blow constantly toward the equator, the year round, in the north and the south, from the northeast or north-northeast, and the south-southeast and southeast. A ship, having worked her way wearily across the calm belt upon the equator and facing the southeast trade winds, would get nowhere if she tried to beat against them. But what else could she do? There was no way to head into the wind. The Portuguese caravels were good, weatherly vessels, which means to say that they could lie up close to the wind and sail like yachts. But even the best of modern yachts will make poor progress *against* a steady trade wind.

The only way to make successful voyages under sail was to *use* the trade winds, not to beat against them. They could be used by accepting the fact that it was impossible to head directly for the wished-for port and, instead, to take the wind upon the beam and snore along with it a thousand miles and more, as far as it would take the ship. Then, having gained latitude this way—for a good ship could make south with the southeast trade or north with the northeast—the bold mariner could turn his prow eastward in the zone of variable winds and make such way as he could, sometimes with the wind in his favor, sometimes against him. The first man to make voyages of this kind, as opposed to coastal crawling, was a great discoverer indeed, and the first man was a Portuguese.

And still, beyond all the region of the southeast trade wind and down into the variable belt, was the formidable coast of endless Africa. As ship after ship, having made the wide-circle course forced upon her, sailed eastward to round the land, her mariners found the great mass of Africa blocking their path, three thousand, four thousand miles from Portugal. No end, no end! And the south winds blew in their faces as they approached the land. The wind blew from the direction in which they must sail, as if determined to thwart them and to destroy the Navigating Prince's great beliefs. Go back, go back! It was always easier to go back than to sail on, for wind and current alike were adverse for continuing, but favorable for going home. It was obvious that a greater and a bolder sailor, taking his courage in his hands, must sail fearlessly farther to the south than any had gone before. When his ship emerged from the trade-wind belts, he must still press southward and not turn east until he had gone another 500 or 600 miles.

This constant ocean voyaging by the Portuguese had made them skilled and fearless navigators. There are, unfortunately, inadequate records of the pioneers who blazed the way toward the southern tip of Africa. No certainty exists as to who among their captains first sailed out into the open sea, who first made a bold board through the southeast trades. There was, of necessity, strict secrecy about much of the voyaging. There was trouble with Spain. It was imperative that both the Venetian middlemen and the Indian Ocean Moors themselves should have no inkling of what was at stake. Records have been lost. Prince Henry died in 1460, and the records of his navigation school were removed to Lisbon, where they were lost, probably deliberately. By that time, cartographers and pilots from many nations had learned to seek information in Portugal. It was easier to copy charts than to make voyages, and Portugal, though already enriched by the slowly increasing West African trade, was not strong enough to stand up to real rivals. The best policy then was to keep potential rivals in ignorance. Knowledge was carefully guarded and myths were fostered, to keep the ships of rival nations in their accustomed trades.

It was more than a quarter of a century after Prince Henry's death before the great continent was rounded and the Indian Ocean reached. The navigator Diego Cão was at Walvis Bay, at the tropic's edge, in 1485, but the Cape was then another 750 miles away. It remained to an obscure seafarer named Bartolomeo Dias, of whom we know little, to make the final great voyage which reached the Indian Ocean and brought Henry's work to a successful fruition. Dias and the others had found much to encourage them. They knew they were on the right track, though they had been compelled to accept so many disappointments.

There had been for many years persistent reports of a Christian monarchy lost in the great land of Africa somewhere, ruled over by a kingly cleric known as Prester John. This Prester John is frequently dismissed as a myth, but there is no doubt that there was a basis of truth in the reports of his existence. Time and again, Portuguese navigators and explorers heard something of a spiritual monarch, as they moved down the west coast of Africa or struck into the interior. The main fact which emerged was that somewhere in Ethiopia there ruled a Christian king whose subjects held him in similar reverence to that in which Catholics held the Pope. Obviously, this man and his kingdom should be powerful allies to the Portuguese plan of outflanking the world of Islam.

In 1486, King John of Portugal heard what he took to be convincing reports of the existence of this Christian monarchy in Ethiopia. Efforts to establish contact were redoubled. The very next year, two great expeditions left Portugal, both quietly, without fanfare of trumpets, without anything to mark them. These were the expeditions by sea led by Bartolomeo Dias, which was to round the Cape of Good Hope, and the party of two men which, proceeding as best they might, was to reach the court of the Christian King of Ethiopia and to sail in Moorish ships to the very land of India.

These two men were Pero de Covilhão and Affonso de Paiva. Their mission was to provide intelligence. Dias was to find the route by which Portuguese ships and seamen could profit, and by which the Christian message could be brought more surely to all who lived in the lands washed by the Indian Ocean. Some contact had been established with Abyssinia before the two Portuguese adventurers set out on their quest, and plans had been formulated to make Prester John into a formidable ally of Christian Europe. But unless European ships could reach the Indian Ocean in strength, it was obvious—at any rate, to the Portuguese sailor-princes—that such efforts were futile. Hence the quest of the Cape, and hence, too, the secret mission of Covilhão and Paiva, which was jointly to examine the trade and the wealth of the Indies, to inform the real Prester John of the Portuguese King's intentions, and to gauge the probable amount of assistance that Prester John could give, if any.

Covilhão and Paiva were alike experienced agents. They spoke fluent Arabic and could pass as Arabs. They also spoke Spanish and Italian, and they had a mastery of the general lingua franca of the Mediterranean used by merchants who wandered here and there in ships, taking their goods with them. The plan of these two was to pass themselves as merchants and, gradually, using what means of conveyance they could find, to work themselves half across the world, from Portugal to India. On the seventh of May, 1487, they were given a Royal audience, in secret, before their departure.

For many, many months and even years afterward, these two strange wanderers were to make their adventurous way about the world—to Valencia first, then Barcelona; thence by sea to Naples and on to Rhodes; thence, with a shipment of honey in which they invested, the better to carry their guise as merchants, by ship again to Alexandria. Here both almost died of fever, and recovered to find their goods and wealth had been seized, as was the local custom when any foreign merchant was about to die. They then went to Cairo, where they learned the way to the farther East. They crossed the Isthmus of Suez and shipped down the Red Sea— probably from Suakin—in a small dhow, which eventually took them to Aden. At Aden they learned almost all they had come to find, for they arrived during the northeast monsoon and the bustle of the Indian trade was in full progress. Here they separated. There were dhows going to the Red Sea coast near Ethiopia, landing goods at ports from which caravans continued toward the court of Prester John. Paiva shipped in one of these and was never heard of again. Covilhão, still posing as a merchant in Eastern goods, took passage in a large dhow bound for the Malabar coast.

He had no difficulty in taking passage in such a dhow, for no one knew him as a Portuguese, and merchants from all the countries of the Indian Ocean and from Egypt and Greece, and even from Venice, were no strangers in the port of Aden. Covilhão was well practiced then in passing as a devout Moslem and his Arabic, though obviously tainted by its Mediterranean origin, was perfect. One pictures him seated with his goods upon the high poop of a big dhow similar in most respects to the double-ended *booms* of today, while the quiet monsoon wind blew the stately vessel on a way strange to the Portuguese but familiar enough to everyone else aboard. He would take part in the general yarning, which was the main way of passing the time, and use the discourse, no doubt, to improve his knowledge of the trade. Whence came the spices, which were so valued in all Europe? Where did they grow? Who controlled the trade? In the big dhow were many merchants, men who knew the Eastern seas and all their trade. Among them, the mission of Pero de Covilhão prospered.

Day after day, the sun shone and the dhow sailed eastward. They lived upon the fish of the sea, which were plentiful and good, and rice, served with herbs and ghee. Dried fruits kept the scurvy at bay. Strong curries kept their stomachs in order. They washed in the sea, and their loose robes of cotton were kept clean in the same manner. A man could have his servant wash out a gown and hold it in the breeze to dry again and be fit for wearing in ten minutes. By the time landfall was made on the Mount of Delli behind the port of Cannanore, King John's special agent knew precisely where to look to round out his knowledge of Eastern trade. He went to Calicut first, and decided that this was the place to make for. Cannanore was itself an important port, but Calicut was greater.

There he found a considerable Moslem colony and, in his guise as a fellow "Moor" from the Mediterranean, there was little difficulty in discovering all he had come so far to know. And so to Goa (which later was to become the very font of Portuguese power in the Indian Ocean) and, ever in quest of more knowledge, he passed on to Hormuz by another Arab dhow, and thence by the great and ancient sea road down the east coast of Africa as far as Sofala, where there was trade with the interior in gold. From here he made for Aden again, and thence to Cairo.

His report was complete. His work had been well done, and he looked forward to returning to Portugal to deliver his report. But at Cairo he learned of the disappearance of his companion, and he received secret orders from his king to return to Abyssinia and establish contact with Prester John. Poor Covilhão! He had a wife and children in Portugal. He had then been away from home four years. He had such a store of knowledge of the Eastern seas and all their trade inside his clever head as, probably, had never been contained in one brain before. His quest had been accomplished, and magnificently. He was tired, and weary for the sight of his own Portugal. Yet now he must set off again. He wrote all he had discovered, in a letter to King John, and started out once more on his travels. First he made his way to Hormuz again, taking with him the King's emissary who had brought his secret orders to the rendezvous in Cairo. From Hormuz he made the pilgrimage to Mecca, the better to continue his disguise as a devout Moslem. From Mecca he went to Medina and to Sinai. Early in 1493, he reached Abyssinia and established himself at the court of the Emperor. If this were Prester John, the contact was not much use to the Portuguese. The Emperor had no ships. But Covilhão was not allowed to leave again; now and then, he could send intelligence to Portugal. He lived in Abyssinia, a hopeless exile, for the following thirty years, and there he died.

There have been many great European wanderers, and Arabs, Persians, and Chinese, in the Indian Ocean, but there has been none greater than this obscure Pero de Covilhão. His whole life was an incredible adventure. In whatever he undertook to do, he was successful. He never wearied, never lost sight of his goal. Turning back from Cairo to begin again the dangerous and exhausting quest upon which he had already done sufficient for one lifetime, was the act of a truly brave man. In the ranks of the Indian Ocean pioneers Pero de Covilhão deserves to rank high.

But he had been overshadowed, long before he was back in Cairo, by the successful voyage to the Cape and around it by Bartolomeo Dias, Knight of the Royal Household and experienced navigator in the southern seas. But Dias, like Covilhão, was doomed to bitter disappointment and frustration when he should have known glory. Success was his, but glory never.

Bartolomeo Dias had made several West African voyages before being selected to command the important expedition of 1487. Three ships went, two being caravels of about a hundred tons and the third a small storeship. A caravel was a vessel corresponding, roughly, to the later barquentine rig, which is to say that she had two or three masts carrying fore-and-aft sails, and one or two large square sails on the fore. She was therefore able to take best advantage of both leading winds and fair winds. The fore-and-aft sails were big lateens, than which there is no better sail, and the big square sails forward were real pullers. These caravels were far from being the clumsy, basinlike vessels, called round ships, which were still in general use from European ports other than the Portuguese, and Dias and his shipmates well understood how to get the best out of them.

On the great voyage, Dias left the storeship, apparently, at Walvis Bay, having come in upon the land there, and then sailed toward the south. One story goes that a strong wind drove the ship for thirteen days toward the south. There are no reliable records of the Dias voyage, and even the precise dates are unknown. It is difficult for a sailor to credit that such a man could have been *driven* to the south for as long a period as thirteen days, in an area where the preponderance of winds is from that direction. It is probable that, determined to come to the end of the continent somehow, he deliberately sailed south as long and as hard as he could, and allowed his crew, perhaps, to believe that there was no alternative.

The ships were small and the weather, we are told, very cold (which it certainly would not have been there with a northerly wind), and the mariners "suffered greatly." After the thirteen days,

Dias turned the prows of his two caravels toward the east. East he sailed and eastward the small ships rolled through a waste of waters, and now the seas were high and the wind tumultuous. But the wind was from the west and the stout caravels, dipping and rolling, ran as fast as small albatrosses. East! East! And there was no land. They ran for many days, and there was no land at all. Africa had gone; they were around!

But now the mariners began to mutter, and there was serious disaffection. "Turn north! Turn north!" they cried, fearful of being lost in the waste of gray waters where no ship had sailed before. Dias had to turn toward the north. The ships made landfall by Mossel Bay, well to the east of Cape Agulhas, in the waters of the Indian Ocean. What Prince Henry had set out to do had now been done. The way to India was clear. The great pioneering had born fruit of untold value.

But Dias's mariners refused to sail on. They had come far enough, they said. They had good tidings to take back to the King. Why seek more? Dias could induce them only to sail onward a few more days and then, sick at heart, knowing that the great honor of being first in the Indian Ocean was his and yet that he was permitted barely to stand upon its threshold, Dias had to put about and sail for home. On the homeward voyage he passed close by the great cape. The legend is that he named it the Cape of Storms and that King John changed the name to Cape of Good Hope. But there is reason to believe that Dias gave it this latter name, which it kept. It was to him the Cape of Good Hope to which he might return upon another voyage, and on this next occasion, reach India.

This he never did, though he was selected as one of the commanders with the later Cabral fleet. Upon a stormy South Atlantic day when Cabral's fleet was making toward the Cape of Good Hope which Dias had discovered, Dias's ship was overwhelmed in the sea. A great squall struck her, and she was not seen again. So Dias perished, taken by the sea one of whose greatest secrets he had

An Indian type of monsoon dhow

The *Keyling*—a Chinese junk that sailed to Europe

Vasco da Gama

Affonso d'Albuquerque

l'Infant Don Henri

Henry the Navigator, Prince of Portugal

Old Portuguese fort, Muscat, on the Gulf of Oman

discovered; and now his homeland cannot find as much as an authentic likeness of him.

Through Bartolomeo Dias and Pero de Covilhão, Europe had acquired a new dimension. The economic and social structure of the Middle Ages were alike at an end, and the Modern Age was about to begin. Though she had known torment and had approached perilously close to being lost, Europe, the guardian of civilization, was about to extend her power and influence to the ends of the earth. The sea washed exultantly over the bones of Bartolomeo Dias, and Covilhão lay in an unmarked Abyssinian grave; but their work was done. The Moorish flank was turned. It had taken a long time, but at last the way was open for European ships to sail to the Indian Ocean. They had had to be better vessels than the monsoonal dhows and junks, to sail so far, and they had to be commanded and manned by able and resolute men. It was inevitable that control of the new ocean would pass into their hands. The Asiatic powers had not had the vision, the knowledge, or the organizing ability to keep the Europeans at bay. Now it was too late.

CHAPTER X

Vasco da Gama

The examination had been satisfactory and the members of the council were unanimously impressed. Admiral Vasco da Gama, talking the matter over quietly with his brother Paulo in the stern cabin of the comfortable *San Gabriel,* allowed himself to venture the hope that the major troubles of the expedition were over. They had been many and serious. Success, he knew, might hinge on the abilities and integrity of this pilot which the Sheik of Malindi had at last provided. The Sheik had said the delays were in part due to his desire to find the best man available. Maybe this was true. At any rate, no captain or pilot of any of the Portuguese vessels had been able to flaw the knowledge of the tall, bearded man whose examination had just been concluded in the main cabin of the flagship. His collection of charts was complete and impressive. His knowledge of such instruments as the Portuguese had with them was obviously thorough; indeed, it was *he* who had asked the more searching questions, and not the Portuguese. He had shown them copies of several oceanic directories which he said he had produced himself. He had answered all queries in a direct and straightforward manner. His air of authoritative knowledge, his quiet gentlemanly bearing, the respect with which he was held by the others from the shore, and his obvious complete familiarity with ships and ocean seafaring, were alike impressive.

"I want the fellow only for the identification of our landfall in

134

India, and to bring us to Calicut," the Admiral was saying. "We can make the passage across this ocean well enough ourselves."

"Indeed we can," said Paulo. "Pero de Alemquer is a first-class navigator. And you know we have others."

"I was especially pleased with the success of our long run in the Atlantic Sea. We have Pero to thank for that. But I do not care to make toward a strange coast with no knowledge of its landmarks," the brother continued, "or at any rate, not enough to be sure. The trouble with these landsmen's reports is that they never see a place the way the seaman is going to see it, when he's coming on the land from a long voyage. I'm glad to have Covilhão's screed—it's useful enough, in other ways."

The two da Gama brothers were discussing the arrival aboard the *San Gabriel* that day of the famous Arab pilot, Ahmed Ibn Majid, who was to pilot them to their destination on the far side of the Indian Ocean. It was more than ten years since Bartolomeo Dias had rounded the Cape of Good Hope, but in all that time there had been no Portuguese or any other European ship in the Indian Ocean. Meanwhile, Columbus had blown across the North Atlantic westward before the northeast trade wind and had stumbled upon the outlying islands of the new American continent. It took time to verify that this was not Asia and that there was no way to India by the west.

Columbus's discovery had put Portuguese plans back, but it had made no real difference to them. The existence of a great land in that direction had been frequently discussed among the pilots. Pero de Alemquer knew of it, and he knew Brazil. How else would the da Gama expedition have dared to go that way? The ships had been able to strike directly through the southeast trade winds, and to make a passage toward the Indian Ocean such as was rarely bettered even in the later days of ocean-going sailing ships. Dias knew of it; Dias had designed the special ships—big, beamy *navs*— for da Gama's voyage. Dias had designed them to run with beam and fair winds, and not to beat. They were large ships, not low caravels; the swift caravel had played its part in the opening of the Indian Ocean. Now the big fellows could come. But Dias would never have rigged the ships with the great square sails if he had not been sure of their capacity to run without danger through the trade-wind zone. Da Gama's two *navs* were large ships because they were going to bring back valuable cargoes. Da Gama was the King of Portugal's Ambassador, and his mission included the establishment of trade.

And now on this balmy evening the big *navs* swung quietly at anchor off the pleasant East African town of Malindi, not far north along the Kenya coast from Mombasa, a handy place for arrivals and departures in the Indian trade. It was already many months since the expedition had left the sunny Tagus, in distant Portugal. The Admiral still remembered the jeers of part of the crowd, shouting stupidly to his men that they were sure to lose their lives. His men were well chosen. None paid the least attention to the silly jeers. Many had been with Dias and upon other long voyages, and all felt now that this fleet would reach India without fail. The Admiral knew that even in high quarters there had been opposition to the idea of sending the ships to India. When King Manoel the Fortunate had called a Royal Council to debate the matter within a few months of ascending the throne, in 1495, almost two years before the vessels finally sailed, the majority of the councilors were against the enterprise on the grounds that Portugal had insufficient resources to undertake a venture so costly and difficult, and that it could not fail to cause trouble, and possibly war, with other powers. But the King knew that the Venetians were already in serious trouble with the Turks and were in no position to oppose him by open warfare. The prize was great. His kinsmen had expended vast sums upon pioneering voyages, and now one last voyage would bring fruition—and profit—to all. Some councilors favored the enterprise, and the King listened to them eagerly. The ships were already under construction and his mind was made up.

There were four ships altogether—the two *navs*, *San Gabriel* and *San Rafael,* a caravel from Lagos called the *Berrio* for her owner, and a storeship. The caravel was a scout, and the storeship was broken up and her stores and crew distributed among the other vessels, once the fleet was safely past the Cape. Vasco da Gama was in command of the expedition, and his brother Paulo in command of the *nav San Rafael.* Nicolas Coelho was in command of the *Berrio,* and Pero de Escolar was his pilot. Pero de Alemquer was chief pilot of the expedition. Another pilot, John of Coimbra, was with Paulo da Gama. These pilots were the best who could be found in Portugal, which is to say that they were without peer in the European world. All the selection of personnel and plans for the ships and the expedition had been looked after with the utmost care. Interpreters were carried who spoke Arabic and many African dialects (which were, however, useless on the East Coast). The ships were stored as well as they could conceivably be, and the 170 mariners had been offered special bonuses to add to their skills. They were good men and good sailors. Also carried in the ships, but apart from the ordinary crew, were ten or twelve men who had been condemned to death for criminal offenses. These were taken along with the idea of using them for especially dangerous enterprises of which there were plenty. This was a custom of the times, and many such men had been landed at odd points in Africa—and Brazil—in order to learn the language and gather intelligence, throughout the preceding half century. Vasco da Gama asked especially for convicts with some knowledge of Arabic, and had received several of these. They were most useful men. Thankful to be spared their lives and to be out of jail, they were content with the enterprises assigned to them.

One had been ashore in Malindi that day, in the month of April, 1498, as his admiral waited impatiently for the pilot promised by the Sheik. It was the same man who had first unearthed the plot against the ships at Mombasa, farther down the coast. The Arabs there had feigned friendship, at first, and da Gama was on the point of shifting his fleet into the inner harbor at their invitation, which would have been fatal. The weather was good and it was quite safe to anchor off. But the Arab Sheik of Mombasa had especially requested that the ships be brought closer in, under guise of being able to assist them better. At the time, many of da Gama's men were down with scurvy. The Admiral had weighed anchor and stood in, with flags flying and the great drums going, and his men lined up in their jerkins and breastplates, although their crossbows and pikes were handy in the shadow of the bulwarks. The fleet made a stirring scene in the African sunlight, and the palm-fringed beach, where the Sheik stood waiting under a crimson canopy, was most inviting.

But the convict had spoken of treachery. Da Gama was on the alert. On the way in, the ships going under easy sail with Arab pilots aboard to guide them, the two *navs* came into slight collision. They had little way and there was no damage. But da Gama anchored at once and the Arab pilots, whose nerves must have been on edge, took immediate alarm and leaped into the sea, striking out for the shore. At the sight of this, the Sheik and his huge party, thinking their designs discovered, rose and shouted, and all guise of friendliness was dropped. At midnight that night a large party of swimmers, armed to the teeth, was apprehended, making for the ships to cut their cables while the tide set in. But da Gama's men were on the alert and the design was thwarted. The Portuguese had known the same kind of thing at Mozambique, where earlier Arab pilots had done their best to wreck the ships.

It was with great relief that the Admiral had brought the ships to the pleasant roadstead of Malindi, with its many-storied houses standing high and white along the waterfront, and the background of gardens and orchards adding to the pleasant view. Many of the houses were flat-roofed. There was a definite aspect of southern Portugal about them and about the town, at least when viewed from the sea. The da Gama brothers marked this resemblance, which was due to the fact that the Moors had had much to do with both countries. The fleet was served well at Malindi. Food supplies were good and abundant. Fat-tailed Somali sheep were especially plentiful and mutton had become a dish served daily in the Portuguese vessels. But the Sheik, who professed friendliness, had been dilatory in the matter of providing the wished-for pilot. The Sheik came aboard the *San Gabriel*, dressed in a satin-trimmed robe of costly damask with a jeweled turban on his head, and seated on a graceful throne underneath a large crimson canopy, while his musicians played for him on instruments made of ivory, silver, and gold.

Da Gama confided to his brother that it was greatly to be regretted that the high cost of fitting out the expedition had left no margin to purchase gifts fit for such a potentate, to whom he could offer only such paltry things as were usually exchanged as trade goods on the other coast of Africa. However, the Sheik accepted these gracefully. Perhaps he had heard of the effectiveness of the Portuguese artillery, from reports of its use farther down the coast. Vasco da Gama was a commanding, almost a dominating figure, and the friendship of a king who sent such a man and such ships on so long a journey was worth while. What was not available in the matter of presents was made up for in a show of good will, and the Sheik was treated to salutes from the bombards and an impressive display of bunting and arms drill.

But after a week of courtesies da Gama, never noted for his patience, had had enough. He knew that the southwest monsoon could not then be far away, and he was well aware that the ports of the Malabar coast would be useless, once the monsoon set in. So he seized a confidential servant of the Sheik and held him until the promised pilot was provided. The very next day this Ibn Majid had come aboard, and the fleet could sail. It was April 24, 1498.

The date could scarcely have been better chosen. On the advice of the Arab pilot, the fleet first ran along the African coast for three days, gradually hauling off the land. The winds were good and favorable, and the weather was delightful. It was the period just prior to the onslaught of the southwest monsoon, and there was generally enough southerly in the wind to let the ships run. Sometimes the wind was from the northeast and from north, but by first running along the coast of Africa toward the north, they were able to use any wind except an easterly. No easterlies blew. Da Gama remarked to the pilot that, if these were the sort of passages to which Indian Ocean vessels were accustomed, then it was not to be wondered at that sewn ships were thought to be adequate in those waters.

As day followed day and week followed week, da Gama found himself more and more impressed with this pilot. So were the professional seamen aboard, Gonzalo Alvares, the captain of the *nav,* and Pero de Alemquer. Through one of the convict interpreters, the Arab explained the best way to make the passage—indeed, the only way. His chart showed two large groups of coral islands in the path of the ships, the groups now known as the Maldives and the Laccadives. The visibility was good and the weather continued excellent. To avoid these dangers, which were practically the only ones, all that was necessary was to know the latitude and to keep a good lookout. So long as the ships were kept to a latitude where there were no islands, they would be all right. They would see the coast of India before they ran ashore there, for the place was high enough. Ibn Majid and the Portuguese pilots made their daily observations for latitude and computations of the ship's run.

Reckoning the run, at first, was a source of worry to the Arab, as he was unaccustomed to such slow vessels. Bartolomeo Dias's roomy design meant plenty of beam, but this in turn meant that the ships had to push a lot of the Indian Ocean out of their way as they sailed along. Their best speed was perhaps eight knots. Any ordinary lateen-rigged Arab vessel would be doing eleven or twelve, under the same conditions. But when he understood them, Ibn Majid admired the Portuguese ships. They were magnificently strong, and he did not fail to notice that they made admirable gun platforms for the heavy ordinance they carried.

When they passed close to the southernmost atolls of the

Laccadive group, although only a few outrigger canoes were to be seen fishing, Vasco da Gama caused the bunting to be flown and a light cannon fired, in salute. At this the fishermen, startled by the great ships, made off for their lives. Ibn Majid had instructed the Portuguese in the art of trolling for succulent fish as they sailed along, and the abundance of good fare caught in this way, together with the fruit and vegetables from Malindi, kept the scurvy down. Nearly all hands slept on deck during this part of the long voyage. The Admiral's quarters aft were light and airy, for he had the magnificent ventilation of the stern windows. The Arab pilot made his home in the open, on the poop, whence he could keep a sharp lookout, but his charts and his instruments he kept below. The soldiers and the sailors, in accordance with the custom of the time, had no proper quarters and no bunks other than such shelves as they cared to contrive for themselves in the upper hold. They were happy to be able to sleep on deck, coiled down anywhere, and a cloth of canvas from an old sail made an excellent couch for them.

As the ships approached the coast of India, everything was prepared for trade and for making an impressive display. Ibn Majid expressed the view that there would be no need for military action. It was known, he said, that strangers were coming, for news of their arrival on the East African coast had swept up the coast by swift dhow and had already been carried across the ocean by Arab and Indian seafarers. There was, said the Arab, trade enough for all, and he was sure the Portuguese would be welcomed, for their feat would be admired and its full import would not be realized. Ibn Majid seemed to have a good grasp of the political situation ashore in India, as well as of the art of pilotage in those waters. Da Gama, he said, was arriving at an opportune time. There was considerable disunity among the states of southern India, and several of the rulers were at loggerheads. Their trade was immense, and so was their wealth, but their military prowess at the moment was not great. They were in no fit state, even if

they wished, to unite to fight such well-armed vessels as the Portuguese. And why should they try? The export trade was in the
hands of the Moslems from Arabia. So long as the Hindu princes
and merchants had their profits from handling Eastern products,
they were not going to mind if competitors from Europe arrived
on the scene to compete for them, and carry them away.

As for the Moslems, it was no use denying that they would *not*
be pleased. On the grounds both of religion and of their own self-
interest, they must become implacable opponents of the Portuguese. But India was not their country. The two strange shipmates,
the distinguished Arab pilot and the Portuguese courtier, often
discussed the probable outcome of the arrival of the European
ships.

"We are coming to share in trade and to spread our faith, but
not to conquer," said da Gama.

"You will find you will have to conquer, whether you wish or
not," was the Arab's counsel.

They were still discussing the matter when, a little over three
weeks after leaving Malindi, the high blue land of India appeared suddenly out of the morning mist. The long-sought land
at last! The Arab's landfall was excellent. As the ships drew in
with the great land, he was able to point out to the Admiral the
various landmarks. It was then May 20, and he was anxious that
the Portuguese ships should find secure anchorage before the
stormy monsoon set in. It was due almost daily. Da Gama, however, was determined to anchor first off Calicut, to make a brave
show as the great ships came into the historic anchorage. This he
did, all the drums and trumpets sounding and the gay pennants
streaming from every yardarm, with the mariners and the soldiery
lined up in their leather jerkins and breastplates, and several of
the guns manned. Every soul aboard felt the drama of this great
occasion, and the chaplains, as soon as the anchors were down,
led a special service of thanks to God. A message was sent to the
ruler, known as the Samuri, announcing the arrival of the Por-

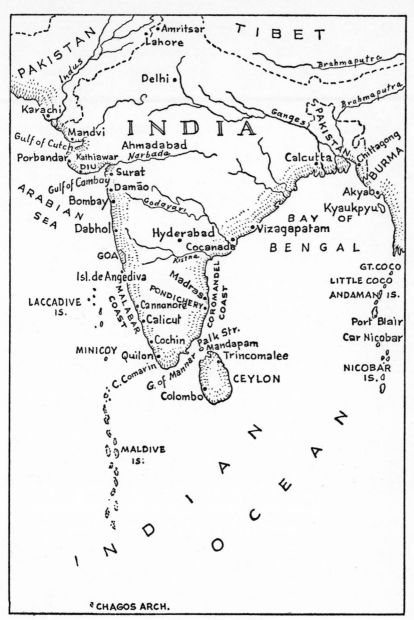

India and Pakistan

tuguese, and the ruler at once sent pilots aboard to shift the ships to a safer anchorage at Pandarani, a few miles up the coast. Within a week, the roads of Calicut would be untenable for shipping.

When the ships were secured, da Gama landed with due pomp and ceremony. He was dressed in his best and most impressive robes, and his haughty demeanor and long, dark countenance well set off the dignity of his attire. The Samuri sent a nobleman to attend him, and da Gama had a full muster of trumpeters, blowers of the Portuguese bagpipes, and beaters of great drums. His soldiers, dressed in their best, fired off their matchlocks every few moments, and a nobleman bore the silken banner of the Order of Christ. The populace of Calicut, unaccustomed to this kind of thing (though they were familiar with processions), crowded the congested streets so thoroughly that it was only with the greatest difficulty the Portuguese could make their way. The people of Calicut seemed pleased to see them. At any rate, they enjoyed the show.

At the Samuri's palace, da Gama found the ruler surrounded by every evidence of tremendous wealth. He sat in scarlet and gold beneath a gilt canopy, spitting betel-nut juice into a golden spittoon, while a further supply of betel was held ready in a large gold basin, in the hands of a liveried servant. The Indian's pearls alone must have been worth a fortune. If da Gama felt misgivings because of the utter inadequacy of the gifts he brought for such a millionaire, he did not show it. The Samuri was obviously interested in him and prepared to be friendly. He entertained the Portuguese with fruit, sweetmeats, and coffee. At a private audience immediately afterward, da Gama dilated upon the power and influence of his distant king, detailing the long record of the efforts to send ships to India. He seems to have been under some delusion that the Samuri, though with imperfect knowledge of its teachings, was an adherent of the Christian faith. He expounded at length on the great piety of the King of Portugal and his long-cherished desire to establish contact with the Christian rulers in

India, declaring that his mission was to spread the faith, and to unite the Christian rulers of West and East.

The Samuri appeared to be impressed. Da Gama and his men found what they imagined to be evidence of the Christian character of the Indians in the local temples, where representations of Indian deities appeared to them to be crude paintings of the saints, and a statue was thought to be Our Lady. To this they knelt and prayed without, apparently, the least idea that they were in a Hindu temple. The Admiral, however, did notice that some white earth which the priests gave him for use consisted of a paste made from cow dung, which struck him as odd, and the pictures of saints in the temple showed some rather hideous fellows, with teeth three inches long and four or five pairs of arms.

However, at the first audience all went well. Still, that matter of presents was a bugbear. Da Gama did the best he could, but his best muster was a poor lot—lengths of striped cloth of no particular merit either in workmanship or color, hoods made from some scarlet stuff to which the same estimates applied, assorted headgear, and coral necklets, a case of basins, some cooking oil, and sugar, and Portuguese honey of a kind much esteemed in Lisbon. The Samuri's factor burst into laughter when he saw the proposed gifts and, after a great laugh, suddenly became serious and refused to have anything to do with them. He would not forward such trash to the palace, he said. Why had da Gama brought no gold? The gifts were left to lie in the warehouse where they were landed. Da Gama was furious, declaring that he was not a merchant come to fawn with gifts of gold. But it was some time before he was granted another audience, and the fact that he declined to offer his gilded figure of Our Lady, which the Samuri requested, put a further strain on relations. In those days, it was an unheard-of thing for any sort of embassy to be sent to the ruler of a rich province—or any other sort of province from which advantage was sought—without bringing a collection of all sorts of valuable things. Da Gama was at a real disadvantage, but he stood his ground. Our Lady, he said, had guided the ships a long way from their home ports, and she must be with them also on the voyage home. The Samuri seemed impressed, but he remained displeased.

Not long afterward, there were demands that the Portuguese ships be shifted to moorings closer to the land and that their sails and rudders be landed, for safekeeping. Though by then the monsoon had broken and the ships would have had the greatest difficulty in sailing, da Gama declined to land anything, except the merchandise he had brought. Permission was given, apparently without enthusiasm, for this to be landed, for the Samuri's factor reported that, like the presents, it was poor stuff and unsuited to the Indian market. The local Arab hostility showed itself openly when it was known that the Portuguese gifts had been spurned. The Arabs were well aware of the importance of this unwanted arrival of European ships in what had hitherto been strictly their preserves, and they set afoot at once a campaign of intrigue to oust the Portuguese before they could become established. When they saw any of da Gama's crews ashore, they spat on the ground before them, shouting "Portugal! Portugal!" But the Hindu populace were friendly and unimpressed by the Arab displays.

All efforts to get some sort of treaty from the Samuri failed, and a demand for considerable customs dues and landing changes met the request for a sample consignment of spices. The Moslem merchants, who were rich and powerful men, had been able to enlist the sympathies of most of the Samuri's closest advisers. They hinted that the Portuguese were probably pirates or, at any rate, more interested in what they could gain than in anything else. They also said that if the Samuri allowed them to share in the spice trade, before long other vessels would shun Calicut, to its ruin. Who knew that any other Portuguese vessels would be able to reach a port so far from their homeland? The Samuri would be foolish indeed to enter into a treaty with a monarch so distant, of whose wealth and power—if any—there had been no satisfactory evidence. No evidence, that is, save the safe arrival of the Portuguese from a voyage greater than any ever before made by man; no evidence, save the obvious superiority of their ships, their arms, their military skills, their cannon; no evidence, perhaps, save the imperious bearing of Vasco da Gama himself.

The Samuri listened to his advisers, but he was a man with some mind of his own. These Portuguese, whoever they were, he reasoned, would be in Indian waters again. A nation which equipped big ships to make so long a voyage was to be reckoned with, and their arms might be of use to him in his troubles with neighboring potentates. He hedged. He supplied part cargo of spices and allowed da Gama to erect one of his precious stone pillars, with which he marked the progress of his voyage. He sent a letter to King Manoel and offered him all the cargoes he wanted in exchange for gold, silver, coral, and crimson cloth.

Nonetheless, there is no doubt that da Gama was fortunate not to be murdered, during his stay on the Malabar coast. Warning of a plot against his life came to him through the agency of a friendly "Moor," a man born in Tunis who, though he was then a merchant in Calicut, had spent years in Spain and spoke both the Spanish and Italian languages. Perhaps with an eye on future good relations, this Moor, whose name is given as Monçaide, several times brought important intelligence to the Portuguese—so much so, indeed, that he dared not remain with his fellows. When da Gama left, Monçaide took passage with him. He knew well that the intention of his fellow Moslems was to cause the destruction of da Gama and his fleet, in order that they could not return to Portugal and so bring further fleets and ruin to the Arabs' Eastern trade.

This Monçaide, like the pilot Ahmed Ibn Majid, is a strange character. Why did he aid the Portuguese? Ibn Majid, perhaps, could scarcely help himself, and even were he minded to wreck the ships, there was little real opportunity on the run across from Malindi. The dangers were obvious, and a sharp lookout would avoid them. Ibn Majid did his job and then melted away. But Monçaide was in a different category. No one forced him to take the Portuguese side. The explanation has been put forward that this so-called Arab was in reality a Spanish nobleman who had been captured at the age of five by the Moors of Tunis, brought up as a Moslem, and taken, eventually, to India. Be that as it may, in any event he abandoned the religion of Islam on his safe return to Lisbon, was baptized, and lived in Portugal as a Christian gentleman until his death.

By early August, da Gama had had enough of Calicut. He had his samples of spices. He knew he would achieve no more until the Portuguese were powerful enough to teach the Moslem merchants a lesson. Some of his people, and his goods, were detained ashore, so when a party of notables from the Samuri were visiting the *San Gabriel* one August day, he seized the lot as hostages. It was still too soon to sail, for there would be no northeast wind until September at the earliest. Da Gama has the name of being an irascible and even a violent man, and the long wait through the humid, wet monsoon had been severely trying. His small stock of patience was gone. But even he could not get the ships out and away from that lee shore. The southwest wind was forcing them upon the coast, though its strength had gone, and their cordage and canvas had suffered from the lengthy lay-up under conditions of great humidity.

Da Gama kedged the ships out of the harbor, but he could not claw off the coast. Calms alternated with heavy thunderstorms, and twice he was drifted back to within sight of Calicut. He had no Ibn Majid to advise him now, and probably would not have heeded any advice. But the fact of the matter was that he had little hope of getting away from the coast for another month. His ships were foul, for he had not dared to careen them for cleaning and repairs while in the Samuri's power. Unless he did clean them, they certainly would not sail. He had not acquired, apparently, sufficient local knowledge to be able to predict the coming of the northeast monsoon, which would have put an end at least to his navigational troubles.

Da Gama was a pertinacious man and he kept to his decision. In this he was the more determined when, on the second occasion of sighting Calicut, a fleet of rovers, in small swift vessels, came out to attack him. "I will teach these dogs who are thieves here!" he roared. "Under God, we will return! And stay!"

Forced again upon the coast to the south of Calicut, he landed and erected yet another stone pillar. Finally a thunderstorm brought some squally wind which was usable, and the big ships stood away. Da Gama stopped at the first useful island, and careened the ships. This done, he took in wood and water and sailed for Malindi. But he was still too early, and the passage was long and exceedingly tedious. The wind was often from the southwest, right in his face. When it was not ahead, it was calm. All fresh food was gone the first month, and before long scurvy made its appearance and gained quickly. In vain the chaplains prayed for the coming of the northeast monsoon. Day after day, the sun glowered behind the leaden sky, the intense humidity seemed to suck the very energy from the wind, and the air hung motionless, like the sails. The sea grew oily, mocking them; and again the grass grew upon the wooden hulls, and the stench from the dank holds was almost intolerable. Men lay about the decks sick and dying, their appearance loathsome.

Before long, less than a dozen men were left fit for work in the *San Gabriel,* and the other *nav* was even worse off. Discipline went to pieces, but the indomitable spirit of the Portuguese kept them going. The ships were worked slowly and painfully along. The water was foul and stank, and there were no more medicines. What winds they had continued to blow from the southwest. Da Gama began to fear that, after all, he might have to return to India, through sheer inability to work the vessels any longer. The fleet had been at sea for almost three months when at last the northeast wind reached them. It was late, that year. Within a day or two, they sighted the African coast—so welcome that it almost looked like Portugal.

It was the end of the first week of January, 1499, before da Gama was anchored safely once more off Malindi, but by that time, almost a third of his men had died. Had the Sheik of Malindi really been bent on treachery, he could have destroyed the Portuguese then. But his friendship continued. Having fresh fruit and food, the surviving men recovered. With the return of the lovely weather of the northeast season, the little fleet sailed steadily toward the south. As if to make amends for its sloth in finding them, the northeasterly blew the ships a long, long way before leaving them—past Mombasa, past Zanzibar, into Mozambique (the *San Rafael* had to be destroyed because there were not men enough to work the three ships, and only the *San Gabriel* and the caravel *Berrio* survived to complete the voyage), and on again down the Mozambique Channel. Everywhere, the Portuguese pilots carefully recorded all the navigational information they could find, for the benefit of subsequent expeditions.

Onward from the Mozambique Channel, the way was comparatively easy. The strong current round the Cape of Good Hope, which had been an insufferable impediment on the outward passage, was now in their favor, and the two surviving vessels passed safely by the dreaded Cape, close inshore, on March 20. From there the passage homeward was almost plain sailing. The wind was in the south, and, though there were squalls and thunderstorms and the usual obstacles before they reached the true trade wind, the rest of the passage was accomplished without incident. A black squall parted the two ships, and the caravel reached Lisbon first, arriving in the Tagus on July 10, 1499, which was two years and two days from the date of her sailing. Meanwhile, da Gama was delayed by the mortal illness of his brother. He put into the port of Angra on the island of Terceira, in the Azores, and there, Paulo da Gama died. It was September before Vasco da Gama finally returned to the Tagus, where a great welcome awaited him.

He had sailed 24,000 miles, to make the greatest voyage then known to history. With a fleet which was minute for the magnitude of the task assigned to it, and a handful of brave men, he had sailed fearlessly across the strange waters of the Indian Ocean, had turned the flank of Islam, had opened up the Eastern trade to Europe, and had brought to the ancient East a new vision. Since then, the wonderful development of the Americas has tended to make the simple voyage of Christopher Columbus outshine all others, but in the measure of hardships overcome, determination and skills involved, and the real results achieved, it was Vasco da Gama whose quest was really successful. He did what he set out to do. Columbus also was in quest of the real Indies, but it was da Gama who found them.

CHAPTER XI

The Struggle for the Indian Ocean

"You may find that you will have to conquer, whether you wish or not," the Arab pilot Ibn Majid had said to Vasco da Gama. These were prophetic words. For at least the following three centuries the Indian Ocean was the scene of conflict, sometimes intermittent, sometimes prolonged. The Portuguese intention to bring about a friendly alliance with the Christian monarchs in India was nonplused when there were no such rulers with whom to form unions. The great subcontinent itself, self-sufficient and rich, could afford not to concern itself overmuch with the arrival of a few ships from hitherto remote Europe, but the Moors very quickly realized that they would have to fight for their lives. They fought back valiantly, but in vain.

Da Gama was followed to India by a fleet of thirteen ships, led by Pedro Alvarez Cabral, who took with him a number of Franciscan monks to convert the heathen and twelve hundred fighting men to deal as necessary with the unconverted. On the outward voyage, Cabral touched on the coast of Brazil, and this was generally recognized as the official discovery of that great country. Since that time, however, evidence of prior discovery by other Portuguese voyages has come to light, and Cabral's must be looked upon as an unveiling, so to speak, of what was already known.

It is possible that an undue proportion of southerly in the southeast trades, or an unusual strength in the west-setting equatorial
current in the doldrums (where the longer a ship was delayed, the
more would she be set to the west, toward the coast of South
America), was really responsible for Cabral's "discovery." In the
later days of sailing ships, when this passage was one of the most
frequently made of all passages under sail, many, many ships
found themselves in the same predicament—forced upon the
coast of Brazil when they had intended to give the place a good
berth, and get south through the trade winds as quickly as they
could. The barque *Penang*, for instance (one of the Erikson line
from Mariehamn, in her last days), was so badly jammed on the
coast of Brazil when trying to make a ballast passage toward
Australia that she got behind Cape St. Roque and had to make a
long board back into the South Atlantic, to try again on the proper
tack.

Cabral detached a ship and sent her back to his king to report
what he had observed of the coast of Brazil. Four more ships of
his fleet were lost when a black southeaster struck them off the
Cape, but the remaining vessels made a good passage of six months
from Lisbon to Calicut, including stops at Sofala, Mozambique,
Kilwa, and Malindi. The Sheik of Malindi was still helpful and
supplied pilots. He had no more of the quality of Ibn Majid, but
those he supplied were quite competent. Cabral, profiting from da
Gama's experience, brought costly presents for the Samuri, but
he had not been long in Calicut before the Moors there gave serious trouble. The Samuri began by being helpful, at least to the
extent of providing a house for a Portuguese factor, or sort of
consul, and this house was gifted with a legal deed engrossed in
letters of gold, and magazines were set up for the exchange of
Portuguese goods for Eastern products. The Portuguese found
themselves harassed by all kinds of restrictions. After three months,
sufficient goods had come forward to provide cargoes for only two
ships, and it was obvious that the others would have to remain

empty unless something drastic was done. The factor did his best, but the Moorish control of trade was too much for him.

In reply to Cabral's protest, the Samuri promised that no further Moslem ships would be allowed to complete until the Portuguese had their cargoes, and Cabral was authorized to seize and examine Moorish ships leaving the harbor, to ensure that they were not carrying cargoes of spices. Within a few days of this arrangement, a big Moorish ship got under way and came ramping through the roads. Cabral seized the vessel, which was loaded with spices for the Red Sea route to Europe. As soon as the seizure of this ship was known ashore, a Moslem mob attacked the Portuguese establishments and murdered Ayres Correa, the factor, and fifty of his men. Despairing then of ever being able to trade fairly at such a place, and losing his patience with the Samuri at the obvious ability of the hostile Moors to control his policies, Cabral got under way, seized ten of the largest Moorish ships in the roadstead, pillaged them and burned them, killed their crews, bombarded the town, and sailed down to Cochin.

Here he was better received. The ruler of Cochin was hostile to the Samuri, and the Moors there, having heard of the Portuguese vengeance, bided their time. Cabral loaded the rest of his ships and sailed back to Portugal with such cargoes as excited the envy of the whole of Europe. Though only six vessels returned out of the thirteen which had sailed from Lisbon, the wealth they brought amply paid for the whole fleet.

Not unnaturally, Cabral left at Calicut implacable hostility to all things Portuguese, but he had in fact merely brought into the open a condition which was bound to exist. Again the Royal Council of Portugal advised the King to have done with the Eastern adventure, and the Pope, moved by Venetian appeals, dispatched an envoy to urge the abandonment of the Cape route. But history was not to be gainsaid. Da Gama himself was recalled to lead a further fleet, this time to teach a permanent lesson to the interfering Moors. He sailed on this second voyage in February,

1502, with a fleet of fifteen ships, followed by Estavăo da Gama with another five. The objective this time was not merely to obtain a load of spices but to leave some of the ships as a permanent squadron in the Indian Ocean for the protection of Portuguese commerce there.

This time, it was a savage and relentless Vasco da Gama who drove his fleet toward the Indian Ocean. He was never a man of gentle nature, and his short temper had been worsened by the slights he imagined he had received from his country. (He had wished, above all, to obtain the overlordship of his home town of Sines as reward for his great voyage, but this was denied him, not by the King but by the Order of San Tiago, which owned it.)

The big fleet sailed out the usual way, from the Tagus Bar with a fair northerly wind down past the Canaries and the Cape Verde Islands, and thence toward the line, with the good trade wind warm and fine and fair; across the line, and on a bowline through the other trade, the ships and the mariners using this time of ease to prepare against the rigors of the west-winds passage, which would drive them around the Cape of Good Hope. They were already learning that it paid to give the Cape a wider berth, to get out of the Agulhas current, which bore ships toward the westward there, and to stay farther from the African coast as they sailed toward the north. Da Gama touched at Kilwa and haughtily demanded of the Sheik there that he should acknowledge the overlordship of the King of Portugal and pay an annual tribute of 2,000 crowns in gold. This the Sheik was glad enough to do, for the fifteen great and well-armed ships were sufficient to strike terror into any East African port. Da Gama, discovering the Seychelles on his way, made thence toward Calicut. He wasted no words on the Samuri, who must have trembled at the sight of the great fleet and have regretted his failure to realize the significance of da Gama's first visit. This time da Gama attacked the port on sight, exacting fierce revenge for the murder of Ayres Correa. On the way, he had intercepted a large Calicut ship homeward bound from Jiddah with pilgrims from Mecca. This ship he burned, leaving the people to their fate. The Samuri tried to retaliate by sending a fleet to attack the Portuguese, but his ships were soundly defeated. Da Gama took two treasure ships containing, it was said, immense riches, which included "an idol of pure gold weighing sixty pounds, with eyes formed by emeralds as large as eggs, and in the chest was a ruby as big as a chestnut."

Scorning Calicut altogether, da Gama freighted his ships at the friendly ports of Cochin and Cannanore. The Rajah of Cochin permitted the establishment of a factory at that port, and both he and the ruler of Cannanore requested that a Portuguese squadron should remain in their waters. This was already intended, and six ships, under the command of Vicente Sodre, remained to show the flag and harass the Moors when da Gama, with his richly laden ships, sailed for Lisbon. Da Gama's fleet returned to Lisbon without incident. On landing, he was received with great joy and made a procession through the town with the tribute of the Sheik of Kilwa carried in a silver basin before him.

Vicente Sodre's squadron were the first European ships to sail the coasts of Arabia and to land at Socotra, which he regarded as the key to the Red Sea. The Portuguese purpose was, as soon as they were strong enough, to seize the whole of the Indian Ocean trade with Europe. Since they could not share it, they would take all. To do this they must control the seas. They would never be powerful enough, nor was it necessary, to exert domination over the vast lands involved. But with their superiority in ships, guns, and seamen, even a small squadron could exercise a great measure of control over the sailing commerce of the Indian Ocean. The ships commanded by Vicente Sodre showed what could be done, though in the absence of a sheltered and secure base, they were battered by the southwest monsoon and Sodre's own vessel was lost.

It was obvious that, in addition to a fleet, at least some secure shore bases would have to be acquired. By 1505, the Portuguese

King decided to send a Viceroy to India, and Francisco de Almeida
was appointed to this important post. Portuguese policy by that
time, quite openly, was to dominate the Indian Ocean. They had
learned that both the Red Sea and the Persian Gulf routes could
be bottled up, for Aden was the key to the one and Hormuz to the
other. There would then remain only the Cape route, which was
theirs, and the overland routes, which with the greater safety and
surety of sea-borne trade, were of less and less importance. Almeida erected a strong fort at Kilwa * and reduced Mombasa. He
thus continued the policy of protecting the Portuguese flank by
establishing bases on the coast of East Africa.

This was a comparatively simple matter, for the Arab states
there were small and not united. If need be, they could be by-
passed; no large-scale attacks were likely to come from them. Their
ports were visited only by trading vessels and none of the city
sheiks was powerful enough to raise an important fleet of his own.
As Portuguese galleons and *navs* began to roam more freely over
the open waters of the Indian Ocean, they discovered that there
were other routes toward India besides the passage of the current-
filled Mozambique Channel. They soon knew Madagascar and
Mauritius and other islands. They could sail where they wished,
so long as they did not overrun the west coast of India. But in
Indian waters they had to fight for it. Almeida soon found himself
attacked by a large fleet assembled against him by the Samuri.

---

* This fort at Kilwa was described by a party of British archeologists who visited
its ruins in 1950 as "the largest and best specimen of sixteenth-century European military architecture on the African coast." According to the Dar-es-Salaam correspond-
ent of *The Times* of London, the party examined ruins covering several acres at
Kilwa Kisiwani and Songo Mnara. Dr. Mathew, of Oxford, said that, when the
Portuguese discovered East Africa, they described the port at Kilwa Kisiwani as one
of the most beautiful cities of the world. It was sacked twice by the Portuguese in
the sixteenth century because the inhabitants omitted to pay the customary tribute.
The expedition found evidence of a third sacking at the end of the seventeenth or
in the early eighteenth century and signs of fire at the sultan's palace. They established the sites of the main buildings, including two mosques, which were the finest
on the East African coast, and a palace of which the walls were 30 feet high, built
round a court or garden modeled on the Arab style of the sixteenth century. There
were also traces of town walls 12 feet high, with towers 20 feet high at intervals.

The Moorish and Indian ships greatly outnumbered the Portuguese, but the Portuguese were stronger, abler, and more heavily armed vessels. They outgunned and outranged both the Hindus and the Moors. Moreover, they gained the initial advantage of getting to windward, and they were able to inflict a crushing defeat on the combined fleets, despite the fact that there were eleven Portuguese ships opposed to more than 200 Moors and Indians, of which 84 were large vessels and the remainder swift *proas*. The slaughter was great, but Portuguese losses also were heavy.

The Moors next sought help from an Egyptian fleet, which was built on the Red Sea and sailed across under the command of an Egyptian admiral named Mir Hosyn. The Egyptians were ready to help their fellow Moslems, as the Portuguese intervention in the rich spice trade had seriously affected their own revenues. In December, 1507, Mir Hosyn's fleet arrived off Diu, on the coast of Kathiawar. Here it was reinforced by the arrival of a large number of Indian and local Moorish vessels, sent by the governor of Diu. Intent upon the final destruction of the Portuguese and the banishment of the Europeans from the Indian Ocean, the great fleet sailed south toward the Malabar coast, where the Viceroy's son Lourenco de Almeida was in command of a handful of ships for the protection of the Portuguese outports. Ignorant of the force against him, Lourenco entered the small port of Chaul (not far from Bombay). Here his enemies found him. The ensuing fight was epic. Though he was caught in narrow waters without room to manuever and was outnumbered by thirty ships to one, Lourenco de Almeida fought so valiantly that it took the combined force of Egyptians, Hindus, and Moors three days to defeat him. This they were unable to do until Lourenco's ship had sunk beneath him, Lourenco was dead, and only two small caravels, locally assembled, survived.

Though the Moors had the victory, it had been gained at such tremendous cost that Portuguese prestige was greatly increased by the action. The vessels from the Red Sea were especially built

for warfare and were large and able ships. After their severe maul-
ing from the handful of Lourenco's ships, the Red Sea vessels, instead of pressing their advantage, retired to Diu. Here Lourenco's
father, the Viceroy himself, pursued them and gave them savage
battle. Again the Portuguese were outnumbered, but the Moslem
force was utterly defeated. Mir Hosyn (or Hussein) was killed,
and Diu surrendered. After this battle, a treaty was made with
Diu, and the Viceroy returned to Cochin knowing that the Portuguese power on the west coast of India, at any rate, was thoroughly
established.

Meanwhile, the greatest Portuguese of all who served their
country in the Indian Ocean, Affonso d'Albuquerque, had arrived
on the scene, and he consolidated Portuguese power over the
whole of the known waters of the Indian Ocean. Almeida had set
up a government at Cochin and a fort, as well as forts at Cannanore
and at Anjediva Island. He had extended the Portuguese power to
Ceylon, and he had sent home cargoes of hitherto unheard-of
riches. He had required that Moorish ships should obtain a Portuguese passport before crossing the Arabian Sea, and any which
were found without such a clearance were immediately seized.
Lisbon, 12,000 miles away by sailing route, had already super-
seded Venice as the market in Europe for the spices and other
products of the East, and Portuguese ships were landing valuable
cargoes of these products as far away as Falmouth, in England,
and in Antwerp, by 1504. Almost on every voyage some new product was added to the already long list of the royal monopolies—
pepper, ginger, cinnamon, mace, cloves, nutmeg; wormwood,
borax, camphor, aloes, musk, civet, spikenard, mastic; and precious
stones, silks, porcelains, fine raiment.

Almeida had also established a base at Socotra, but it was soon
obvious that, despite its location, Socotra was useless as a strategic
base for covering the Red Sea. It was without a harbor, and the
Gulf of Aden was too wide to permit a useful blockade from such

a place. Control of the Red Sea would have to be established from a base which could not be by-passed so easily. The real key was Aden.

Affonso d'Albuquerque had already been in the Indian Ocean. He and his cousin Francisco had led fleets from Portugal to the Malabar coast in 1503, when they had reached Cochin in bare time to save the Rajah there from defeat by the Samuri of Calicut, enraged by the Portuguese successes against him. Francisco d'Albuquerque's ships went missing on the homeward voyage toward Lisbon and no trace of any of them has ever been found. But the energetic and capable Affonso, correctly sizing up the situation, determined that he would thoroughly establish dominion there for God and Portugal. A man of great determination and exceptional vision, he saw that effectively to control the Indian Ocean the Portuguese must hold its four known exits—the mouths of the Red Sea and the Persian Gulf, the Straits of Malacca, and the Cape of Good Hope—and must have a capital of their own in India. Alliances with Eastern rulers would be of no real value, for, he argued, if Portugal were strong enough she would not need them, and if she were not, the treaty of such a potentate would not be worth the paper it was written on. She must rely upon her own strength and that was upon the sea, but there must also be adequate bases ashore, securely held.

It was, moreover, not enough to oust the Moors from the place of middlemen in the spice trade at a few marts along the Malabar coast. They must be driven also from the greater markets farther to the east, and the most important of these was Malacca. As soon as possible, the spices must be traced to their source and control established there. The Portuguese must examine more closely the islands of these eastern seas, and ensure that they could not be attacked upon their flank. Might there not be another route, as yet undiscovered, toward the riches of India?

D'Albuquerque thought of all these things and, as soon as he became Viceroy, pursued a policy to give lasting effect to his

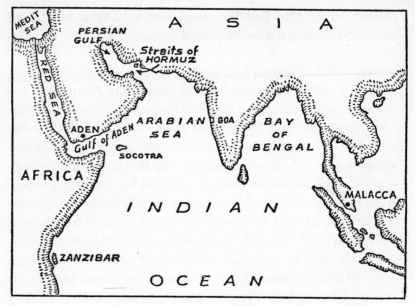

The keys of Affonso d'Albuquerque

ideas. He took Hormuz, and he established a Portuguese capital in
India at Goa, which he converted within a few years from a
heathen outport to "Golden Goa." He tried to take Aden, but was
driven back from that great stronghold; nonetheless, he had effective control of the Red Sea trade in other ways. He captured
Malacca. He sent expeditions to explore Indonesia, and his emis-
saries found the famous Spice Islands of Ternate and Tidore and
the source of cloves at Amboina. What else they may have found
geographers and historians still argue, for there is a reasonable
certainty that some of them at least sailed to New Guinea, and
they may have touched Australia. There is no adequate record of
their wanderings.

From Malacca, d'Albuquerque was able not only to control trade
farther east and to eliminate the Moorish middlemen entirely,
but he could establish relations with Burma, Siam, Java, and

Cochin China. Embassies were sent to each of these countries and Portuguese settled in most of them.

In those days, Malacca was the crossroads of the East, the sixteenth-century Singapore. It was the key to the whole trade of the Far East. D'Albuquerque's embassies traveled thence also to China and finally to Japan. There was practically no end to the great trade opportunities of Asia; but a man of d'Albuquerque's genius and energies was needed to see them and to use them. Such men were rare in the early sixteenth century, as they have been rare all through history and are now. D'Albuquerque could not carry out his great policies without overcoming intense and endless difficulties. He had to fight desperately for Goa and for Malacca. His noblest efforts came to little at Aden, though the valor of the Portuguese there struck such a fear into the watchful Egyptians that they did not again send ships to attack the fearless Portuguese. They remained on the defensive, where they could do no harm. D'Albuquerque was opposed, sometimes treacherously, by his own countrymen. The wealth of the fabulous East was intoxicating. Before long, every fidalgo in Portugal was flocking there, too often intent upon enriching himself by any means possible and with no other ambition. Few realized the full import of their Viceroy's policy or did much to help it. The great majority were intent upon making such efforts as were required to gain wealth for themselves, careless alike of how they achieved this and of their country's future. There was inevitably considerable exploitation and some oppression. There were many who argued that Goa was unnecessary, and the great Viceroy had to defend himself against charges of waste of lives and treasure in the campaign against that city.

In truth, he was straining Portuguese resources to the utmost. The Lusitanian state had, unknowingly at first, taken on a tremendous assignment. Under the guiding genius of Affonso d'Albuquerque its great plans prospered and it was able to dominate, from a faraway speck of storm-lashed land, the vast domain of the Indian Ocean and the infinite wealth of the wonderful East. But Affonso d'Albuquerque, worn out by his great exertions and tried beyond bearing by the fumbling minds of a thousand lesser men, died in harness, in 1515. He was a real empire builder. He had laid the foundations of a great empire, which might have flourished. But much of what he had set out to do was destroyed within a half century of his death, to some extent by his own countrymen. Not for the first time in history, the little men triumphed or, at any rate, were able to bring the vision of great minds to nothing.

Some of the forts which Affonso d'Albuquerque built still exist, noble monuments of their kind. His capital city of Goa survived as a Portuguese outpost in India, even after the British had relinquished their control of that great country. Farther east, at Timor and at Macao, remnants of the Eastern empire which he founded still stand. He was honored by his country and by the Pope. After his conquest of Goa and of Hormuz, he received embassies from almost every important ruler of coastal areas in the East. When news of his victories was received in Rome, the Pope ordered that a solemn procession should commemorate them, and he himself took part in this, for it seemed that such conquests with so little means could only have been made by the direct will of God.

In the story of the Indian Ocean, it is generally acknowledged now that there is no greater name than that of Affonso d'Albuquerque. He had never control of more than 4,000 European warriors and a small fleet of ships. He had to operate at all times thousands of miles from base. Many of his enemies were excellent fighting men, particularly the Turks, who came by sea to oppose him. He was relatively an old man. But he possessed in abundance the great and enduring qualities of integrity, inspired leadership, and indefatigable tenacity of purpose. He was a talented administrator and organizer, as well as a valiant warrior by sea and

At Cochin

Dutch East Indiamen

East Indiamen in convoy

Life on board an East Indiaman as seen by Cruikshank

by land. Even his greatest enemies appreciated his fairness, his readiness to use honest diplomacy when it was possible, and the abiding integrity of his character. His achievements would have been extraordinary had he had the full resources of a great and rich kingdom at his disposal. As Professor Prestage has pointed out in his admirable *Portuguese Pioneers,* when carried out by a small country little more than the size of Wales, they become almost miraculous.

Prince Henry the Navigator's aim had been to open a Portuguese commerce with the East, to turn the flank of Islam, and to spread the word of Christ, but his seamen were forced to found an empire. Their factories could not operate without protection, and there could be no protection without adequate power. The great Portuguese pioneers discovered these things quickly; others, who followed them, were to find that they, too, were caught up in the Indian Ocean's mighty rollers and driven where they had had no wish to go. Their quest for the passage around Africa to India had brought the Portuguese to the uttermost ends of the earth. From rich Brazil to far Japan, the riches of the world were theirs. The Pope had ordained that half the world should be reserved to Spanish domination and the other half to Portuguese. The Spanish conquests were, in fact, largely confined to North America and the western half of South America, and—after the Portuguese Magellan had shown the way—the Philippines. The Portuguese controlled the whole of the Indian Ocean and half the Pacific and the Atlantic besides.

This was magnificent while it lasted. But the empire grew too large, and there were many ambitious and envious eyes upon it. Portugal, valorous and full of vision, was too small a state to control so much for very long. Hers was the inspired leadership; it passed to others to exploit.

CHAPTER XII

The Hollanders

Of the several competitors of the Portuguese in the Indian Ocean trade, at first the most successful were the Hollanders. The Portuguese trade was conducted as a royal monopoly, but the Hollanders and the English were individualists, the Hollanders with state backing and the English, all too often, with state interference. The Hollanders had early experience of the spice trade. They were the great carriers of Europe and they played a large part in distributing the products which the Portuguese imported. Dutch and German sailors served in the fleet taken by the first Portuguese Viceroy to India in 1505, and there was a German ship in this fleet, for there were not enough large Portuguese ships to make up the required numbers.

The Portuguese were not a race of shipowners or merchants, as the Hollanders were. If the Atlantic fisheries of Portugal had bred fine seamen, the herring fisheries of the North Sea were conducted on a much larger scale, and frequently in even worse weather. There only good ships and good seamen could survive, and the Dutch were the leaders in this trade. It would be no exaggeration to say that they rode upon the backs of the pickled herring to the Indian Ocean. Their seafaring and shipbuilding abilities and their business acumen were alike fostered by this important fishery. In Portugal, sixteenth-century historians apologized when they were compelled to mention affairs concerned with trade, or they left such matters out of their chronicles. The Portuguese had gone as crusaders, not traders. But in Amsterdam successful trade was not merely respectable. It was almost a religion. The Hollanders, moreover, understood intelligent cooperation for the common good, and they were highly successful shipowners. This a royal monopoly could never be.

In Holland, as the Portuguese effort inevitably declined, there arose a mercantile class with sufficient wealth, enterprise, and experience to profit by the great opportunities being presented to them. At first, they did well as carriers of the Eastern products in European waters, as distributors and as middlemen. But they began to grope toward the ice wastes of the misty north for a way into the Indian Ocean around the north of Canada or Siberia. If Magellan had found a way through his straits in the distant south and reached the Spice Islands, there might be a way through in the north, which would be shorter. The quest of a northeast or a northwest passage was alike doomed to failure, for there was no practical route to the East that way. But the canny Hollanders profited by exploiting the seal and whale fisheries of the north, so that their efforts and expenditure were not wholly in vain.

The enforced union of Portugal with Spain played further into their hands. King Philip II adopted a harsh policy toward the Netherlands, which was under Spanish dominance. Following the union, he was able to drive Dutch ships from Lisbon and to stop commercial intercourse between the two countries. Dutch ships had brought salt fish to Lisbon and Oporto and carried products of the East back; and Dutch financiers, with Italians and Germans, had assisted to finance Portuguese Eastern expansion almost from the beginning. The independent Hollanders did not accept King Philip's high-handed acts. They threw off the yoke of Spain and decided at once to send their own vessels to the Indian Ocean to secure, at their source, the cargoes which Philip had denied them.

They were in a good position to do this. One of their countrymen, by the name of Jan Huyghen van Linschoten, had served for many years at Goa as secretary to the Portuguese archbishop there. In this capacity he had kept his eyes and ears open and had learned a great deal about Eastern trade. It had not, indeed, been the Portuguese policy to exclude other nationals from their enterprises, and Linschoten could learn all he wished. But Linschoten published a very useful book containing not only the gist of his researches, but translations from all the useful sailing directories he had been able to get hold of, and these were a comprehensive guide to the means of conducting a sailing ship in Eastern waters. Linschoten was in Goa from 1583 until 1592, and he was able to gather information not only about the Indian coast and the Bay of Bengal, but of Malacca and the Malayan and Indonesian trades. His book is interesting reading still.

With Linschoten's *Itinerario* and their own determination, energy, and abilities, the Dutch abandoned the northeast and northwest passages to the whaling industry and sent a fleet of four fair-sized ships out boldly around the forbidden Cape of Good Hope, into the Indian Ocean. These ships were commanded by Cornelius de Houtman, one of many Hollanders who had been in Portuguese employ, who spoke the language and had made it his business over many years to learn everything he could about the ocean to which he was the first to take Dutch ships. This was in 1595. On the advice of Linschoten, Houtman made directly for the island of Java instead of for the Indian coast. Linschoten had said—at second hand—that the Portuguese themselves did not visit Java, since they were able to control this trade from their base port of Malacca. In this the Hollander was wrong, and when Houtman's ships duly arrived at Bantam in June, 1596, the Portuguese were there, well established and intent upon preserving their monopolies. At their instigation, the natives rose against the Dutchmen. Houtman himself was taken and thrown into prison, from which he extricated himself only on the payment of a considerable ransom and upon undertaking to leave. He visited Lom-

bok and the Moluccas, finally doing his best to complete the
cargoes of his ships at little-known roadsteads along the southern
coast of Java, which was an area then thought to be dangerous
because of excessive currents.

Houtman was greatly impressed with all he saw, particularly
with the beauties of Java. His ships had shown themselves well
able to make the long voyage, and if his seamen suffered heavily
from scurvy—of 250 leaving Holland, less than 90 returned—this
was the accepted thing. Houtman returned to Holland after a
voyage lasting twenty-eight months. His ships could have brought
a great deal more cargo, and the expenses had been heavy. But
the profit from the venture was sufficient to encourage the merchants, and Houtman was sent out again before the turn of the
century. On this voyage he lost his life when the King of Achen
rose against him.

Simultaneously, another fleet, consisting of eight well-found
vessels, sailed from Holland under the command of Jacob van
Neck. To finance this venture, the two pioneer Dutch East Indies
companies had amalgamated, for it was obvious that if too many
companies entered the trade their rivalry would do Holland no
service and might bring down the prices of Eastern products. The
Dutch were determined to establish a monopoly in these products. From van Neck's fleet, four ships, all very richly laden, were
back in Dutch ports after the then remarkably rapid turn-round
of fifteen months. At this success, the trade to the Indian Ocean
boomed. Between 1595 and 1601, no fewer than 65 Dutch ships
in 22 fleets sailed for the East. One of these fleets, commanded
by Oliver van Noort, sailed through the Straits of Magellan. The
Dutch were courageous and capable seamen, as well as good
businessmen. Oliver van Noort made a successful circumnavigation.

Van Noort's circumnavigation, together with the success of far
too many other Dutch voyagers, so angered King Philip that he
ordered the seizure of all Dutch ships in Spanish waters, con-

fiscated all the Dutch property he could get hold of, and forbade his subjects to pay any debts they might owe to Hollanders. He sent a squadron of well-armed ships to attack a returning squadron of Hollanders, but the victory was with the Dutch. If Philip's hope had been to ruin the Dutch, it was, unfortunately, Portuguese interests—then bound with Spain's—which were most adversely affected. The Hollanders, having tasted the riches of the East at their source, were in no mood to give up their profitable voyages. The government of the Netherlands, which was an interested shareholder in the Dutch East India Company, retaliated by suspending all commerce with Spain, by commissioning every Dutch captain in command of a ship which sailed for the East, and— more important—by promoting the success of Netherlands ventures by easing the terms on which money was available for seafaring activities. Early voyages were exempted from taxation, and every possible step was taken to see that the individualist enterprise of the companies could flourish. Money for shipbuilding was available at 4 per cent (which compared with 8 per cent in England).

The Dutch government, itself virtually an association of merchant princes, quickly realized that one great corporation of all the companies trading with the East would be in a much stronger position to maintain the costly paraphernalia of that trade, in the shape of establishments ashore and factors to operate them, a fleet of ships to cruise against the Portuguese and Spaniards (and the English too, as these also came upon the scene), and a system of fortresses. So, in 1602, the United East India Company was formed. It was empowered to establish colonies, to make peace or war, to raise whatever funds it might need, and to construct military establishments and fortresses anywhere in the East. Its capital was the hitherto unheard-of sum of 6,500,000 gulden, the equivalent then of $3,500,000 and worth at least $20,000,000 today.

With these resources, and knowing that the government and

the people were behind them, the Company went ahead rapidly. From Hormuz in the Persian Gulf to distant Japan, their ships cut deeply into the Portuguese trade. One after another, the Portuguese outposts fell. The Dutch captured Ceylon, and they established themselves in Java and throughout the chain of Indonesian islands. They occupied ports in India. The first fleet sent out by the new amalgamation consisted of fourteen ships, some of which went to Ceylon and others to Java. In 1603, a fleet of twelve ships, under Steven van der Hagen, was sent out with orders to destroy the commerce of the Portuguese in India, or at least to make it unprofitable. An attack was made, on the way, on the Portuguese fort at Mozambique, but this was defended heroically. Van der Hagen had to content himself with sweeping Portuguese shipping—for the time being—out of the Mozambique Channel. Friendly relations were established with the rulers of Cochin and Calicut. Goa was blockaded briefly and van der Hagen moved on to take the Portuguese fortress at the island of Amboina, while one of his captains reduced Tidore.

Others followed the advantages which had been gained. The Hollanders made bases at the Cape of Good Hope and at Mauritius, which they named, though it was a Portuguese discovery. They attacked Malacca, but failed at first to make much impression there. The Portuguese fleet was weakened by this constant warfare and by the need to provide escorts for convoying merchantmen as well as patrols in the Persian Gulf, Arabian Sea, Bay of Bengal, and Straits of Malacca. In a decisive battle fought in October, 1606, the Dutchman Cornelius Matelief defeated the weakened Portuguese squadron, and again blockaded Malacca and later Goa. The warfare was carried into European waters, and in 1607, a Dutch fleet under Heemskerk defeated a Spanish fleet in Gibraltar Bay. Heemskerk was killed in the action, which was fought furiously. The Spanish fleet under D. Juan d'Avila was destroyed with heavy loss of life, notwithstanding the fact that the Hollanders had to go in under the very noses of the shore-based cannon. Don Juan went down with his galleon, a vessel of 800 tons, and nearly 4,000 Spaniards lost their lives.

After this, a truce was arranged between the Netherlands and Spain, but this made no difference to Dutch plans for expansion in the Indian Ocean. There, their policy was all or nothing, and this they rigorously pursued. The United Company's first governor general, Pieter Both, who was appointed in 1609, went out with instructions "that the commerce of the Moluccas, Amboina, and Banda should belong to the Company, and no other nation in the world should have the least part." This was at least explicit. The English had meanwhile also established themselves, though precariously, in the Spice Islands. The Hollanders now seized them, tortured and massacred them, and carried on a relentless campaign against them also in Java. The port of Jacatra was chosen as their capital and the modern city of Batavia was founded there in 1621, to become the center of Dutch influence in the Indian Ocean for the next three and a half centuries. In 1950, by order of the Republic of Indonesia, Batavia reverted to its ancient name of Jacatra.

The Dutch chose to concentrate their power in the islands of Indonesia for excellent strategic reasons. Lying in the belt of the permanent trade wind and so outside the changeable monsoons, sailing ships could always reach and leave Batavia by using different routes across the Indian Ocean. Homeward bound, they could blow across the ocean on a more or less direct course toward the Cape. Outward bound, they had only to get well to windward in high latitudes before turning north for the Straits of Sunda, and then they could carry the trade wind free on the starboard beam. There were two routes into Batavia Roads, one by the Straits of Sunda and the other down Malacca Straits. Moreover, Java itself was immensely rich, and Batavia was convenient to the Spice Islands. Based on Java, Dutch ships were to windward of the main Portuguese bases in both monsoons and so could always keep the weather gauge, a matter of importance in the days of sailing men-o'-war. Batavia itself was a good deep-water port, as it had to be to offer refuge to the very deep-draughted Dutch ships, which often drew more than 30 feet of water. They were short, deep, and beamy, and they carried large cargoes.

Having established their power in Java, the Hollanders took Malacca in 1641, and the Straits became a Dutch waterway. It took them twenty years to drive the Portuguese out of Ceylon, and indeed they never did succeed in quite removing Portuguese influence. But by the time Portugal was free of Spanish domination in 1640, her Eastern power and prestige had passed effectively to those "most cruel and bloody people," the Dutch. As their power increased, the Hollanders showed themselves capable of ruthless brutalities to forward their ends.

"They have lately in these parts," complained the English factor in the Persian Gulf, "committed such inhuman acts, in murdering all they meet abroad, as well friends as foes, that it is abominable before God and man." "They wrong you in all Parts and grow to insufferable insolences," wrote a contemporary who said he "had tried them East and West, and knew their beastiality and ingratitude."

In the Persian Gulf the Dutch made common cause with the English against the Portuguese for a while, but it was in their own interests. As soon as they dared, they did what they could to oust the English from the Gulf, as well as from everywhere else in Eastern seas, and they nearly succeeded. The English were not helped by the formation, in 1664, of a French East India Company. The Dutch rested their claims on the fact that it was they who ousted the Portuguese, at the expense of Dutch lives and treasure. To them both English and French were nothing but late-coming interlopers, to be treated with the utmost arrogance, and worse.

After Pieter Both, their able Governor Jan Pieterszoon Coen further built up the Dutch empire and continued the policy of implacable hostility to all other Europeans. Under his control, the commercial affairs of the Company prospered to such an extent that it was paying 160 per cent. But the Dutch were laying up a store of hostility toward themselves, in the Indonesian mind, which was to remain and to prove their downfall in the long run. Such wanton acts as the spoliation of Banda, the massacre at Amboina, the destruction of surplus products, the introduction of slavery, and the methods used to exploit the natives and subdue them were not to be forgotten. Coen was quite ruthless. To him, an Indonesian had no rights. Moreover, the effects of life in the East took their toll. The Portuguese, a people used to hot and frequently trying summers in their own country, found the tropics of the Indian Ocean extremely difficult, and did their best to develop a new race of half-breeds, the better to accustom Portuguese blood to such conditions. The Hollanders, from Europe's colder north, suffered greatly, but they were persistent and resourceful. They, too, formed alliances with the native women, and they also did not hesitate to cut themselves off from their distant homeland and set themselves up as colonists in such favored spots as Java and Ceylon. The high lands in these islands were favorable to Europeans. Some brought out wives and founded families. But drunkenness, immorality, and unchecked greed were rife and uncontrollable. Without the iron hand of a Pieter Both, Jan Coen, or Antony van Diemen, the Dutch empire would soon have gone to pieces.

Whatever might have been their shortcomings ashore, the Hollanders continued to show their capabilities and good seamanship at sea. It was not long before they realized that there were better routes to the Indies than the endless groping through the Mozambique Channel and wandering about the Indian Ocean in the monsoonal or the trade-wind belt. Such a voyage was tedious and long, and ships using it could be a year on the way. Its heat and the absence of facilities for fresh stocks of provisions were very trying on crews, and mortality from scurvy continued far

too high. It was an odd thing that such heavy losses from this foul
and avoidable disease continued to be accepted for so many
years after the Portuguese navigator, Pedro Fernandez de Queiros,
had led an expedition across the Pacific from Peru to Santa Cruz
without loss of a single life, and other enlightened leaders were
able to do the same thing. Nor did the crowded Arab dhows suffer from scurvy to anything like the same extent as European ships
did.

The enterprising Dutch navigators soon conceived the idea that
it would much shorten their voyages if they sailed their ships
across to the longitude of Java in the west-winds zone of the
southern Indian Ocean, before standing toward the north, and
this they had begun to do before 1620. Their charts showed nothing there but a great mass of land, vaguely called *Terra Australis,*
to which was generally added the qualification *Incognita.* If the
Portuguese had been upon the west or the northwest coasts of this
strange continent—and there is reason to believe that they had *
—they had left no discoverable record of it. The Dutch were soon
among the shoals and sandy headlands of the barren northwest,
and many a noble carrack, driving east too far in the brave west
winds, turned north to find shipwreck on Australia's inhospitable
shores. Gone were the "knightly mariners, following the gleam of
a golden continent" and the coast of West Australia emerged, apparently useless and certainly unfriendly, from the fascinating
myth of the Great South Land.

It was the Hollanders' misfortune that the Indian Ocean was
reef-strewn on both its western and its eastern shores, unlike much
of the Atlantic and Pacific. The jagged coral reefs of West Australia

---

* Two old guns, of Portuguese origin, are preserved at Garden Island, Sydney,
which were found on Graham Moore Island near Cape Londonderry, on the coast of
northwest Australia. A party landed from H.M.A.S. *Encounter* on the island in 1916
found the guns protruding from the sand. The circumstances in which these guns
(obviously from an ancient wreck) reached the island are unknown, but markings
on them indicate that they were probably part of the armament of a Portuguese
vessel in the early sixteenth century.

tore many a lumbering galleon to ruin, and the Dutch skeletons are still dug up, from time to time, among the cheerless islets of the Abrolhos, Dirk Hartog Island, and the Dampier group. Until such time as a ship's longitude could be fixed with reasonable accuracy, it was dangerous to approach too closely to New Holland, as Australia soon became known.

A few Dutch navigators took time to have a closer look at the place, and though it obviously possessed some good, arable land in the southwestern corner and could scarcely all be the sandy, fly-ridden, resourceless waste it first appeared, Australia was of little interest to mariners bound for the rich markets of the East. To them the place was nothing more than a navigational hazard, though an enterprising governor at Batavia dispatched several expeditions to examine it. What he was seeking was a proper knowledge of the flanks of Indonesia and a possible "island of gold," of which there was much talk in those parts, but which no one ever found. Dutch investigators had a careful look at much of the northern and northwestern coasts of Australia, but they failed to find Torres Straits, the passage between New Guinea and Australia through which Luis Vaz de Torres—yet another Portuguese —had first sailed in 1606. This, indeed, *was* another route toward their precious Indies, but it was a route which was destined to remain unused for almost two centuries.

It seemed to them that they could safely afford to let Australia sleep. It was unlikely that any attack upon their trade could be launched from there, and the continent offered little or nothing worth exploitation. The French, later, gave serious thought to establishing themselves in Australia, but they had been forestalled by the examination of the more fertile east coast by the Yorkshireman James Cook and the founding of a British colony in New South Wales.

The Dutch used some curious ships in their Indian Ocean trade. For a century and a half after they first sailed there, almost every voyage was a perilous adventure. The practice of allowing masters and officials to carry their own private ventures caused many a vessel to sail for home grossly overloaded. Many were lost, from this and other causes. There were still reefs and atolls lying unknown in the Indian Ocean. Almost each of these claimed a ship before being added to the charts, often in an erroneous position. Coastal navigation in the waters of Indonesia was perilous, and was bound to remain so for clumsy vessels which were dependent solely upon their sails. As C. Ernest Fayle has pointed out in his excellent *Short History of the World's Shipping Industry,** there is evidence that they deliberately sent out old and worn-out vessels, time and again, to save the cost of replacing them. Some of their masters were incredibly old. One was a "good old Man near ninety years of age." Good he might have been, but an alert master mariner he certainly was not.

No wonder the casualty returns were dreadful. When the accepted risk of loss was so high, it is not to be wondered at that such old ships were retained. They had as good chance of getting home again as new ships, perhaps. Passages by both were very long. The sailing ships of those days, used for deep-sea voyages, were slow, cumbersome, and awkward. They were built of wood exclusively, and length of timbers kept them short. What they lacked in length they made up in excessive beam and great depth. Their sail plans were often inadequate, and ancient masters, intent upon a night's sleep, frequently snugged them down every night at sea, even in the trade winds. Passages of more than six and even seven months, between Holland and Java, were the accepted thing even by the new route using the west winds. In such conditions the mortality was terrible. The ships were crowded with men, who were often recruited from the slums of half Europe. Dirt abounded and was the accepted thing. There is a record of one of these outward-bound Dutch East Indiamen throwing overboard sixty-two corpses in a week's delay in the Atlantic doldrums.

The loss of life on the long voyages was so bad that many

* George Allen & Unwin, Ltd., London, 1933.

men, once having arrived safely in East Indian waters, were loath to leave again, and saw out their days in ships which traded locally. Of these there was a huge fleet, for the Dutch commerce prospered despite, in due course, the loss of their position in India and their expulsion from the Persian Gulf and from Ceylon.

"The Prodigious increase of the Netherlands in their Domestick and Foreign Trade, Riches, and Multitude of Shipping is the envy of the present, and may be the wonder of all future generations," wrote Sir Josiah Child in the seventeenth century, in his *New Discourse of Trade*. In the Indian Ocean, at any rate, this "prodigious increase," impressive as it was, was made at the cost of many lives both Dutch and native, and some oppression.

But there were others besides the Hollanders and the Portuguese who were sailing the Indian seas. The mariners and the merchant-adventurers from the stormy British Isles were there as early as the Dutch, if not earlier, and they were destined to know the greater power. There was to be a "prodigious increase in their domestick and foreign trade," too, and it would last.

CHAPTER XIII

John Company

The first Englishman to sail a ship across the Indian Ocean was Francis Drake, returning in the *Golden Hind*, ex-*Pelican*, from his voyage through the Straits of Magellan, up the coasts of Chile and Peru, the west coast of North America, and across the North Pacific to the Spice Islands. Drake sailed from England in 1577 and was back in 1580, the year of Portugal's ruinous association with Spain. His voyage had angered Spaniard and Portuguese alike, not merely because it was quite unauthorized and was regarded by them as a contemptuous infringement of their rights, but for its ruthless piracies and pillage.

Drake had come very near losing his own ship, on the threshold of the Indian Ocean. Homeward bound from his successful call at Ternate (of which his knowledge was gained from Portuguese charts and the Portuguese pilots he had kidnaped), the *Golden Hind* first touched at an unknown island, to careen and clean. This took the best part of a month. She had scarcely been able to resume her voyage when she struck a reef and began to heel over. The little vessel was deeply laden with stolen treasure, rich plate, silks, and all kinds of valuable goods, in addition to 6 tons of cloves, which she had just embarked at Ternate. (The fact that cloves were worth loading by the ton in a vessel already freighted with treasure is an indication of their worth in those days.) When the ship struck, the wind got up and the sea with it, as they always seem to do when a ship is at their mercy. Drake ordered 3 tons of cloves to be thrown overboard, as well as some of the guns. The reef was in the open sea, and if the wind really got up, it would be the end of the *Golden Hind* and, very likely, of all aboard her. Where could they go? She had only one boat. She was little more than a large, decked boat herself, by modern standards. Some Atlantic liners of the 1950s carry lifeboats of practically the same dimensions.

Fortunately for the *Golden Hind,* she appears to have been caught by a projecting horn of reef while sailing on a parallel course with the main reef, in the night. She was not athwart the reef, and she was not impaled. There was plenty of deep water all round, save where the coral held her. In the morning, Drake tried to carry out an anchor to heave the ship off, but the sea was so deep that this was impossible. The wind was blowing right on the reef. When it looked as if the ship must be lost, a sudden shift of wind saved her. The wind swung through eight points of the compass. Drake immediately set sail aback on his foremast. Her head slewed round, and she was off. His sigh of relief must have been profound. She had been twenty hours on the reef, but the vessel had taken little serious damage and was making no more water than before she went up. Drake was a very lucky man.

His luck stayed with him until he had safely threaded his way through the maze of islands, reefs, sandbanks, and twisting channels of the Eastern Archipelago. At last, more than five months after first sighting the islands of Indonesia, he was safely anchored off Java on March 11, 1580, and there he was very happy to stay for a fortnight while his shipwrights made sure that everything was in as good a state as possible for the long passage across the Indian Ocean, around the Cape of Good Hope, through both Atlantics, and home. Drake sailed from Java on March 26 and, with his ship full of "joyful minds and thankful hearts," was off Plymouth six months later. He had put in at Sierra Leone in West Africa for water and provisions, but it was a long passage.

Pirate though he undoubtedly was in more senses than one (for he also pirated his navigators), Drake's circumnavigation was a great achievement. He showed the way to other English adventurers and when, within the decade, the Great Armada was soundly defeated, his countrymen began to send ships toward the wealthy East. Like the Dutch, they had sought at first to find a way around the north of North America or around Asia, reasoning that since passages had been found already around the south of Africa and of South America, there were just as likely to be navigable routes to China and India north-about, as south-about. They were wrong in this, but it took a long time to find out. Drake had sighted Cape Horn, which was yet another route toward the Indian Ocean, albeit a long and a hard way round. He had gone through Magellan Straits and been driven back to within sight of the Horn, but it was left to the Dutchman le Maire actually to establish the route that way. From Cape Horn to the Spice Islands, however, for a sailing ship, was all of 9,000 miles. The monopoly held by the Portuguese kept other ships from the Good Hope way, which was the only really useful route into the Indian Ocean or, for that matter, toward Australia. The Cape Horn route had to wait for the development of the powerful clippers of the nineteenth century, and then it was of real use only to shipping bound for the west coast of the Americas. The Straits of Magellan were of no use to anybody in a square-rigged ship. They were navigable only to a Magellan or a Drake.

A translation of Linschoten's *Itinerario* into English, published in London in 1598, was a considerable service, but before this a group of London merchants, elated by the defeat of the Armada, had obtained a license from the Queen to send ships to the East Indies, and a small squadron was sent out in 1591. This was more than sixty years after the first attempt, in 1527, to find a passage round the northern way, and in the meantime a number of Englishmen had sailed in Portuguese and other ships, under Portuguese charter, to India. The expedition of 1591 set out boldly to round the Cape of Good Hope. There were three ships. Their passage out as far as the Cape was so tedious and their provision for the voyage so poor, that one ship had to be sent back from there with the sick, and a second went down off the coast of Madagascar with all hands. The third, which was commanded by Captain James Lancaster, reached the East Indies in no state to fight or to try to trade. The principal object had been to capture Portuguese or Spanish ships, but Lancaster arrived scarcely able to take a Malay proa. On his return voyage he put in at the West Indies. His ship by that time was so ripe, and his crew in such a state of ill-health and insubordination, that the ship was cast away. Only a handful of survivors reached England finally in a French privateer.

But a disaster of this kind did not deter the merchant-adventurers. Others came forward, and more ships were sent. The leading merchants of London were determined to have their share of Eastern trade, and the Queen granted a charter to a group of them at the end of the year 1600. This group was known as "the Governour and Company of Merchants of London trading to the East Indies," and that was the beginning of the great East India Company, called later the Honourable Company, and many other names besides.

The Company began operations by sending out Captain James Lancaster with a fleet of six ships. Intending to profit from the experience gained by Lancaster's previous misfortunes, these ships were as well chosen, manned, and stored as they could be. The Company put $350,000 into the venture, which was a large sum in those days. Lancaster's flagship was an 800-tonner called the *Red Dragon*, bought from the Earl of Cumberland for $17,500. With her went the ships *Hector, Susan,* and *Ascension,* of about 300 tons, and the *Quest,* of 100 tons, called a pinnace. Lancaster was styled General. John Davis was the Pilot-Major, and John Middleton the Vice-Admiral and Principal Factor. The object of the voyage was frankly to engage in commerce, but it was the intention to respect both Portuguese and Spanish rights in places where these were properly established. What was not proposed was to allow these countries to continue their Pope-given monopoly, for Lancaster's report, Linschoten's *Itinerario,* and ample other evidence existed to show that there was trade enough for all. So the ships dropped down the Thames on a February day in 1601, "to bring into this realme spices and other commodities" of the East, and passed out into the North Atlantic from a port in Devon, a month or two later, with the east winds of Spring. They took with them cargoes worth nearly $150,000, including iron and tin, good English broadcloth, lead, cutlery, glass, and silver, as well as handsome presents intended for friendly native rulers. All the ships were well armed.

The pinnace did not get far, for her stores, tackle, and people were taken out of her on the coast of Brazil, and the hulk was turned adrift. Scurvy again took dreadful toll, though Lancaster kept it down in his own ship by an issue of lemon juice as a compulsory antiscorbutic. He tried to enforce this in the other ships, but the people laughed at him. Long before they reached the Cape, however, they were so short-handed that "the merchants took their turns at the helme and went into the tops to take in sails, as the common mariners did." The common mariner was regarded as a lowly type in those days, and the ships must indeed have been hard pressed. However, a month at Table Bay put things to rights, and the surviving ships went on to a highly successful visit.

Lancaster was well received by the King of Achen, who had heard of the defeat of the Spanish Armada and was glad to welcome Englishmen. Lancaster had a letter from Queen Elizabeth for the King, and suitable presents. He was able to negotiate a satisfactory treaty, despite the fact that the Dutch were already established there. He then went on to the Moluccas and to Bantam, and shared with the Dutch the capture of a rich galleon in the Straits of Malacca. His ships were able to load good cargoes, and by the end of 1603, the fleet was back in the Thames. The profits from the voyage were enormous, but in the meantime London had been paralyzed by the plague, and it was some time before the weakened market could absorb cargoes so large and valuable. The Company found itself in difficulties, and its expansion hindered. Sir Henry Middleton was sent to the Moluccas to establish a station in 1604, but despite the fact that Captain Keeling—the same who discovered the islands which now bear his name—was able to make a voyage a few years later without the loss of a single man to scurvy or dysentery, on the whole the English ships suffered dreadful losses through these causes, so much so that the efficiency of both ships and shore stations was often seriously affected.

The English, moreover, had neither the resources of abundant cheap money nor the help of a sympathetic state to assist them, and though English ships and seamen were as good as any and better than most, at first the Company made slow progress. England's peace with Spain compelled a policy of at least noninterference with Spanish shipping in the Indian seas, but the Hollanders were bound by no such restraint. Dutch ships abounded, and Dutch policy was trade first and politics afterward—long afterward. The English claimed prior rights at the Spice Islands, in view of Drake's alleged treaty there with the Sultan of Ternate, but the sultan's successors said plaintively that for one English ship they saw twenty Dutch; what were they to do when the English ship was not there? The King of Achen, too, was prepared to be friendly; but the Dutch were not, and they predominated.

Dutch shipping and Dutch shipowning alike had thrived on the Indian trade and, at first, the English lagged. The Dutch governors applied ruthlessly their policy of military domination, and they steadily and rapidly increased their influence, and their trade, throughout the East Indies. Before long, the English factors were thrown out of Jacatra and were murdered in the Spice Islands. The Company, unable to induce the King to do anything to uphold English prestige so far from the Court of St. James, sent out an armed expedition of its own. But dissensions in the command brought this to nothing. Sir Thomas Dale, who had been Governor of Virginia, went as "general," but his ship was wrecked on the voyage out, and the result of the expedition was merely to strengthen the Dutch position.

Meanwhile, the Company had established itself in India and in the Persian Gulf and, though there were difficulties, here it prospered. Portuguese squadrons were defeated or driven off. By 1612, the English had a factory at Surat and were established at other places on the Gulf of Cambay. In the Persian Gulf, they captured Hormuz from the Portuguese in 1620, and from this date Portuguese power in the Indian Ocean declined. The struggle then was between the Dutch and the English. In 1665 Bombay Island was handed over to the English Company. It had formed part of the dowry which the Portuguese Princess Catherine of Braganza brought with her on her marriage to Charles II. Bombay then was "a very pleasant place and a good ayre," which, however, yielded "nothing but a greate quantity of Coco Nuts and Rice, with other necessary Provissions." The name Bombay is said to derive from the Portuguese *Bom Bahia*—a good bay. Charles II having no use for it, and the Honourable Company having a great deal of use for it, it was rented for a loan of $250,000 and an annual rent of $50, and the Company moved its headquarters from Surat to the new port of Bombay, which, from a group of seven swampy islands, was destined to grow into one of the great ports of the world.

This was a great achievement, and it was the East India Company which fostered it. Within ten years of the Company's move, the population of Bombay had increased to 60,000, and the building of magnificent teak ships was already an important industry. From its founding, Bombay prospered, and so thereafter did the affairs of the Company. The policy of peaceful trading paid in the long run. "Let this be received as a rule, that if you will profit, seek it at sea, and in quiet trade," wrote the famous Englishman, Sir Thomas Roe.

But it was not always possible to take a profit from "quiet trade." There were to be many troubles with the Dutch and at least two periods of open warfare with them. The French, too, had founded an East India company, first in 1604, and they wanted their profit from "quiet trade." They did not become active in the Indian Ocean for more than a decade after the first company was formed. A Frenchman named Francis Pirard de Laval, in a ship from the famous fishing port of St. Malo, had sailed around the Cape with an English pilot in 1601, but he was wrecked on the Maldives and spent five years in captivity there. Pirard de Laval left a narrative of his experiences. Apparently the sailors got uproariously drunk when the ship struck. "This filled me with horror," says the narrator, "and convinced me that sailors leave their souls and consciences ashore." When M. de Laval was rescued, he saw to it that he made no more voyages with any such wretches.

It was not until 1664 that the French became serious competitors for Eastern trade. They established trading posts in the Persian Gulf and in India and, in due course, were able to seize Mauritius, which became a valuable base during the Napoleonic Wars. Bonaparte's invasion of Egypt was to coincide with French dominance in the Indian Ocean, and for more than twenty years French privateers and war vessels made themselves great nuisances to British shipping. But all this came to an end when Mauritius was taken in 1810. French expansion later took the form of colonizing Madagascar and extending trade in Cochin China and Indo-China generally, and in the establishment of such colonial possessions as Djibouti in Somaliland, on the Red Sea, as a coaling port on the route to the East and an answer to the British occupation of Aden. French influence, too, was important in Oman for many years and, to a less extent, in Persia, and the French colors were abused a great deal in the notorious slave trade between Arabia and East African ports.

The British occupied Aden in 1839, but its importance as the "Gibraltar of the East" had long been appreciated. It was one of three great Indian Ocean ports which were the keys of Eastern trade, as d'Albuquerque had pointed out several centuries earlier.

The first is Malacca, at the exit of the Straits of Singapara [he had written]. The second is Aden in the entry and exit of the Straits of the Red Sea. The third is Ormuz at the entry and exit of the Straits of the Persian Sea. . . . And if the King of Portugall had made himself master of Aden, with a good fortress, such as those at Ormuz and Malacca, and so held the sway over these three Straits, he might well have been called the lord of all the world.

It was not so much its importance in controlling the approaches to the Red Sea which finally induced the British to occupy Aden, as its value strategically and as a coaling station and port of refuge on the shortened route to India. Aden's close connection with India was marked until very recently by the use of the Indian rupee as the local currency.

Before Aden was occupied, another of d'Albuquerque's famous "keys" had been improved upon by the East India Company. Instead of being content to control the Straits of Malacca by the acquisition of the island of Penang—an unsatisfactory substitute, though a good port in its own right—which the Rajah of Kedah had ceded to the Company in 1786, a farsighted and most brilliant man had conceived the idea of founding a new great port on Singapore Island. This man was Sir Stamford Raffles. Raffles, who was born at sea, joined the service of the East India Company as an "extra clerk" at the age of thirteen and was only forty-five when he died. His extraordinary vision and organizing, military, and administrative abilities had made a conspicuous success of his new "key," and he would undoubtedly have achieved a great deal more had he not been hindered by the Company. For a time, Raffles was Governor of Java, when the English defeated the Dutch in 1811. In 1816, by an agreement at home, the rich island of Java again reverted to the Dutch, but some of Raffles's reforms were permitted to continue. A few years later, in 1819, Raffles arranged the lease of the island of Singapore from the Sultan of Johore, on behalf of the Company. Singapore was then little more than a fishing settlement and a nest of pirates, the bones of whose victims littered parts of the foreshore. But it had once been a great port, and it could become so again.

"I have declared that the port of Singapore is a free port and the trade thereof open to ships and vessels of every nation, equally and alike to all," declared Raffles. This was a new doctrine and not at all that under which any of the great national companies had labored. But it was immensely successful from the beginning. Within a few years Singapore was prosperous, its trade second only to that of Calcutta; within a decade its trade was worth more than $20,000,000 and its population, a few years later, was equal to that of the whole Malayan Archipelago. Singapore was more than a "key" and an invaluable halting place at the crossroads of the Eastern world. It *was* the crossroads.

There was only one Stamford Raffles. Men of vision were as rarely encountered in the employ of John Company as they were anywhere else, and some of his greater ideas were brought to nothing. By its very nature, the Company was conservative, hidebound, and completely monopolistic. By its nature, too, it could not help but grow far from the original ideas of "quiet trade." Before the seventeenth century was out, it had been forced to develop as a territorial power, with the rights to coin its own money and command its own fortresses and troops, who were both European and Indian. Very soon it had to found its own navy, and this—the Bombay Marine—was to become famous in Eastern waters. The Directors had been compelled to confess that they could not "trade boldly, or leave great stocks where we have not the security of a fort." Before long, they sought "to establish such a politie of civil and military power, and create and secure such a large revenue, as may be the foundation of a large, well-grounded, sure English Dominion in India for all time to come."

Just as the Portuguese had found before them, and after them the Dutch and the Spaniards elsewhere, some sort of flag *had* to follow trade, and that quickly. If the flag could not be England's, then it had to be the Honourable Company's. This was a distinctive ensign, consisting of the red cross of St. George on a field of red and white stripes. This flag already flew from the peaks of a great fleet of ships of all sizes; now it flew ashore over forts and encampments as well as factories, magazines, and trading centers.

The monopoly granted to the Company was the cause of considerable envy. Pirates, including the notorious Kidd, Avery, England and company, sailed to the Indian Ocean to prey on the fat ships homeward bound, bulging with riches. In England, fierce opposition developed from time to time in the Parliament, and in consequence there were several far-reaching reorganizations. The Company's charter had to be renewed at stated periods, and when Parliament took a hand in this there was bound to be trouble. But year after year, and even century after century, reorganized or not, John Company lumbered profitably on. The astonishing growth and development of the British Navy, and England's assured dominance of the sea, were, however, the real keystones of its success. The Company's own Bombay Marine could deal with the pirates of the Indian coast and of the Persian Gulf, but without the strong arm of the Royal Navy there would have been no Bombay Marine and, indeed, no Company.

The French had line-of-battle ships in the Indian Ocean at the beginning of the eighteenth century when De la Hayes' squadron was sent there. However, they did not achieve much, either then or later. The Company's own ships were heavily armed and well able to give a good account of themselves in action, even against French ships of the line. This was shown in the historic action—perhaps masterly lack of action would describe it better—between a group of sixteen East Indiamen, returning heavily laden from China through the Malacca Straits, and a squadron of four French warships under Admiral Linois. The warships should have had little difficulty in taking all sixteen ships, and a tremendously rich prize-fleet they would have been. But the Indiamen at once formed line of battle in close order, their ensigns and battle colors flying, and signals passing between them. They *looked* like men-o'-war, with their towering hulls, their long lines of gun ports (mostly unmanned), their spotless white canvas, and their perfect maneuvering. But a hostile admiral should have known them for what they were. East Indiamen were a common enough sight. At any rate, Linois kept his distance, and there was no action at all, the first day. The East Indiamen continued steadily on their course, looking ready for anything and making a brave show. Their commodore was Nathaniel Dance, a merchant seaman well known for his coolness and daring.

The following day, after lying to all night, they found the French warships also lying to, to windward. The fact that the Indiamen looked so much like warships, and that there were so many of them, had caused the French admiral to believe that he had encountered not a group of more or less peaceful merchant ships, but a well-armed and warship-protected convoy. The fact that some of the ships showed red ensigns and some others blue further deceived him. He was hesitant about coming to blows at all, and when he did, it was in a halfhearted fashion. After a very brief period, the French admiral broke off the engagement and fled! Dance gave chase to give, perhaps, the appearance of overpowering belligerence; but after three hours he resumed his course, doubtless much relieved. Not a ship was taken.

This, perhaps, is an early instance of the importance of a proper mastery of the subject of ship recognition on the part of professional naval officers, a matter which was brought out on several occasions of importance during World War II. But indeed Commodore Dance and all the captains in that brave fleet must have been skillful and courageous seamen. The French admiral's ship alone had a weight of metal on the lower deck which gave her superiority over *all* the Indiamen which could, at any one time, have brought their guns to bear on her. And well did Dance know this. He was knighted for his bravery and for the exhibition of excellent discipline which stood behind it, and received a pension of $2,500 a year from the Directors of the Company. Such a sum was real money then; and he deserved it.

The Company was by no means always so fortunate or so well served. It lost many ships, and it suffered some fools. But on the whole, it played a great and invaluable part in the remarkable increase in British trade which took place almost continuously from the time of Queen Elizabeth; and it was, for at least two eventful centuries, the font and expression of British sea supremacy in the Indian Ocean. The tremendous distance of India from Europe in the days of sail and the power and prestige which the Company had built up, not alone in India but in the Persian Gulf, Arabia, Burma, the Malay Archipelago, and China besides, were considerable factors in permitting the continuance of its monopoly, despite ever-growing opposition. To those who had no capital or interests in it, it could do no right. Charges were made against it that it strangled trade and held back the science of naval architecture, that it held the kingdom to ransom for the exorbitant prices charged for the products it brought from the East, and that the continuance of its gigantic monopoly was morally and politically indefensible.

By the beginning of the nineteenth century, it was obvious that the giant monopoly could not continue. It had served its purpose. The great developments brought about by the industrial revolution in Britain made it archaic and unnecessary. The long period of European wars had brought not only France, but most of Europe with her, to her knees. Dutch interests had received such heavy blows that their full recovery was unlikely, if not impossible. There had grown up a new race of British shipowners and merchant-adventurers, with vastly increased fleets and resources on a scale hitherto unheard of. The Honourable Company could no longer hope to defend its enormous rights. In addition to all India and China and the East, there was now the new continent of Australia to be reckoned with and the great Pacific, for the Company's monopoly of the Good Hope route was held to give it effective control of the Pacific, as well. It took better ships than the eighteenth-century sea-soaked wagons to make a commercial route of grim Cape Horn.

The clamor for a share in ocean trade beyond the confines of the Atlantic, intensified by the loss of the American colonies, whipped by the vast increase in British shipping, could no longer be withstood. By 1814, the Company had to bow to the inevitable. Its Indian monopolies were taken from it in that year and the Indian trade was thrown open, though the Company held all rights in the China trade for almost twenty years longer. These were rescinded in 1833, and then the Company sold off its ships and went out of business.

It had a great record. Blemishes there certainly were, but considered as a shipping business alone, without regard to its many other activities, the Honourable Company was perhaps the greatest and the most successful maritime enterprise the world had known. Nor is it probable that its like will be seen again. It had inherited the great mantle first worn by da Gama and the illustrious d'Albuquerque, and it had stretched this gold- and jewel-encrusted cloak to cover half the world.

CHAPTER XIV

The Ships and the Men

If the warships of the period were wooden walls, the ships of the Honourable East India Company were more like wooden barrels. Little attempt was made to get any speed out of them. Great carrying capacity, a good gun platform for fighting, roomy decks, and an official tonnage kept for many years to a rigid 499 tons, to save the expense of carrying a chaplain, were the main requirements. An old regulation was that the Company's ships of over 500 tons should carry a chaplain, and this was not popular. The diversity of size among the Company's ships of 498 and 499 tons became so marked that at last there was a storm about it, in Parliament, and when, afterward, the ships had to be properly measured, some of them leaped at once to the 800-ton mark and some were over the thousand.

They were picturesque vessels and, under a press of snow-white sail, even beautiful. Their lofty masts and slim yards, their comfortable great apple bows, their enormous poops with built-up tiers of windowed gracefulness on the decorated counters, their lines of gun ports and their great bowsprits and long jib booms, growing from the curved cutwaters, made them ideal subjects for marine artists of the day, and a fleet of them getting under sail from St. Helena must have been a stirring and magnificent sight.

But a contemporary speaks of them as being "a cross between a castle and a floating warehouse," their best speed was about six knots, and some of them were so unwieldy as almost to be unmanageable. They could carry big cargoes and they could fight, and—provided that their navigators kept them off the reefs and the navy's press gangs left them crew enough to survive the scurvy, dysentery, and fevers—they could waddle outward to the Indian Ocean around the Cape of Good Hope and waddle home again and earn satisfactory profits. They were, indeed, astonishing vessels. They were passenger ship, mail ship, cargo ship, and warship, all in the one hull. On occasion—many an occasion—they were ships of discovery as well. They were in many ways the most interesting fleet the world has seen and, in spite of their imperfections, they were also probably the most successful. Scions of the nobility competed for service in them, for the rewards of command were tremendous and the Company's service was often ranked ahead even of the Royal Navy.

Of the two services, [wrote the great geographer James Rennell in a letter of advice to a noble family considering where best to place a son destined for the sea] I should prefer the India Service for a Boy at his first going to sea. He has there less chance of being corrupted than in the Navy where there is such a parcel of idle young Fellows in every ship: he will also probably make a swifter progress in learning his Duty and will be much closer overlooked by the Captain, or whoever has charge of him, than the nature of the other Service will allow. . . . After he becomes Master of his business, he can still choose which Service he will follow. The officers of India Ships are known to be in general thoroughbred seamen, and are seldom refused preference in the Navy after being a very short time in it.

The officers in the Company's ships were an elite of the merchant navy such as has no existence today. They wore uniform, were entitled to carry swords, and were received with deference and afforded proper dignity when they went ashore. A captain of an Indiaman landing at any of the Company's stations had to be received with a salute of thirteen guns, and the guard had to turn out whenever he visited a fort. The Company had a proper appreciation of the importance of its ships and the senior officers aboard them. No captain was ever required to skulk round a shore office waiting to be received, even by the marine superintendent. Several captains were peers of the realm, and many were or became baronets and knights. A captain had valuable privileges. He could, if he were fortunate, make $50,000 out of one Indian voyage, and even as much as $150,000 was not unknown. He had the right to certain cargo space for his own "ventures," and whatever he could make out of the passengers was his.

His personal accommodation included the airy and comfortable great cabin in the poop, with its attractive stern windows, and he had plenty of room to spread himself there. It was easily the best place in the ship. Indeed, it was often the only decent quarters in the ship, everyone else putting up, at the best, with small and stuffy cabins, ill ventilated, noisy, and frequently awash in bad weather. A captain could easily sell half the great cabin or three parts of it, for a passage, and make a very good thing out of it. He sold the places at his table, and only those who bought these places were allowed to take the air on the poop. For the rest, there was the crowded main deck.

Catering was another of the captain's perquisites out of which he did extremely well. He ran a good table, but he charged heavily for it. Even to sit at it might cost a passenger $500, and as many as a score of assorted humans would be crowded there, the two senior ladies seated carefully at the captain's side. The captain himself sat in the center of the table, whence he could see through the large windows over the deck. The mate and the second mate ate at the captain's table, and the third mate ran a mess of his own for the lesser passengers. Even in the third mate's mess, a place could cost the India-bound adventurer $350 or more. Passengers provided all their own furniture, and as they were sometimes a year and generally half a year aboard, their needs were extensive. A "good" passage out took six months. Prodigious quantities of livestock and poultry were carried, so much so that in many ships it was impossible to use parts of the main deck and even of the poop, for the cattle stalls, rabbit hutches, chicken houses, pig sties, and sheep pens crowded everywhere. Chickens were wedged like bottles in a rack and sheep were jammed together. Rich hams, wines and beers in abundance (charged separately, of course), plenty of fresh fish caught over the side at the slovenly rate of the ship's speed, ducks, fowls, roast mutton, and steaks were commonly on the menu. One dinner for sixteen persons—not at all an unusual meal—which is recorded by a passenger as having been served in the ship *Sir Edward Hughes* (Captain James Urmston) in 1797, included pea soup, roast leg of mutton, hog's puddings, two fowls, two ducks, two hams, corned round of beef, mutton pies, pork pies, mutton chops, cabbage, and potatoes, followed by an "enormous plum pudding." Many captains grew their own salad stuffs and even mustard, in tiny plots in the quarter galleries or slung in the skylights (this was commonly done, almost to the last days of big deep-sea sailing ships).

Making money from everything he touched, cashing in on the passengers and all their needs, overloading the ship to make more room for his ventures out and homeward, sometimes doing handsomely out of smuggling as well, no wonder captains were able to retire ashore with their fortunes, after a few voyages. The greatest number of voyages which any captain made, according to the records, was thirteen. Most were well off after four or five. Anything at all did for outward ventures. The captains were all experts in the Indian trade, and they knew what to take. Some specialists kept the better class millinery shops stocked, and the arrival of an East Indiaman would be followed by an announcement in the press that Madame So-and-So, in Calcutta or Madras or Bombay, now had an ample showing of the very latest modes (ten months on the way) which were available for ladies of discrimination, at a price. One captain became such an expert in the millinery business that he forsook the sea, married his milliner, and doubtless lived happily ever after. Some brought packs of hounds, and the muttered oaths of the crew who had to clean up after the "damned dogs" did not matter in the slightest. Hounds were popular and sold well, and that was all that mattered. Cut glass, silverware, porcelain, even furniture and grand pianos, horses—anything and everything which would sell—formed part of these ventures. One hundred per cent was generally regarded as the lowest acceptable rate of profit. But the investors sometimes failed, as on one occasion when freakish weather brought the entire outward-bound fleet of the year into a few ports of India at the same time, and there was—for once—a buyers' market in European productions for a month or two.

Ventures homeward were on the same scale and were even a surer means of profit, for Eastern products—thanks to the Company's monopoly—still brought fabulous prices, though the consumption everywhere was rising. Such commodities as spices and drugs and tea were coming into wider and wider use. By 1805, for instance, East Indiamen brought 23¼ million pounds of tea to England, of which 1¼ millions formed captains' and officers' ventures. These ventures were then computed at roughly 8 per cent of the Company's total trade, and both the Company and the venturers were profiting exceedingly well. By 1805, however, there was a serious competitor in the shape of the fine ships from the new American colonies. It was the Company's tea which—though not then in the Company's ships—had figured in the famous "tea party" at Boston, which touched off the Revolution. The New Englanders soon came looking for some tea of their own, and they showed that they were not going to be kept out of the Indian Ocean by any old-fashioned monopoly granted by England. Their increasing and virile competition had something to do with the loss of the Company's monopolies.

Some of the Company's captains were remarkably young. The regulations required that they be at least twenty-five years of age, and mates had to be twenty. Mortality was heavy, and promotion came fairly fast, though influence had a deal to do with selection for command. There was a definite captain class, and though it was possible to reach command from the lower deck, only a most unusual man could achieve this, and then he was frequently not confirmed in his command. His path was thorny because of his lack of friends at court, and he could be removed to make way for one of the more favored, almost at any time. The ships generally carried six mates and crews of about a hundred men, including gunners, sailors, stockmen, cooks, servants, midshipmen, boys, and everything else. Captains were entitled to two servants, and mates to one. Surgeons were not ranked high and were usually required to do all the barbering fore and aft, as well as the bloodletting and distribution of pills. Surgery was rough and only for the really fit. High mortality was accepted as a matter of course. Sailmakers, caulkers, coopers, shipwrights, bakers, poulterers helped to swell the ship's company. All were required to fight, and one of the first things done on leaving port was to assign every man aboard to his action station. Pirates were a real menace in the Atlantic and the Indian Ocean. In the Atlantic, the corsairs from the Mediterranean came out into the shipping routes between the Channel and the Cape Verde Islands. In the Indian Ocean, the European pirates based on Madagascar and the Indians based on the Malabar coast were rival menaces. Ships bound for China had to work their way through the treacherous Archipelago, where fleets of swift and deadly *proas* often combined to attack them.

Action stations were no sinecures. In the very early days there were frequent actions with the Portuguese, and later with the Dutch and the French, which did not always go in the Company's favor. There is at least one case of a magnificent East Indiaman's being snapped up by a French raider at the very Sandheads, just as she left Calcutta with a valuable cargo and a large passenger list of distinguished persons. This ship, the *Triton,* was taken by the famous French admiral Surcouf and spirited off to Mauritius.

In addition to peril from pirates, privateers, and hostile frigates, there was the very real danger of shipwreck. Even when the actual

wreck was survived, castaways were sometimes murdered by natives. There is the classic case of the ship *Grosvenor*, wrecked
somewhere near the Cape in 1782. The *Grosvenor* was a popular
ship, full of passengers from Calcutta and Madras, who included
many persons of distinction in the Company's employ and an
exceptional number of women and children. Out of the 135 persons
who survived the wreck and reached the shore, only 4 lived to reach
Cape Town. These were 3 sailors and a deck boy. Native attacks
accounted for most of the others. Though a tragedy on this scale
was unusual, far too many ships were lost. There were many reefs
to strike, storms to survive, unpredictable currents to contend with.
Years after the Company had gone out of business, the waters in
which its ships operated were most inadequately surveyed. On
almost every voyage, the ships had to go through the cyclone belt
in the area of Mauritius and Madagascar and the hurricane belt
of the Bay of Bengal. Navigating methods were still imperfect. In
addition to navigational dangers, there was always the most alarming risk of fire. The ships were built of good wood for burning and
they all had large powder magazines. Many which sailed and were
never heard of again were probably lost to fire and subsequent
explosion. It is no cause for wonder that, between 1750 and 1800,
more than 160 of the Company's valuable ships went missing or
were lost by wreck, fire, or capture.

As for navigation, that was by no means the precise science it has
since become, at least in theory. It was not uncommon for ships to
be 100 miles and more out in their reckoning. The greater part of
an Indian voyage was usually made in good weather, both outward
and homeward, with bright sunshine and good visibility. This may
have made some captains careless. There was the case, for example,
of the ship *Doddington*, which struck a rock off the Bird Islands in
Algoa Bay and went to pieces within twenty minutes, with heavy
loss of life. Her reckoning had placed her nearly 100 miles offshore,
and the captain had supposed he was taking every reasonable pre-
caution to avoid the coast, as indeed he was enjoined most rigor-

ously to do in the Company's instructions. For over a century prior
to this wreck, the Company had been consistently drawing attention to the danger of that very rock, near which sets and currents
could put a vessel dangerously out of her reckoning. Some captains
were notoriously pigheaded and overconfident navigators. The Indian climate, apparently, turned out a fair proportion of peppery,
red-faced sea captains, as well as colonels.

Loss by foundering, too, was all too common, and overloading
had certainly a great deal to do with this. The Company, after some
early bad experiences, did not usually own its ships but had them
built to order and chartered them. Such as they were, they were
good ships, and they were well maintained. But even the best
wooden ship could not stand up to a succession of black south-
easters off the Cape, if she were loaded down with an excessive
quantity of her peoples' ventures, in addition to her proper cargo.
Even a well-loaded ship could succumb to the terrible storms, and
some did. The four ships *Lady Jane Douglas, Calcutta, Bengal,* and
Jane Duchess of Gordon, which went missing on the homeward
passage in March, 1809, could not all have been grossly overloaded.
They were last seen off Mauritius, and nothing from any of these
ships has ever been found. The Cape took them, without a doubt.
The previous year, the three ships *Glory, Lord Nelson,* and *Experiment* had similarly gone missing. The *Prince of Wales,* hove to in
the middle of that year's fleet of Indiamen off the pitch of the
Cape upon a black night of June, 1804, simply disappeared from
the face of the sea, and not so much as a chicken coop from her was
ever found, though there were ships all round her. She was the
commodore's vessel, and in the middle of the fleet. Even when a
captain arrived "safely" at his destination, his troubles were far
from over, especially if he were to discharge at one of the open
roadsteads along the Coromandel coast. Madras anchorage was
particularly dangerous, and so many ships were driven ashore there
that captains were forbidden to lie there at all over certain periods
of the year.

What with the trials of their long voyages—the risks of mortal illness, of shipwreck, of capture by pirates, and the extreme slowness of their wooden ships—there is no cause for wonder that captains were likely to become fiery, pigheaded, or morose. It was no joke to rule over anything up to a couple of hundred passengers, cooped up for so long in ships so comparatively small. Strict rules were laid down for the passengers' behavior. Young women, of whom a good many went out to India in search of suitable husbands, could cause a lot of trouble, though in those days they were generally accompanied by some flint-faced and hardhearted relative or other chaperon whose main duty it was to see that they formed no damaging shipboard friendships and that they preserved a proper decorum.

"We were only five times on deck during the voyage," wrote one of these flint-hearts proudly home, after safely delivering a brace of husband seekers in Madras, "to guard against imprudent attachments which are more easily formed than broken." It must have been a dreary voyage for the unfortunate young women. Many young women went aboard with a veritable sheaf of instructions as to what they were to do and not to do, the whole being aimed against these "imprudent attachments," which nonetheless remain a hazard of shipboard life to this day, particularly in cruising liners. Today, however, the aim seems to be to seek them.

One reason for avoiding going on deck was that, in the unwieldy garments of those days, young women could not walk the deck properly or keep their stance at all, without the support of a gentleman's arm. Young ladies were particularly enjoined to see that they "never walked for long, let the conversation be general, and always have one of your sisters on your other arm" and, if possible, another in the cabin. Those were the days of many sisters. Dancing, wine at table, and going on the poop at any time were alike forbidden. Laundry must have been a serious problem, both because of the general shortage of fresh water and because chaperons were strictly enjoined to see that no vestige of their charges' garments should ever be so exposed to the public view, or even trailed overboard in the dead of the night from an open window of the great cabin, or from their own ports.

However, life cooped up in this manner had a few compensations. It was the custom for the well-to-do to settle themselves aboard ship with every conceivable comfort, before setting out on such a long voyage, even in quest of a husband. There is a record of the directions given by Mr. Peter Cherry to a group of his daughters coming out by Indiaman, from which the previous quotations have been made.

I will suppose, my dear children, [writes Mr. Cherry] that you are properly supplied with every necessary for the voyage and provided with a comfortable cabin: half the roundhouse of a regular Indiaman of not less than 800 tons, wherein will be abundance of room for your piano, harp, etc., hanging lamp and candles, two or three small bureaux with bookshelves on them, two or three sea couches with drawers to convert into sofas in the daytime, a wash-hand stand with two pewter juglets and two pewter basons, foot tub and three chairs, all well cleated and secured before you proceed aboard. . . .*

But despite harps and grand pianos and plenty of furniture, there were many occasions when the women aboard were at loggerheads with each other and there was relentless, continuous, and destructive warfare among them. There is a recorded case of an Indiaman arriving at Madras in 1780 with eleven young husband seekers aboard whose warfare had been so prolonged and successful that not one had a stitch of untorn clothing left to land in, nor a hat! But they all gained husbands, without difficulty. Nor were all the carefully planned schemes to avoid "imprudent attachments" successful, by any means. Many a duel was fought over some lovely woman passenger, and many a quarrel raged for years. Duels were forbidden on shipboard, so the contestants had to wait until the ship touched at the Cape or arrived at her destination. More than

* Quoted by Sir Evan Cotton in his *East Indiamen*, The Batchworth Press, London, 1949.

one gravestone in the English burial ground at Madras records the fact that the occupant met his death while dueling, probably over a woman. Sir Evan Cotton tells of an instance when three men all fell violently in love with the same young woman on the voyage from London and landed at the Cape to fight it out. But the lady broke up the bloody business by rushing in and declaring that she would marry each in turn if they would only stop stabbing at each other's vitals. This she was able to do, for the fever took her first choice within a year of their arrival, and dysentery got the second a year or so later. So she retired to England with the third and a comfortable fortune.

Sometimes there were suicides. Death stalked the wake of many an Indiaman. For sensitive souls such a voyage could impose intolerable burdens. Some captains were boorish fellows with whom the passengers could not get on, though such commanders were in the minority. When a captain was doing so well out of his human cargoes, it paid him to look after them and establish his reputation. Junior officers and midshipmen were kept very much in their places, and the crew were just necessary labor. In those days, conditions afloat for the ordinary seafaring man were appalling. It must be remembered that they were equally bad, if not worse, ashore. The laborer was little better than a serf and was worse off than many slaves, in that no one had a proprietary interest in him or capital invested in him. The seaman could be impressed (though the Company was against this), die like a dog, be flogged unmercifully and even round the fleet, as in the navy. He had no claim upon his wages until the freight was earned. Whoever else made a fortune, he never could. He was a lucky man if he lived to be forty years of age or survived half a dozen voyages. If he were impressed for the navy, which was simply a form of slavery, he had no redress. The press gang made a habit of boarding homeward-bound Indiamen (and outward-bounders as well) and taking off the likeliest fellows, no matter what illnesses or crippling ailments they tried to pretend. They could be taken in Eastern waters also.

A sailor's soul was never his own. If he was forced into the navy, there was not the slightest guarantee that he would ever receive his pay from either the navy or the Company.

Several useful records survive that show what the life of a foremast hand was like aboard an Indiaman. Of these, the best is a journal written by Edward Barlow, who was in eight of the Company's ships between 1669 and 1703. Barlow's journal was edited by the late Basil Lubbock, the sailing-ship historian, and published in London in 1934.* It throws a lurid light on the conditions, and Barlow is a reliable informant. He was a decade at sea before shipping in an Indiaman, and he was an outstanding man who was able to rise to command, despite the disadvantages of lowly birth and his advancement "through the hawsehole" (as sailors used to say). In his first Indiaman, his pay was only 22 shillings a month, which was about $5. He became successively quartermaster, gunner, boatswain, second mate ($10 a month) and mate, at $30. He is scathing about conditions at sea as he knew them.

We seldom in a month got our bellyful of victuals, [he writes] and that of such salt as many beggars would think scorn to eat. [Regarding a Christmas dinner, he records] we had nothing but a bit of old rusty salt beef which had lain in pickle eighteen or twenty months, and a piece of it for three men, about three-quarters of a pound, which was picked out of all the rest, for the officers having the first choice always, nothing was left for the poor men but the surloin next to the horns.

Some ships provided only one meal a day for the mariners, and that of execrable stuff. The usual fare served aboard Indiamen for those before the mast was ship's biscuit and ancient salt beef or pork, deliberately chosen from the worst and cheapest cuts off the most inferior beasts and kept in pickle for years. As for the surgeons, they did not trouble themselves about the men, for they commonly waited until a man was half dead before going near him, "and then giving him some of their medicines upon the point of a knife, which doeth as much good to him as a blow upon the pate with a stick."

* By Hurst and Blackett.

If the cargo was damaged, the unfortunate seamen were held liable, and though their pay was the least on board, they were commonly mulcted the most, nor had they any chance of redress. Captains were complete autocrats. In addition to the power of flogging a man nearly to death or ducking him from the yardarm, they could turn men and officers out of the ship, destitute, anywhere they chose, and Barlow was twice turned out of Indiamen in Eastern ports. Barlow was forty years at sea, despite his complaints, and managed to put by a competence for his old age.

Despite the hardships of the sailor's lot and the tyrannical powers which his officers held over him, the Company received devoted service from many of these men. A portrait in the National Portrait Gallery in London shows John Dean, sailor in the Company's ship *Sussex*, a strong-featured, intelligent man of perhaps thirty years of age. Dean owes his distinction to his own heroism when the Indiaman *Sussex* was partially dismasted and abandoned near the Cape, when homeward bound with the usual valuable cargo from China. A storm had whipped the main and mizzen out of her, but she had masts enough left to be manageable and a moderating of the weather had permitted her to be pumped dry. Nonetheless, her commander, officers, and the greater part of the crew left her and made off in the *Winchester*, a sister ship, which was in company. Dean and sixteen other mariners refused to leave the ship, saying she could be saved. The captain declined to let Dean have the longitude and saw that the longboat was stove in, so that, whatever else happened, the salvage party could not survive—he hoped—to report him to the Company. Then he made off.

The *Sussex* floated quite well, for the hull had not been strained, and Dean and his mates were able to get enough sail on her to manage her. The accident happened not far from Madagascar, which is a high island. Dean made for the island and eventually worked the ship into the safety of St. Augustine Bay. Here her rigging was put to rights for the homeward voyage. All went well, and in three weeks she was able to sail again. Neither Dean nor any other of the plucky fellows who stuck to the ship could navigate, unfortunately, and they had not gone very far before the *Sussex* took the ground on an offshore shoal. They could not get her off, and she soon began to pound to pieces. The only boat left was a small pinnace, and this was stove in while leaving the ship's side, spilling the men into the water. Only Dean and four others survived. Again they reached Madagascar, after a passage of seventeen days in the open sea, during which some of them died. This time they struck the coast at an inhospitable and fever-ridden spot, and they all died there except Dean. He eventually was picked up by another Indiaman, the *Prince William,* and taken on to India. From there he sent a narrative of his proceedings to the Court of Directors, who had already heard something from the *Winchester* of the hasty abandonment of the *Sussex* and had suspended the captain. On Dean's evidence, they filed suit against this captain, and eventually recovered $100,000 from him.

Dean received a gift of $250, a pension of $500 a year, and the post of head porter in one of the warehouses; and he had his portrait done in oils, to become the only likeness of a sailor in the National Portrait Gallery.

Aye, the Indiamen were indeed astonishing vessels, the like of which the world is unlikely to see again, lumbering under a press of snow-white sail through the trade-wind zone of the blue Indian Ocean or storming eastward in a Good Hope gale. The long sea grass trailed from their wooden undersides and their apple bows pushed stubbornly through the gurgling water. In good weather, as in the quiet stretches of the Mozambique Channel and the Indian Ocean in the northeast monsoon, the great stern windows would be open, with perhaps the ship's orchestra playing to beguile the time for the captain and his table mates (at $500 a seat), while from the decks came the clucking of a vast horde of cooped-up chickens, the bleat of goats, and the noise of cows. The great barrel hull creaked on beneath its spread of glorious canvas, and the only other sounds were from the creak of well-seasoned timbers, the slow gurgle of water at the bows, the gentle hum of the warm wind in the taut rigging.

There was something valid in the charge, so often made, that the Honourable Company retarded the development of ship design in the English merchant service. In two centuries there was remarkably little change, and a crew resurrected from a ship of the early 1600s would have been equally at home aboard an Indiaman of, say, 1790. So long as any ship which could make the voyage at all could do so at a substantial profit, there was little incentive to provide better vessels. British, French, Portuguese, and Dutch East-Indiamen were much of a muchness, wind-blown old wagons which were content to make slovenly passages, to sail with a comfortable sloth aimed at arriving somehow, sometime. It took the virile competition of the new Yankees, with their unlimited pine forests and their abundant energies, to jolt the science of naval architecture with the startling innovation that a merchant sailing ship should not merely sail but sail rapidly and well, *all the time*, day and night. The coming of the early Yankee clippers in the Eastern trade was a bit of a shock to European shipowners and seamen. Then came iron, with all its great improvements—at first, the strong composite hull, built of wooden plank on an iron framework; and then the long, lean iron hull, with strong iron-wire rigging, which could stand nobly up to gales.

But the sailing ship by then was already doomed. The first steamer burst upon the Indian Ocean scene over a century and a quarter ago, when the little *Enterprise* arrived at Calcutta on December 9, 1825, one hundred and fifteen days out from Falmouth, direct. The *Enterprise* was only a sailing ship with a weak and unsatisfactory steam engine as an auxiliary, and she had made most of the passage under sail. But she brought with her a threat which drove not only the big-hulled Indiamen, but every other European sailing ship, from the waters of the Indian Ocean so completely and so finally that seamen of later days might wonder that wind-driven vessels had ever been there.

CHAPTER XV

The Oldest Profession

In the Indian Ocean, the profession of piracy is as old as seafaring itself. The first man who ever straddled a drifting log probably knocked the second man from another log. So piracy began. It has been going on ever since. The Trucial Coast of Oman in the Persian Gulf, the reef-strewn waters of the Red Sea, the Indian coast especially in the region of the Gulf of Cutch, the Andaman Islands, the Malacca Straits, the island of Madagascar, the Comoros and all the Mozambique Channel were notorious as the hotbeds of ferocious pirates, some of whom marauded well into the nineteenth century. In the period of lawlessness immediately following the Japanese capitulation in the Malay Archipelago after World War II, pirates began again to operate in the Malacca Straits, seizing junks laden with rice. There are still antipiracy patrols carried on by the Royal Navy in the waters of the Persian Gulf. If these were to cease—and effective control with them—there is little doubt that piracy there would quickly return.

There have been two kinds of pirates operating in the Indian Ocean, the local and the imported. The locals include Beduin, who are still prepared to reenter the business. One of the oldest industries known to Bedu tribes in Arabia has been to "protect" land caravans taking goods through their territories. When the rich goods from Eastern markets were transported by land, obviously every petty chieftain on the route, every wandering tribe could and would take toll, unless they were first bought off. They had to be paid to protect the caravan and its merchandise against themselves, a "racket" which is still far from unknown, even in a country like the United States of America. The bigger the chief or the bigger the tribe, the bigger the "racket" they were able to exploit. From time to time efforts were made to avoid their rapacity by transferring the carriage of goods to ships. This, naturally, made the racketeers extremely angry, and they attacked the ships whenever they could and took their vengeance on ship-wrecked persons.

For instance, more than two thousand years ago, when a people known as the Nabataeans controlled the northern end of the caravan route up the west coast of Arabia and earned their living from the "protection" they gave to merchants using it, navigation was reopened on the Gulf of Suez, and much of the rich commerce took to the sea. The port of Alexandria was founded, and this was more easily reached by sea, as there was an elementary Suez canal across the isthmus. The reaction from the Nabataeans was immediate and thorough. Every ship they could attack they did attack. Anyone cast ashore they slew at once, if he was not worth holding for ransom, and stole his belongings. The historian Agatharchides speaks of their "ferocity and lawlessness" and says that a fleet of quadriremes was sent through the canal to deal with them. They were caught on the open sea and "properly punished," for the swift quadriremes could overtake their vessels in calm waters. But before long, the canal silted up again and the quadriremes could not pass through it, and piracy flourished once more.

It was the same story in the Persian Gulf and, every now and again, rulers of the rich area in the valleys of the Tigris and the Euphrates had to send out fleets to deal with the pirates farther down the Gulf. Those whose lands were poor preyed on the goods from richer areas for so long and so successfully that—in their view, at any rate—to carry on such raiding became a right.

There were rules to govern it. A great deal of the coastal area, both of the Red Sea and of the Persian Gulf, was poor land, and the fierce coastal peoples thought it only proper that Allah should send fat argosies from richer lands to offer tribute for their sustenance. When they took too much sustenance they were sometimes punished, but here and there they became so powerful that they forced trade into other channels altogether. Both the Red Sea and the Persian Gulf sea routes were closed at different times, sometimes for as long as a century.

The Indian coast was no better, and the whole Arabian Sea was a great net for the pirates, wherein they caught many valuable "fish." The ancient historians make many references to this menace. Pliny speaks of companies of archers being carried in all ships crossing the Arabian Sea, to fight pirates. Ptolemy recounts the pirates' extreme ferocity. Marco Polo gives a factual account of something of their activities.

There go forth every year more than a hundred pirate vessels on cruise [he says, speaking of the coast of Gujarat in western India]. They take with them their wives and children, and stay out the whole summer. Their method is to join in fleets of twenty or thirty of these pirate vessels together, and then they form what they call a sea cordon, that is, they drop off until there is an interval of five or six miles between ship and ship, so that they cover something like a hundred miles of sea, and no merchant ship can escape them. For when any one corsair sights a vessel a signal is made by fire or smoke, and then the whole of them make for this and seize the merchants and plunder them. After they have plundered them, they let them go, saying, "Go along with you and get more gain, and mayhap that will fall to us also!"

Marco Polo records other interesting customs of the well-established pirate fraternity, including the habit of looking upon any vessel forced by stress of weather or other circumstances into their harbors as fair prey. These worthies at least had the grace —according to the great traveler, at any rate—of addressing the masters and merchants of such afflicted vessels in the following terms: "You were bound for somewhere else, and 'tis God has sent you to us, and so we have a right to all your goods," which they promptly took. But if any vessel ever brought a cargo which was intended for the port in the first place, she was "received with all honor and given due protection."

There were other well-established pirates at the mouth of the Red Sea, where conditions were ideal for swift descents upon merchantmen, and there were plenty of safe harbors to run for, behind the reefs and among the shallows. But the worst of all were the pirates of the so-called Trucial Coast in the Persian Gulf, particularly those led by the sheiks of Sharja and of a place called Ras al Khaima. The Trucial (formerly Pirate) Coast stretches from Ras Musandam, at the turning point into the Persian Gulf proper from the Gulf of Oman, along a sandy, shallow maze of largely useless land toward the peninsula of Qatar. Roughly 150 miles in length, it offered the ideal base from which to sally out and attack ships passing through the Straits of Hormuz. The pirates used particularly fast dhows, of shallow draft. Local knowledge was necessary to approach any of their ports, for a regular labyrinth of reefs and sandbanks lay off them, and a race of curious tides and sets streamed in and out among them, defying prediction to any but those who were born there. Local knowledge could not be acquired by any others, for all strangers were murdered on sight. Here the pirates reigned for centuries. There is a record that they preyed upon the Children of Israel when the ships taking them from their Egyptian bondage passed by. Later, they preyed upon the Portuguese and upon the English.

Even in the nineteenth century, they were able to operate a fleet of 63 large vessels and more than 800 smaller ones, manned by 19,000 bloodthirsty and voracious warriors. They took ships belonging to the great East India Company and defied pursuit. They spread at various times to the islands off the nearer coast of Persia, where they set up warlike establishments. When things were slack in the Gulf waters, they were not afraid to make long voyages round the southern coasts of Arabia and as far as the Malabar coast. Fanatical Moslems at one stage, they cut their captives' throats, remarking that the Koran forbade them to plunder the living but said nothing about the dead. In truth, however, they required no precepts from the Koran or anywhere else to bid them carry on their business of robbery with murder.

For a time, they were able to defy attacks by large assault forces sent against them by the British in India. One of the East Indiamen they captured was the *Minerva,* which fought them for two days. There were too many of the pirates, and she had no chance. The master of the *Minerva* tried to blow her up, knowing full well the kind of fate his people would suffer. Unfortunately he failed. According to a contemporary account, the infidel ship was then "purified" by a ceremony of water and incense, and all hands were bound and taken singly to the gangway, where one of the pirates slit their throats, piously exclaiming over each that he was acting in the name of God. An Armenian lady, passenger in the ship, was spared, for it was not their custom to molest women. The *Minerva* herself the pirates pressed into their own fleet, and they made good use of her.

This was in 1808. Elated by his success, the Sheik of Ras al Khaima sent an impudent demand to the Bombay government requiring a large sum in tribute, offering if this were received to allow the Honourable Company's ships to pass unmolested in the Persian Gulf. The answer was to institute a convoy system and carry the war right to the Trucial Coast. At this time the mighty Arab warrior Saud, from whom the present King of Arabia * takes his name, ruled all Trucial Oman with his intractable Wahabis. Saud was an organizer of genius. He brought about a union of the various pirate chiefs and set up an organization which was authorized to prey upon all shipping in the Gulf without exception, and one-fifth of the proceeds were to be his. The other

* His Majesty King Abdul-Assiz Ibn Saud.

four-fifths went to the pirates. This organization rapidly became so strong that it threatened to make the waters of the Persian Gulf impossible for shipping, altogether. The British government, always slow to act, at last decided it was high time that such practices were brought to an end. The *Minerva* and the Honourable Company's cruiser *Sylph* were sailing about the Gulf as part of a force of some 70 large and well-armed vessels, with crews averaging between 80 and 200 men, based upon secure and almost impregnable ports upon a flea-bitten coast that had not even been surveyed. So an expedition was sent from Bombay in 1809, having as its main object the destruction of the forces and the power of the pirate sheiks once and for all.

But that was not so easy, though the British ships reached Ras al Khaima safely and, after furiously bombarding the port, destroyed it and all the ships in the roads, which numbered more than fifty. The pirates fought fiercely but in vain. They were driven into the interior, but were not followed, for the instructions for this amphibious operation—like too many others—tied the hands of the commanding officer. He was forbidden to pursue operations by land "otherwise than might be momentarily necessary for the more effectual destruction of the pirate vessels in their harbours." So the ships were burnt and sunk and the waterfronts destroyed, but the pirates watched grimly from just out of range, and when the expedition departed, they began immediately to build more ships and more forts and to plan further depredations.

Within a few months, they were attacking vessels again. Six or seven years later, in 1816, a considerable fleet had to be sent to Ras al Khaima, but this attempt also proved abortive. As soon as the force had withdrawn, the pirates went to work once more. Success bred success, and the Sheik of Bahrein was known to intend to establish piracy from that island as, he said, this was "the surest way to make a fortune." Pirate strongholds flourished on the Persian islands, and the wild men of Trucial Oman again had a fleet of more than three-score large vessels hailing from Ras al Khaima alone. British cruisers were out hunting the pirates, but they could never come to grips with more than a handful of them. There were never enough cruisers. So once more, in 1819, a large amphibious expedition was mounted, and the Imam of Muscat came to its assistance. The Imam had a fleet of frigates of his own (relics from some of these were still in Muscat when I was there immediately prior to the recent war) and he had his own grudges to settle with the Wahabi pirates.

This time, Ras al Khaima and every other stronghold along the coast was razed and *every* pirate vessel was destroyed. Ras al Khaima put up a stout resistance which lasted almost a week, but the end was inevitable. This time, too, the British followed up their blows by beginning at once to make a comprehensive survey of the coast itself, and despite the jealous, sullen, and often murderous opposition of the inhabitants, this was carried through to its conclusion. Antipiracy patrols were established, and in due course, these were supported by the system of British political agents which, gradually but effectively, secured control of the important sheikdoms all round the Gulf and, by so doing, controlled the Gulf itself. The Royal Navy kept order afloat and British agents, appointed from the army in India, "advised" the leading sheiks, emirs, and other rulers ashore. The Pirate Coast became the coast of truce, the Trucial Coast, which it remains to this day, sometimes under an uneasy truce and often with internecine wars both afloat and ashore. But never again, after that truce in 1820, did great fleets of well-organized pirates sweep out from behind Ras Musandam and murder, rob, and burn all shipping in their path.

Oddly enough, the worst of the Gulf pirates was not from Trucial Oman. He was a Kuwaiti, by name Rahma Ibn Jabir, and he was generally recognized—and is still—as probably the most successful pirate who ever operated in those or most other waters. He led more than two thousand fierce freebooters and commanded a fleet which included at least six ships with crews of more than two hundred men. He had a system of forts ashore. He carried on his own wars, as well as piracies. He held a considerable part of the Hasa coast, over which he ruled with a ferocious efficiency. His wealth was fabulous and, at one time, he was said to have more than two hundred wives.

These must have found him difficult to put up with, for a contemporary describes the archpirate as a man of disgusting personal habits. A garment, once on, he never removed or suffered to have washed until it fell off or was cut off, or blown off in battle. His appearance is described by the same informant in most unflattering terms. "Rahma ibn Jabir's figure presented a meagre trunk with four lank members, all of them cut and hacked and pierced with wounds of sabres, spears, and bullets, in every part. . . . He had, besides, a face naturally ferocious and ugly, and now rendered still more so by several scars and by the loss of one eye."

In the end, this monster, finding himself facing hopeless defeat in a sea fight somewhere off Bahrein, put a match to his powder magazine and blew himself, his ship, and all his companions straight to the devil.

But the real fiends were the pirates from Europe and North America, who flocked into the Indian Ocean before the end of the seventeenth century, when stories of its vast wealth became known. The area and the trade lent themselves almost ideally to the pursuit of piracy. Great, lumbering ships, full of the richest cargoes, came sailing year after year from the Malabar coast and from the Persian Gulf and from Malacca toward the Cape of Good Hope, around which lay the only useful route to Europe. The island of Madagascar with its many creeks, lagoons, and harbors might have been designed as a pirate lair. All shipping *had* to pass it, either to the east or to the west. On the west lay the Mozambique Channel, where at the northern end the Comoro Islands offered safe bases and admirable lookout points from which to watch for ships. Just as on the Trucial Coast, the coast of Madagascar abounded in natural retreats which were perfect for shipping with local knowledge and impregnable to outsiders. It was a simple matter to move a few guns ashore and make a fortress out of a pretty bay, whence it would take a major assault to dislodge the defenders.

In the sixteenth, seventeenth, eighteenth, and part of the nineteenth centuries, small European sailing ships were mobile and easily maintained vessels. If the Arabs and the Indian seamen could do their own cleaning, careening, and ordinary repairs, so could the Europeans. Their principal needs were wood, water, and some fresh food, and these things were plentiful at Madagascar. They could lay up coir rope from the coconut as well as the local seamen could and, though it was very hard on the hands, coir cordage was much used in big sailing ships up to the end of the era of sail and was quite satisfactory. They could soon steal from other vessels what stores and ironwork they might require. At Madagascar or anywhere else in the Indian Ocean, they were a long way from authority. There was, moreover, an abundance of slave labor available, which they used. The climate in selected spots was tolerable enough, and, altogether, a pirate could lead a fuller and far happier life than any he might then know in the merchant service.

Those were the days of intense brutality in far too high a proportion of the European merchant service. It was customary to recruit crews from the slums, or worse, and to treat them like beasts. Low, brutish masters, quarrelsome despots who seemed to delight in the oppression of their men, sailed too many an English ship then on long and short voyages. The intelligent man before the mast had little to hope for. In narrow waters the press gang awaited him, and service in the navy could be almost as brutal and, far too often, was also unpaid. At a time when, in the main, ne'er-do-wells, prison scourings, and slum dwellers formed the greater proportion of the crews in far too many vessels, perhaps some despotism among the afterguard was to be expected. The wonder really is not that the pirates were so brutish but that there were not more of them. Many men were forced into piracy by being given the choice of going "on the account" or walking the plank, when the ships in which they served were taken. It is astonishing that there were men who refused to enlist.

For many years now, a stupid glamour has been cast over too many pirates' memories and, in the popular conception at any rate, they are frequently regarded as colorful and even romantic figures, led by thwarted heroes who, in the main, were iron-willed and lionhearted mariners, of real worth. But on the whole the record of piracy is a despicable one. Meanness, debauchery, the foulest kind of double-dealing, sneaking treachery, stabs in the back, and unrelieved brutality mark the careers of most pirates— leaders and men. Some of the very worst roamed the Indian Ocean. Though they roistered a while and had their "fun," in the long run few profited from their murderous profession, and only fools would ever equip an expedition to go in search of their alleged buried "treasure" now. Most accumulated little treasure and did well to make a nefarious living. They were outlaws, who could be hanged summarily by any ship which performed the good service of taking them. It is true that, at times, a few of them captured cargoes, even vast cargoes, of riches, jewels, gold, and the like. But these were always shared out, and the pirates were compelled to dispose of these things at ridiculous rates. Middlemen established themselves at Madagascar to buy the pirates' loot. It was they who collected treasure, and they did not leave it around.

Consider, for example, the case of the so-called Captain Avery, or Ivory, or plain Long Ben Bridgman, as his real name appears to have been. Avery, England, Tew, Roberts, and Kidd were the "great" pirates of the Indian Ocean, and they all came to bad ends. A seventeenth-century ghost writer has turned us out a juvenile which does the scoundrelly Avery proud. The poor boy, we read (broadsheets about pirates sold well when they were executed), was born at Cat Down in 1653, the son of a man of wealth. Orphaned at the age of ten, the story goes that a rascally uncle stole his inheritance and apprenticed him to sea in the hope that the well-known rigors of that profession would lead to his early death. But he survived to join the Royal Navy, in which—we are told— he did well. It was while he was a merchant captain of a logwood trader in the West Indies that he decided to become a pirate, and the decision was entirely the fault of a worthless wife, who was unfaithful in his absence. He then became a slaver and a buccaneer.

Other biographers failed to note any gentle birth in the career of Cut-throat Avery, alias Bridgman. If ever there was a pirate born, it was he. Quite early in his career he sailed as mate with a notorious pirate known as the Bloody Hand, who gave no quarter. Avery succeeded the Bloody one, who was killed in action. Before long, he had run off with a fine vessel, which he had helped to commission as a coastguard on the Spanish Main. This vessel was the *Charles*. Avery seized the captain and made off. Renaming the *Charles* the *Fancy*, he sailed to Madagascar and to Johanna in the Comoros. At these places he recruited a crew, for plenty of villains were offering there.

Avery left a strange epistle for commanders of English ships calling at the Comoros, in which he declared that he would not attack English or Dutch vessels. "But my men are hungry, stout and resolute," he continued, "and should they exceed my desire, I cannot help myself." He signed himself "Henry Every, *As Yet* a friend to all Englishmen."

The date of this strange document was February 18, 1695. Avery seems to have kept its terms, in general. His prey was the rich pilgrim trade of the Moslems from the East toward the Red Sea and Mecca. Here his first sally was astonishingly successful, for he took—with the help of some other pirates—the great ship of the Mogul, which was returning from its annual voyage to Jiddah. The name of this vessel was the *Gang-i-Sawai*. She was well armed and carried 500 soldiers, in addition to her regular crew. There were several hundred passengers aboard, including more than

200 women, and one of these was the daughter of the Grand Mogul. Such a party carried immense riches. Gold, silks, richly embellished ornaments of all kinds, including a ruby-encrusted saddle, and jeweled arms, diamonds by the sack, bales of silk and precious goods were among the cargo, the worth of which even then was estimated at over half a million pounds. The capture of this ship should have meant wealth beyond their dreams to the pirates who took her. But it meant other things, for the Mogul was incensed when he learned of it, and swore vengeance. This was to catch up with Avery, in due course.

But for the moment he was in clover. The rich prize was taken to Socotra and looted, all the pirates taking it, by turns, to go aboard and rape any woman who caught their fancy. Some of the women killed themselves with daggers and swords snatched from the pirates' belts. Others leaped overboard. Among them, in addition to the Mogul's daughter, was a party of Turkish virgins traveling from Mecca to India, apparently as part of the captain's "venture." Doubtless they were to have been sold as concubines. When the ship was attacked, they wrapped turbans round their hair and fought furiously. The more fortunate among them were killed in the action. The others were taken on to remote Indian Ocean islands where individuals among the *Fancy's* crew chose to retire ashore, with their share of the gold and jewels, rather than take a chance on returning anywhere in Europe.

On the way from Socotra toward a rendezvous at Madagascar, Avery gave the slip to his confederates in the other ships. A sly rascal, he first induced them to put their share of the loot into the *Fancy* (on the reasonable grounds that their own vessels were leaky and unseaworthy). Then he changed course by night and did not keep the rendezvous. Where exactly he went is not now known, but the *Fancy* turned up some months afterward in the island of St. Thomas, where Avery, mean to the last, paid for his stores with a bill of exchange drawn on the Bank of Aldgate Pump. He had plenty of gold to pay for his needs, but that was not his way.

The *Fancy* then sailed for the Bahamas, but the uproar raised by the Grand Mogul had reached the islands before the pirates did and, despite a present of the ship and of $20 a man, the governor dared not openly assist them. Before the governor could take possession of her, the ship drove ashore during a drunken orgy aboard and became a total loss.

Not only were Avery and his companions wanted for taking the Mogul's ship, but the stealing of the *Chance* was enough to hang them. After the loss of their ship, they tried to infiltrate into various islands and some reached the mainland of America, where they very wisely disappeared. Avery changed his name back to Benjamin Bridgman and took a party of some eighty of his men into Providence. There he bought a sloop for the passage to England. Others in the party quietly dispersed and did the same thing. Before long, half a dozen tiny vessels full of dark-jowled, suspicious, and silent men, whose chests clanked with gold and precious jewels, slipped out from Providence, bound east. Several of these vessels were not 40 feet long, but the pirates were rarely troubled about the size or seaworthiness of their vessels. All safely crossed the North Atlantic, only to find a reward of £1,000 ($5,000) a head against the apprehension of each of them, for both the Admiralty and the East India Company were determined that they should be punished. Avery landed his party at a remote spot on the coast of northern Ireland, not far from Londonderry. In Dublin they learned that a free pardon awaited any among them who would turn informer. But Avery had melted away.

He is next heard of in the pretty old town of Bideford, in Devon. Here, hugging in his chest treasure worth possibly $500,000, and fearful of spending a cent of it lest his identity be suspected, he led a miserable life, scarce able to pay for his bread. Suspicious of every stranger, starting at every sound, at length he was prevailed upon by some relatives to hand his jewels and gold over to a party of close-lipped merchants in Bristol, to dispose of on his behalf. But the merchants kept the loot and gave him nothing. When he visited them, they threatened to expose him as the notorious pirate, "for they were as good pirates on land as their client had been at sea," as the chronicler reports it.

This broke Avery's heart and he fell ill and died "not worth so much as would buy him a coffin." His bones were lowered without honor into a pauper's grave somewhere in Bideford.

Another of the same sort was Captain Kidd. Kidd was a Scot from Greenock, who disclaimed Scotland; and he was sent out to destroy the pirates of the Indian Ocean, only to become one of the most notorious of their number. The halo of romance round the name of the useless Kidd is heavier even than that round the thick head of the scoundrel Morgan. In the year of grace 1951, an expedition was organized to seek his "treasure," alleged—then— to be buried on an island in the China Sea, despite the fact that there is no evidence that Kidd ever was in the China Sea. He had no reason for going there, and there is plenty of evidence that he could have had little treasure to bury, if he had any at all.

Going to the American colonies as a young man, Captain Kidd did well there, especially in command of a privateer against the French, in the West Indies. He came to the favorable notice of the governor of New York, Lord Bellamont, and various other gentlemen, and others, prominent in that state. This Lord Bellamont appears to have had much the same piratical inclinations as the merchants who marketed Avery's jewels, for under the guise of organizing a cruise to suppress the pirates of the Indian Ocean, there is little doubt that his real objective was to seize the enormous wealth supposed to have been accumulated and hidden by that fraternity in the less frequented harbors of Madagascar. Lord Bellamont was a pioneer seeker of buried treasure, and he knew where it should be. What he ought also to have known was a little more of the character of Captain Kidd. At any rate, Kidd was appointed to command the Bellamont expedition's ship. His backers included the First Lord of the Admiralty and the Lord High

Chancellor, among others, and he carried a Royal commission dated December 11, 1695. His ship was named the *Adventure Galley*. She had 30 guns and 150 men, and she sailed from Deptford on the Thames in April, 1696.

Kidd went first to New York, where he recruited further crew to replace 80 men taken from him by the naval press gang in the Downs. New York was a good place to recruit pirates, then and later, and with a "villainous herd of men" (as Governor Fletcher described them) Kidd sailed for the Indian Ocean. He put in at the Comoros and tried a bit of piracy there against an East Indiaman, but there were too many ships there for him and he moved on to the Red Sea. He was in the mouth of the Red Sea too soon after Avery's success with the Great Mogul's ship, and the pilgrim fleet was then being convoyed. A halfhearted attempt upon an Arab ship in the convoy was beaten off and Kidd, now openly a pirate on his own account, cruised along the Malabar coast. Here his reputation had preceded him, for news traveled fast in those waters, even in those days.

The chief factor at Karwar, where he touched, had nothing good to say about him.

This captain is very severe to his people by reason of his commission, and carries a very different form from what other Pirates used to do, this commission procuring him awe and respect from his men, and to this is added his own strength, being a very lusty man often calling for his pistols and threatening any that durst speak to the contrary of what he desireth, to knock out their brains. . . . They are a very distracted company, continually quarrelling and fighting among themselves. . . . We were informed that at St. Mary's in Madagascar is settled great abundance of these villainous people with their families, yearly supplied from New York with liquors, provisions and other goods, so that any ship which desires such men may obtain as many as they please there.

Shortly afterward, Kidd fell in with his only good prize, a large Indian Ocean trader named the *Quedah Merchant*. This vessel hailed from Surat and was richly laden, but he had to dispose of her cargo the best way he could, selling a lot of it to the local inhabitants along the Indian coast. The share-out afterward was about $1,000 a man, and Kidd's own portion was $40,000. With this he sailed to the Laccadives, where he amused himself and his crew by permitting the rape and torture of the islanders. His next stop was Madagascar, where he transferred the guns and people of the *Adventure Galley* into the *Quedah Merchant*. Many of the people refused to continue with him, taking their share and going to other pirates, several of whom were acting as minor kings along various stretches of the coast. Kidd lost nearly a hundred men in this way and, very shorthanded, sailed from Madagascar for the West Indies.

Here he is supposed to have landed some treasure and to have buried it. The *Quedah Merchant* was abandoned at Curaçao and burned there, after which Kidd sailed for his favorite New York. Here also he is supposed to have buried his treasure on Governor's Island. Apparently, he was relying on the high standing of his backers in New York to save him from the consequences of his acts of piracy. In this he was wrong, for his backers were under suspicion too. He was promptly arrested and sent to England for trial.

That was the end of Captain Kidd. He was hanged at Execution Dock, Wapping, on May 23, 1701, and as if in expiation of his crimes, the rope broke under his weight twice and he had to be hanged three times. He had, at any rate, a kind of courage, for it was related of him that on the scaffold he kicked his shoes off, remarking that he was damned if he would die with his boots on. His body, with the boots put on again, was hung in chains by the riverside, where it swung for a long time as a warning to other intending pirates not to try operations under a Royal commission.

As for that fabulous treasure which has been hunted in places as far apart as Hispaniola, New York harbor, and the shores of

Madagascar, the only certainty is that Kidd could have left little treasure, if any at all. His only worth-while prize was the *Quedah Merchant,* and her value was placed by the East India Company at less than $100,000. Her owners refused Kidd's offer to ransom her back again for $80,000. They offered, instead, twenty thousand rupees, which at the rate of exchange then was little more than $15,000. Where Kidd could have collected any great treasure no one has explained, for he had to share his takings with his crew. He could scarcely have amassed, at any time, a fortune in excess of twenty thousand English pounds, and more than six thousand pounds (about $30,000, then) was taken from him on his arrest. The balance of his estate, which totaled £6,473–11s., was paid over to the Greenwich Hospital in 1725. These were comfortable sums in those days. But they represent no fortune, then or now. Ships and persons in quest of the Kidd Treasure would be well advised to stay home.

A good many of these Indian Ocean pirates originated in the West Indies. Pirate settlements at Madagascar existed for several centuries, and throughout that time there were well-maintained communications both with the West Indies and with New York. There was a regular American depot at St. Mary's, and a great deal of the booty found its way to New York. Piracy became an established industry on the island, and pirates passed between the West Indies, New York, and Madagascar almost as they wished, for more than a century. Slave trading was a side line, for there were plenty of slaves to be had. The pirates helped petty chiefs to make war on one another and accepted slaves in payment from both sides. These brought a good price in America and the West Indies, and furnished as well a legitimate cargo for their vessels. After all, treasure did not occupy much space. One of the more successful middlemen for the New York houses was Adam Baldridge, who had been a pirate himself in both the West and East Indies. Baldridge made a fortress out of St. Mary's. His agents in New York were the firm of Phillips (or Philipse) Brothers; or more likely, he was Phillip's agent in the Indian Ocean. Baldridge became a sort of minor king in Madagascar. Most of the buried treasure found its way into his (or the Phillips's) New York bank account, where there is no use digging for it now. Baldridge spent his declining days at New York, a respected citizen.

Other reigning monarchs in Madagascar were a mulatto named Abraham Samuells, who had once been a quartermaster in an honest ship; a ship's carpenter named Tom Collins; and a villain named—or known as—Jack Plaintain. This Jack Plaintain amused himself by forcing his captives to dance upon red-hot ashes while natives practiced throwing spears at them, and all hands laughed at the fun. A Dutchman named Ort van Tyle and a Dane named Hans Burgen from Copenhagen, a Scot named Adair, and an Irishman known as King Kelly were also in the business. Another was said to be the son of Captain Avery and the daughter of the Great Mogul, but there is considerable doubt about this. This individual, it is said, looked like Avery and had the long, dark hair of a "Moor."

Plaintain tired of his kingship at Madagascar after some years of profitable existence there, and built himself a sloop in which he embarked his wives and children, loot, and some companions and sailed for India to join forces with a famous Indian pirate by the name of Angria, with whom he got on very well. Most of his fellow kings came to violent ends, though a few managed to drink themselves to death. Most of them were butchered in wars with one another.

Among the buccaneers from the West Indies who came to try the Madagascar pirate trade was a man whose only name is given as "Edward England." He is said by some authorities to have been an Irishman but, by others, to have been a Scot. He was engaged, apparently lawfully, in the West Indies logwood business in the early years of the eighteenth century but soon

joined the nest of pirates then on Providence Island. Here, he
quickly became so notorious that his name was expressly exempted
from the Act of Grace (which purported to allow other pirates to
give up that calling and escape the gallows, if they surrendered to
the proper authority). But it was said of him that "he was not
avaricious and was always adverse to the ill-usage prisoners received." A captain of pirates had to be the most bloodthirsty of all,
lest the others fear his softness was intended to buy him a pardon
at their expense. When all were lawless, only the greatest outlaw
could command.

By 1720 this "England," whoever he was, was in Madagascar.
Whether or not he was personally inclined to show mercy to prisoners, foul acts of the usual barbarous kind were permitted under his
command. The record of his first Indian Ocean voyage speaks of
an unfortunate captain named Skinner who was brought aboard,
triced to the windlass, pelted with broken bottles by the drunken
crew, and then whipped about the decks as long as they had
strength enough to raise a whip or a rope's end against him. Then
after a night of this, he was shot dead.

England, with another miscreant named Taylor (concerning
whom no authority ever said a good word), was soon after East
Indiamen and "rich Moors' ships." He made a successful cruise
and took many prizes, one of the last of which was the East India
Company's chartered ship *Cassandra,* which was carrying money
for the factors on the Malabar coast. The *Cassandra* was commanded by a noble Scot named Macrae, who fought the pirates so
well that he nearly defeated them. When Macrae was captured,
England seems to have gone to considerable trouble to see that
his life was spared.

Later, when the pirates learned that Macrae had made his way
safely to Bombay and was bringing a squadron against them, they
marooned Captain England on Mauritius. Though he made his
way in a home-built boat to Madagascar, he died there shortly
afterward. It was said of him that his death was hastened "by

the severe stings of his conscience for his wicked course of life."
If this was so, he was a most unusual pirate. He may have represented the one genuine case of an able man forced into the dastardly profession and, once committed to it, unable to leave.

As for the fiend Taylor who took over his command, he cruised with more success than enough for a number of years, once taking a ship in which the Viceroy of Goa was embarked, with a cargo said to have been worth $5,000,000. From this ship Taylor took so many diamonds that the share-out for each of his 300 men included 42 stones. One pirate, receiving, instead of 42 smaller stones, one very large and beautiful brilliant, became incensed at what he regarded as his poor deal, and taking a hammer, smashed the priceless diamond until it split into his 42 parts. Some, at least, of this loot found its way back to the West Indies, and Taylor met his death, shortly afterward, commanding an armed ship in the Spanish service.

One day Taylor's cook burned the soup. Remarking that so fat a wretch would burn well, Taylor thereupon triced the man up and burned him to death. This was regarded as a great joke.

The last of the European pirates to prey upon Indian Ocean shipping on a large scale was the notorious Benito de Soto, of the ship *Black Joke,* who operated in the 1820s and early 1830s and was distinguished for a ferocity toward captives which was almost unparalleled, even in pirate annals. De Soto's aim was to sink without trace, murdering everybody and scuttling ships. With a rich cargo from the East Indiaman *Morning Star* under hatches, at length he made for a port in Spain to realize his riches and enjoy a spell ashore. But unknown to him, the *Morning Star* had not sunk, though the pirate crew had left her with auger holes everywhere and making water enough to sink within a few hours. All the women were locked up aft, where they had been treated with unspeakable ferocity, and the few surviving men and boys were locked up for'ard. The masts were sawn through, the boats destroyed, the food and water flung overboard, and the charts and compasses removed.

But the women broke out and freed the men, and the *Morning Star* was saved by the superhuman efforts of both. After having lost his ship conveniently on the Spanish coast, deeming it prudent to hide himself in Gibraltar, de Soto was swaggering along the main street there, dressed in the murdered captain's clothes, when an invalided soldier who had been in the *Morning Star* recognized him. De Soto was at once arrested. Search of his room soon proved his crimes. After a summary trial, he was sentenced to be hanged. When he reached the place of execution, he observed that the halter was too high. He could not reach it from the cart. He leaped nimbly atop his coffin, which was in the cart, adjusted the noose, and as the first rumble of the fatal wheels came to his ears, kicked himself away.

CHAPTER XVI

Slavers, Pearlers, Whalers

When I was at Zanzibar in a Kuwait *boom* one day in 1939, the captain of the port was worried by a message from the nearby island of Pemba to the effect that a young African child was missing there, believed to have been kidnaped by a Suri dhow to be carried off as a slave to Arabia. The slave trade was even then not quite dead, though a cathedral had stood on the site of the notorious Zanzibar slave market for many, many years. There were still Omani Arabs, especially from the more or less uncontrolled port of Sur, who were capable of picking up a healthy young boy and carrying him off for sale. There were plenty of "wild" young boys serving in the dhows, either as ship's boys or as servants for petty merchants, who traveled up and down the coasts of Arabia and monsoonal East Africa. There were several such boys in the Kuwait *boom*, but they were not slaves. They had been engaged by merchants from the beach at various Arab ports. Though they appeared quite capable of looking after themselves, I wondered whether they would not be better off if they were slaves. Their masters could let them go at any time, and then they would have to fend for themselves.

There were then still plenty of slaves in the Oman and in Kuwait, and elsewhere in Arabia, and they were treated very well. The religion of Islam recognizes the state of slavery as being legal and proper, and the sacred book charges masters to treat slaves fairly.

They must feed, clothe, and maintain them until death, and provide them with wives. The life of a slave was no harder than the life of an ordinary Arab. Many of them, I knew, had become more Arab than the Arabs themselves. They were devout Moslems, good citizens, and perfectly happy. Complete "freedom," after all, is a state not often achieved and, indeed, little understood. Slavery need not be the worst form of human relationship, or the worst condition. All slavery is relative, and the slave in Arabia had compensations that the nonslave could not have. Relieved of all worries about his home, his sustenance, his health, his future, and his children, the slave in the homes of Arabia could indeed be the happiest of men. As for the European version of "freedom," whatever that might mean to him, he could have it by presenting himself formally at the establishment of any British Agent. Few ever did.

Like the pirates, there were two kinds of slavers and two sorts of slave trades in the Indian Ocean, the local and the foreign. Again, as with the pirates, the foreigners were infinitely the worse. The districts of East Africa were never raided for the dreadful slavery trade to the West Indies and the Americas to anything like the same extent as the African west coast was. East Africa was farther away. But a good many cargoes of slaves were taken from Madagascar, especially by returning pirates who were anxious to have a "clean" manifest of ordinary goods, and some were taken from the coast. It was the European slave trade which was really horrible. The unfortunate Africans were seized, netted, stolen, snared, lured, or kidnaped anywhere, and loaded into old ships under truly appalling conditions. It was the custom in European ships to put them down in the holds, stacked like sardines, shackled, and ironed together, and there they remained for the long voyage around the Cape, through the trade winds, through the dreadful calms of the doldrums, and on to the ports of the West Indies or America. They were never taken up on deck unless they died. Food, water, and even air were at a minimum. The slaves' masters and transporters felt no obligation toward them, and they were given no consideration which was not based on the value they represented, as money. They were black heathens, regarded as worse than animals.

When they reached their destinations, they were sold to the highest bidders and began at once lives of degraded labor under conditions which were usually wretched and frequently were quickly fatal. They had no rights. If they escaped, as some did, it was the common thing to advertise for them to be brought back "dead or alive." They could be whipped for the slightest offense and have their noses and ears slit or cut off. Families were broken up, often wantonly. The long coast line of East Africa provided more than enough cargoes of poor wretches destined for this really horrible trade, but no Arab ship transported Africans to America or the West Indies. The big Arab slave centers were at Kilwa, Zanzibar, Juba, and Brava, and they catered to the Indian Ocean trade. The whole of the Negro population of East Africa was regarded both by the Arabs and Europeans as fair prey, except that Somalis were declared free and unenslavable by the Koran. Wiry, agile, and intensely independent, the average Somali made a poor slave. He was a fierce warrior, a good trader, a man able to look after himself. Whether the Koran forbade his capture or not, he would have been left alone.

On the whole, the African was fortunate who was enslaved by an Arab rather than by any European. The conditions of capture and the long and arduous march to the markets on the coast were undoubtedly very bad for both, but once he was aboard a dhow, he was generally little, if any, worse off than the average migrant who traveled by such vessels on the southbound voyage.

Except that they are more crowded, I have not perceived that the condition of the slave, in transit across the Arabian Sea, is very different from that of his master [wrote Captain Colomb, R.N., who was in command of H.M.S. *Dryad* operating against the slave trade in 1873]. The Englishman would probably succumb to the privations of the journey, but I have often heard it said on the spot that no one should talk of the cruelty of the Arab to his slaves on the northern voyage, unless they were acquainted with the conditions under which he and his family performed the voyage of business or pleasure from Arabia to Zanzibar. . . . We must not suppose that crowding, by itself, affects the Negro as it does a European, or indeed an Asiatic. We shall meet with at least one cargo of slaves, plump, well-favoured, and not unhappy, with the worst of their journey to Arabia over. But if disease, want, and crowding come together, then God help the wretched items in that crowd. Yet again, I have to say that I could not choose offhand whether I would rather spend a fortnight in the conditions of a slave in an Arab dhow not overcrowded, or the condition of a peasant in some cabins I have seen in the south of Ireland, whose masters were said to possess a considerable balance at the bankers'. . . . I speak of what I have seen, and judge to be the average condition of things.*

No less an authority than the British Resident in the Persian Gulf added his testimony, in 1844, to the reasonable conditions of the slave in Arabia. Slavery was an accepted condition of life and well conducted. It was never the cold-blooded importation of cheap labor which it was in the West Indies and the Southern states of America.

The treatment of the African slaves is at no time either severe or cruel [wrote the British Resident]. During the sea voyage they are not bound, or kept under particular restraint. Rice, dates, and fish, in sufficient quantities, form their food. . . . From the moment of their purchase at their eventual destination, their condition is materially improved and . . . they are comfortably provided for and amply fed by their masters. They, in return, work hard, willingly and well, and are apparently happy and contented.

I have lived in Arab households where such slaves were kept and have noted the fullness and real usefulness of their lives. In a large Arab household the children generally mix freely together, the little sons of slaves playing merrily with the sons of the richest

* Quoted by Sir Arnold Wilson in his *Persian Gulf*, Oxford, 1928.

merchant, and no one is conscious of any oddness, or so-called class distinction. The merchant's son may go off to college in Iraq or to a university in Cairo, to be educated; but he is just as much the friend of the slave boy when he comes home again. Indeed, he might be envious of the young slave. There was not the slightest sign that anyone regarded the slave as a degraded person. He could, and often did, rise to positions of the greatest responsibility, in both private and public life.

I often thought of the great crowds of pale-faced men I had seen in England, in cloth caps and wretched clothes, waiting outside the Labour Exchanges for a pittance called a "dole," because there was no work for them to do, and of the choirs of Welsh miners with their magnificent voices singing in the gutters of London. I saw no slave beg for alms in the bazaars of Muscat, Kuwait, Bahrein, or any other Arab city. Such a thing was unheard of and would have been regarded as a most serious reflection on his master.

As Britain took the lead in the suppression of the slave trade to the Americas—the British Parliament passed an act to abolish the slave trade in 1807, and the condition of slavery itself was done away with in 1834—she led in attempting to regulate, if not to abolish, the Arabs' trade in slaves in the Indian Ocean also. This trade was formerly on a considerable scale. At least 10,000 slaves a year used to reach the Zanzibar market alone. There was no one central slave mart in the Gulf. Sur and Muscat, on the Gulf of Oman, were perhaps the principal ports. No statistics were kept at Sur, but it was estimated that of the 13,000 slaves annually reaching the Gulf from East African ports in the sixties and seventies of the last century, at least 4,000 or 5,000 were landed at Sur or at Ras al Hadd, close by. When the slave trade as conducted by Europeans was abolished, the British joined with other nations to put a stop to what might be called the wholesale trade in the Indian Ocean. The retail trade, in small parcels, continued for a very long time, well into living memory.

As a first step, it was enacted that any slave was free who requested his freedom anywhere on British soil or at any British agency; but in the first five years, less than 80 slaves sought their freedom in this way. Enlightened Arab rulers helped the British to remove the worst abuses of the trade. Prominent among these Arabs was the great Seyyid Said, whose dominion in Africa extended from Lamu in the north to Kilwa in the south—the very heart and arteries of the slave coast. As early as 1822, Seyyid Said had agreed to prevent the sale of slaves to Christian nations, and in 1845 he prohibited entirely the transport of slaves across the Indian Ocean—across, that is, and not along his own coasts.

These treaties caused Seyyid Said a great deal of trouble, for they were most unpopular with his subjects. They also caused him serious financial loss, as slaves had been subject to considerable import and export duties. After the treaties, they were smuggled. The British government kept a squadron of cruisers off the coast of East Africa to intercept slavers beyond territorial limits, but the big *baggalas* of Sur promptly sprouted French flags and could not be molested. The slave raiders, too, were invariably very fast dhows, and they could outsail any sailing vessel from Europe. Nor were the early auxiliary cruisers more effective against them. After Seyyid Said died, his son Seyyid Barghash carried on his work, and slowly, step by step, the wholesale trade was brought to a stop.

In the middle of 1940, when German bombers were attacking the London docks, I was appointed to H.M.S. *Aberdonian* lying there at the time, undergoing conversion to take a flotilla of motor torpedo boats on a raid to the coast of Norway. One of the last items of war equipment to be sent from Admiralty was a case of books. I had been appointed, among other things, the Books Officer. Among those books was a little black volume bound in morocco, with a title picked out in letters of gold. It looked interesting, and I took it up.

Slave Trade, [it said] Instructions for Officers Employed on Detached Boat Service [and, inside the cover] East African Slave Trade.

Admiralty, October, 1892. The Lords Commissioners of the Admiralty are pleased to issue this Manual of Instructions for the guidance of officers when detached on boat service on the East Coast of Africa for the suppression of the Slave Trade.

The little black book gave in great detail directions for boarding vessels, how to tell whether or not they were carrying slaves or fitted for such cargoes, how to distiguish genuine French papers from ungenuine, and how to carry on an interrogation among the passengers in the Swahili tongue, with useful phrases. I was never able to make use of the little book, but it may still be in the *Aberdonian.*

Service for those who really did need that little book could be extremely hard. Since their ships could not overtake dhows or follow them into shallows, the navy had to stalk them in small boats. It was not uncommon for dhows to show fight, and several graves on Grave Island in the harbor of Zanzibar contain the remains of British sailors killed in this manner. Some dhows were well armed, carrying cannon, and they did not hesitate to fire on boats seeking to board them. Even without warfare, life in a small naval cutter, undecked and primitive, compelled to cruise for days beneath the hot African sun, must have been trying. It took years to put a stop to the trade. The coast was long and dhows were fast. Nor were there ever enough cruisers. Even when it became unprofitable to try to import large numbers of slaves from East Africa, swift small dhows could still steal across the Red Sea by night laden with boys and virgins, and it was impossible to stop them.

There were slaves and there was slave trading elsewhere in the Indian Ocean, in the islands of the Dutch East Indies, in Malaya, in India itself. The Dutch East India Company made considerable use of slaves, often under harsh conditions. There was for years a well-organized slave business on the Persian coast, and many Baluchis were carried off, but it was the trade from Africa which was always of prime importance.

There slavery was as old as trade itself. It is true that the great export and import business built up in Negro lives has been brought to an end. But it is perhaps also true that the end may be merely temporary. It was imposed from outside the powers of the Indian Ocean itself. If some of these again reach a state wherein they may regard themselves as free from outside regulation and interference, the slave trade may be reborn. After all, we have seen in recent years that not only native states could condone such practices. In the past decade, slavery far worse than anything conceived by Arab minds has been commonplace in parts of Europe.

The main centers of pearling in the Indian Ocean are in the Persian Gulf, the Palk Straits between southeastern India and Ceylon, and off the northwest coast of Australia. There is also some pearling in the Red Sea. The best pearls come from the Persian Gulf, where the island of Bahrein was formerly the headquarters of the trade. For centuries the main trade of Bahrein was pearling; but with the coming of the modern oil industry, this has now seriously declined. The waters of the Persian Gulf are rich with pearl oysters, particularly on the chain of reefs and banks near Bahrein, farther up the Gulf not far from the bay of Kuwait, and off the coast of Trucial Oman. The best banks are on the Arab side of the Gulf. The season lasts for four months and ten days in summer, when the water is hot, for all diving is without gear other than a sort of clothespin nipped on the nose and a stone to go down with. In 1905, there were 4,500 boats and 75,000 men employed in Gulf pearling, according to statistics kept at Bahrein.

The greater part of the pearls taken are of poor or indifferent quality, as they are everywhere else, but now and again the Gulf yields a truly magnificent gem. One worth $40,000 was found in 1807, and this eventually became the eye of an Indian idol. The Arab pearl traders believe that pearls are coated with luster, and they rate Indian Ocean pearls as follows: Karachi, one coat; Ceylon, three coats; Red Sea and Socotra, five coats; Persian Gulf, seven coats. These traders grade pearls into more than twenty different kinds. They weigh them by "chows," and grade them by sieving and by careful and prolonged examination.

When my voyage in the Kuwait *boom* was ended in the summer of 1939, the considerable fleet of pearling vessels out of that port were getting ready to go to sea. They were of all sorts, from converted *booms'* longboats to handsome *sambuks*, of perhaps 75 tons. There must have been more than 200 of them altogether, but the great majority were small vessels with only a handful of divers. I spent some time with them on the banks, pearling, and also made a buyer's run among the fleets of Kuwait and of Bahrein, with the expert buyer Sheik Mohammed Abdul-Razzaq, who had with him interesting paraphernalia, consisting of pieces of red flannel, a minute pair of scales which he held by hand, a large box of silver rupees, his brother, a clerk, a servant and a handyman, five sheep, several goats, and a large supply of sherbet, rice, ghee, and other necessities. We traveled in a small motorboat, and it was our custom to spend the day among the pearling vessels and the nights at anchor close off some pleasant beach, where we drew up our carpets out of the reach of the tide and slept on the sand, beneath the stars. It was a good life.

The aim was to acquire as many large pearls for as few silver rupees as possible, and the sheik spent a deal of his time with one ear on the sand, trying to learn in which vessels good pearls were to be found. Who was in luck this season? Who had pearls worth buying? There were other buyers on the grounds, and if a really good gem turned up there would be wasteful competition. So his ambition always was to learn about some wonderful pearl, preferably found by a small vessel, and then to race to this vessel and buy the pearl before competitors could arrive. We never did this, but we did get some lovely pearls.

Another of his quests was for pearls of lumpy, irregular shape, which were very cheap and on which he "operated" by peeling off skins, hoping to find a perfect gem beneath. The sheik was buying

for the Bombay market, and we heard plenty of rumors. When he
bought pearls, he had to buy the entire take of a vessel. He could
not just shop round for the pearls he wanted. If a ship had some
which he wished to add to his collection, then he had to buy her
whole catch. In this way he soon had a great many pearls, perhaps
enough to half fill a bucket. He was trying to match a necklace
with exceptional pearls, but he told me he had already been buying for that necklace two seasons and, though the market was
depressed, he had had to buy at least 10,000 rupees' worth of
pearls to get a round dozen for the necklace. He expected to be
buying pearls for that purpose for at least two more seasons, and
already his castoffs almost covered a small carpet.

The sheik practiced a most curious method in his bargaining.
When we approached a little pearler or a big one, we would go
aboard with quiet and unhurried dignity, be received with coffee
and sweet confections, and discuss all manner of things for an hour
or so before the subject of pearls was mentioned. Then in due
course, out would come a piece of red flannel or an old black sock,
and the nakhoda would carefully untie the bundle to display his
take. They were always a lovely sight, and the sheik's eyes used
to gleam, though he would invariably begin by decrying the gems
and lamenting that the waters of the Gulf no longer produced
pearls worth a buyer's attention. Then, in another hour or so, he
would condescend to examine the take properly, sieving it and
weighing the various grades, and examining some through a small
magnifying glass. Only after several hours would the subject of
price be mentioned. Then would follow the usual sparring, always
cheerful and conducted according to rule.

If he really intended to buy the pearls, the sheik would at last
grab a spare piece of his red flannel, throw it over his right hand,
grasp the right hand of the nakhoda beneath this flannel, and
conduct the final negotiations by manipulation of fingers, according to some ancient code, in solemn and complete silence. Sometimes he varied the procedure by grabbing his brother's hand in

the same manner, and working on his fingers, but this was when he wanted to get his brother's idea of the value of the parcel he was considering. I could not get the hang of this finger manipulation, but they were experts at it and it was, I was told, commonly practiced among the Gulf pearl merchants. At any rate, as soon as we got to the finger-play stage, the parcel was quickly bought, or we were off in our dugout canoe back to the launch. Usually the parcel was bought.

Interesting as this trading was, it was the actual diving and the life aboard the pearlers themselves which was really fascinating. Though the year was 1939, there had been no change, of note, since Biblical times, apart from the fact that the vessels were then iron-fastened and not sewn. Each ship used sails and sweeps as well, in the manner of the old Mediterranean galleys. All were decked, even the longboats having a sort of false working deck built on them for the season. Everyone lived in the open, as in all dhows. Each vessel, large or small, carried a crew of two divers for each sweep, and one man for each sweep to tend the lines, and, in addition, a number of ship's boys—up to six or eight in the really large pearlers—a cook, and a nakhoda in charge. They worked in groups, anchoring on a bank shortly after dawn and working slowly across it on a long kedge line and with the sweeps. They generally tried to stay in water of less than five fathoms' depth, for there were strong tides at times, and diving without gear was difficult and dangerous. All the divers wore loincloths of cheap calico, dyed black because they believed the sharks did not care for that color. There was a long line with a stone on the end of it round each sweep, and when diving was in progress, the sweeps were run out horizontally from the ship in order to keep these lines clear. A group of divers, one to each sweep, went down on the stones, each taking a small wickerwork or coir basket with him, attached to a second line. When they reached the bottom each tender at once hauled up his diver's stone and then stood carefully holding the line to which the basket was attached.

Meanwhile, the diver groped on the sea bed, tearing oysters from rocks and coral with his bare hands and filling his basket as quickly as possible, the clamp on his nose keeping the water out of his nostrils. When his basket was full or when he could stay below no longer, he gave a tug on the basket and was at once hauled rapidly to the surface, one hand still grasping the rim of the basket. I counted dives of eighty seconds, but generally they were a little less than a minute. Each man did ten dives, which were carefully tallied. Then, the ten dives completed, the group came at once inboard, to be replaced by a second group, which had been warming itself round the little brushwood and camel-dung fire at the firebox. These made ten dives, with rests between; and so the process was repeated hour after hour, all day long, with breaks only while the vessel herself was moved across to new ground. These breaks came fairly often.

As the divers brought their baskets up, the line tenders took them from them and held them ceremoniously until all were aboard. Then, with a concerted cry to Allah, they dumped the oysters onto a general heap. This heap grew all day, and the oysters were not opened until the following morning, immediately after the dawn prayer. Everything was done with rhythm and, frequently, also with song. The plying of the sweeps, the hauling in of the kedge line, the hoisting of the lateen sail (if this were done at all), the emptying of the oyster baskets—all these necessary procedures were done with great style. Indeed, there was frequently so much noise and stamping of great, horny feet and clapping of enormous, powerful hands, and throaty bellowing and singing, that orders could not be heard, and the larger vessels employed half a dozen boys to stand together by the foot of the mainmast and shrill the nakhoda's orders, in their piercing trebles, so they would penetrate the orderly din.

I saw among the divers many sailors that I knew, but there were also Beduin with long hair, who did not go in the deep-sea vessels. There were many slaves. Slave or free man made no difference.

Diving was not a popular occupation and the whole business was honeycombed with a system of debts and alleged debts and sundry sharp practices. All the divers, apparently, were in debt. They always would be in debt, through a system of advances which was rigidly enforced. All the nakhodas were in debt. Whoever was going to make a fortune out of pearls, it rarely was a nakhoda and never a diver. But the hope of finding some fabulous gem helped to keep them at work. The divers, having to spend in the aggregate many hours groping at the bottom of the sea, did not dare to eat a good meal, from the time the season began until it ended. They kept life going on a diet of coffee flavored with cardamoms or cloves, and ate the minimum of fish and rice. The contrast was great between them, thin and gaunt, the fat and bulky tenders of their lines, and the sleek, piping little boys. The merchant was sleek enough, too, but the nakhodas were almost as gaunt and thin as the divers.

It was a tough life. But they were all set against the introduction of diving gear or fostering the artificial or cultured pearl businesses. Anyone who tried to introduce a parcel of cultured pearls into the bazaar at Kuwait would probably have lost his life. The expert merchants there knew cultured pearls quite well, for their business had been gravely upset by them. The cultured pearls came from Japan, and they lacked the luster of the Gulf varieties. For that and other reasons, the Kuwait merchants could detect them almost at a glance, but I confess I could not, not even after three months with the excellent Sheik Mohammed Abdul-Razzaq.

There was in 1939 an admiral of the Kuwait pearling fleet who was responsible generally for discipline and for settling disputes, if any. He was Sheik Sabah bin Nasir al-Mubarak al-Sabah, and he was a relative of the ruling Sheik. His authority was absolute, and he kept good order. His *sambuk* was a beautiful large vessel with exceptionally fine lines. He did not sell his pearls to merchants on the banks, but kept them until the end of the season, when they were forwarded to Bombay or to Paris for disposal.

Some of the Kuwait divers used formerly to spend the summer diving in the Persian Gulf, and then would dive for another season in the Palk Straits. One of the sailors in my *boom* had done this. The methods of the fishery off Ceylon were much the same, he said. He displayed no enthusiasm for the industry in either place and confided that if he had not been in hopeless debt to his nak-hoda, he would have finished with it long ago.

The coming of the oil industry on a large scale to Kuwait, with its inevitable upset of the ancient economic and working conditions, largely put an end to this sort of pearling. But it is still, in 1951, practiced to some degree. No longer do fleets of a hundred and more little vessels, brown and slight and swift, run for the sandy coves in the evenings and, by a miracle of seamanship performed daily, come to a hundred anchorages without as much as a collision or a stove-in dugout canoe. No longer do the two or three thousand men manning such a fleet join on the beach for the evening prayers, to drop into sleep immediately afterward, buoyed up by hopes of opening some great oyster in the morning, to find it bulging with a priceless pearl. A few still go to the banks, for the lure of the lustrous pearls is great.

As for whaling in the Indian Ocean, the industry was never on the same scale as in the more prolific Pacific grounds, in the days of the old sailing whalers. But there were fat sperms to be taken in the Mozambique Channel, round the Comoros, and off the Chagos Archipelago. Many a Yankee whaler drifted about these grounds, her hawk-eyed Azoreans and Cape Verde Islanders ever ready to lower the swift whaleboats and do battle with whales. That sort of whaling went out three-quarters of a century ago. The island state of Tasmania, south of Australia, was one of its last bases. Tasmanian whalers and sealers were noted for their audacity and their toughness in an audacious and extremely tough profession. They used to go to the stormy islands of the Roaring Forties in quest of seals and, later, when the seals were all killed, for sea-elephant oil.

Sealing for oil or skins was a bloody and reprehensible business, as it still is in those few parts of the world where it is practiced. It was in the main a matter of endurance, but the stanch and stubby little wooden barques and brigs which were the sealers' floating homes must, in their way, have been brave and able vessels. To beat into the westerly gales of the southern Indian Ocean was no fool's pastime, and considerable skill was needed to find desolate anchorages year after year in such abodes of mists and gales as the Kerguelens, the Crozets, or Heard's Islands. It was a hard way to make a living.

It was the custom for both American and Tasmanian whalers and sealers sometimes to leave parties of men to winter on these sub-antarctic islands. There is a case recorded in the Tasmanian state archives at Hobart of the barque *Offley*, out of that port, where the captain of that vessel, finding his carpenter's hands very badly frostbitten after a winter sojourn, chopped them off with an ax.

They must have been a crew of real "hard-case" whalers. Whales were sighted one day and, as one was a big bull, a boat steerer was told off to load a bomb gun. This he was doing on the small poop when there was a sudden explosion, and the lance with the bomb on the end of it went into the mate's side. The boat steerer tried at once to haul it out, but the bomb exploded. It took the mate—his name was Thomas Cracknell, of Hobart—twenty minutes to die.

"I knew those damned bombs never were no good," he muttered in his agony.

The Indian Ocean whalers of today are vastly different from the 376-ton wooden barque *Offley*. Now great fleets of factory ships and diesel-engined whale chasers go out annually from Norway and from Britain, to hunt the blue whales and fin whales by the pack-ice rim round the Antarctic continent. Some of these factory ships are over 20,000 tons, carrying 400 or 500 men, and using fleets of eight and ten whale chasers, assisted by towing vessels, which are often converted corvettes, to bring in 20 or 30 whales a day. The chasers are larger than the *Offley* and her kind. They are wonderful vessels and are among the most seaworthy small ships in the world. They hunt by means of modern harpoon guns on platforms in their bows, and use every modern aid. Asdic to "ping" for sounded whales; helicopters to spot them; radio telephony to call for a tug to relieve the chasers of the duties of towing, in order that they may be free to hunt to the limit while their fuel lasts; radar to ward off collision with growlers and 'bergs—most of these things are standard equipment. The factory ships can turn out whale meal and canned whale meat, as well as get the last drop of oil from every carcass brought to them. The dead whales are hauled bodily aboard, up huge rampways cut into their sterns, and are flensed on a working deck as large as a ball park. So rigorously are the whales hunted while the short Antarctic summer lasts that special oil-tankers (which often are 12,000 tons and more) are sent down, halfway through the season, to take off the oil then ready, and the meat and meal, in order that the factory ship may fill herself to capacity twice if the hunting will stand it.

Some of these vessels touch at Cape Town on their way to and from the Indian Ocean's Antarctic grounds. Many operate in other sectors. In 1951, twenty such fleets were at work. Despite international conventions and agreements to limit the number of whales taken, and much shaking of scientific heads, statistics show a marked decline in the sizes of whales now being taken, despite the fact that there was an enforced closed season in the war.

With organized slaughter on such a scale and of such unparalleled efficiency, the days of the unfortunate whale would seem to be numbered in the Indian and all other oceans. His only chance is the very scale of the attempt to exterminate him, for fleets so vast, complicated, and costly will be unable to hunt to the last whale, as the southern sealers took the last seal. Such expeditions must find whales by the thousand, or they cannot go at all.

CHAPTER XVII

The Tragedy of Houtman's Abrolhos

In the annals of the Indian Ocean there have been many tales of shipwrecks and tragedies at sea. Perhaps the most dramatic of these is the wreck of the Dutch East Indiaman *Batavia*, which occurred off the inhospitable coast of northwest Australia on the eastern side of the ocean. Because of its many extraordinary features and its lessons on the inevitable fate of dictatorship, I think the story is worth giving in some detail here.

Well out to sea off the coast of West Australia, between the latitudes of 28 and 29 south, lies a group of coral reefs, banks, shoals, and small islands known as the Abrolhos Group, or Houtman's Abrolhos. The Portuguese derivation of this name is plain. *Abrir os olhos* is the Portuguese expression meaning to open the eyes, and the name may derive from the first recorded visit of the Portuguese to the coasts of West Australia in 1527. When the Dutchman Hendrik Brouwer, in 1611, found a new way to sail to the Indies by sailing due east from the Cape of Good Hope until he reached the longitude of Java and then turning north, it was inevitable that the Dutch East Indiamen should, sooner or later, come upon the coast of Australia.

By 1616, another commander of a Dutch Indiaman, Dirk Hartog,

had given his name to an island off the continent. In 1619, Frederic
Houtman was on the coast in latitude 32½ degrees south, not far
north of the Swan River, on which the pleasant city of Perth now
stands. When he came upon the dangerous group of reefs and islets
as he sailed north toward the East Indies, he gave them the name
of Houtman's Abrolhos, or at any rate they were given that name
afterward. It is possible that some such group, with this name, was
already on a chart in his possession. He was a fortunate navigator
to come upon the group in daylight, for they lay athwart the track
of Java-bound ships. They began to claim the first victims on their
long list very soon afterward.

The group is of interest for other reasons than that so many
vessels have been lost there. Some of the unattractive, sandy cays
act as bird sanctuaries, principally for Pacific gulls, Caspian terns,
silver gulls, pied cormorants, and noddy terns, including the rare
lesser noddy tern, which makes nests of seaweed in the branches
of the mangroves. Ornithologists have described the group as probably the greatest sea-bird rookery along the whole Australian coast,
offering good breeding conditions for a greater number of species
than any other comparable spot in the world. Fish and lobsters
abound in the surrounding waters, and on some of the islands there
are wallabies, snakes, and lizards. Just how the wallabies reached
the Albrolhos nobody knows, but an ancient connection with the
mainland seems to be indicated. They certainly were not brought
there, for their presence was noted by the first shipwrecked party
to reach the islands. These were Hollanders from the Dutch East
Indiaman *Batavia,* which drove up on a reef off the group on the
night of June 4, 1629.

The *Batavia* was one of the Dutch East India Company's fleet
of eleven vessels which sailed together from Holland in 1628, bound
outward for a cargo of spices and other rich products to be loaded
at Bantam, Banda, Ceram, and wherever else they might be found.
It was late October when she sailed, and she had to beat down the
Channel against a succession of westerly gales. Her captain was

named Francis Pelsart. He was an experienced shipmaster, whose home was in Antwerp; and her crew of about a hundred included some excellent men, besides more than a few of the sweepings from the worst waterfronts in Europe. Service in East Indiamen was not popular and mortality was high. In addition to her crew, the *Batavia* carried a number of passengers and soldiers for the garrisons in Java. The passengers included several families, among whom were women and children. One of the families was that of a Lutheran preacher named Gysbert Bastians, who had with him his beautiful eighteen-year-old daughter Judith and her maid. All told, there were well over 200 persons embarked, though the *Batavia* was not a large ship.

She had also a valuable cargo, which included several chests of treasure worth perhaps $500,000, and she carried regalia for setting up an impressive and colorful Dutch court to impress the rich potentates of Java. Looking after this cargo was an officer known as a supercargo. This man was a Haarlem druggist named Jerome Cornelius, who had been a seaman in his youth. Rumor alleged that he was leaving his country in a hurry for his country's good, and his own. It seems scarcely likely that the Company would have selected a man whose reputation was in question to go as supercargo in so valuable a ship, but perhaps recruitment for supercargoes was difficult, as well as for crews.

The *Batavia* had not gone very far before this Cornelius showed himself in his true light. He had deliberately worked his way into the ship in order to seize her and turn pirate, and he soon began to work among the crew and the soldiers to gain the necessary handful of fanatics to put his schemes into effect. There were plenty of men aboard with nothing to lose. Death by scurvy, dysentery, or fever, or a miserable lingering death in the East awaited the majority of them, and the prospect of going "on the account" appealed to several. But the *Batavia* was in company with the other ships, and since Pelsart was senior captain and acted as Commodore, the other ships kept close to him when they could. There was no opportunity for Cornelius to operate his scheme. He was hindered, too, by the obdurate honesty of the great majority of the ship's people, poor as they were, and by the general happy spirit aboard, which was largely due to the good influence of Preacher Bastians and his daughter. Cornelius bided his time.

He was still biding his time when the fleet touched at the Cape and sailed again. No matter, it would be better to let Captain Pelsart sail the ship almost to the East Indies before seizing her, for the most difficult navigation would then be over and the richest prizes in Cornelius's grasp. What might have happened aboard the *Batavia* had she continued without accident toward her destination there is no saying. Hers might, in any event, have been added to the long list of names of missing ships. But not long after she had run her longitude down in exceptionally severe weather—for it was winter in the southern Indian Ocean when she raced across from the Cape—and had turned at last toward the north, she sailed right into the Abrolhos reefs. It was a bright, moonlit night and there had been no sign of land. As soon as she struck, the ship began to pound, and the breakers were soon making a clean breach over her. The noise of the coral grinding through her planks was dreadful to hear. Her masts began to go by the board, and the furious flapping of her torn canvas and the groaning of her timbers, the smash of the seas, and the swirling of the foam all round her, set up a frightful cacophony. Some of the children began to cry, for they were wet through in the driving spray and thoroughly alarmed by the suddenness of the accident and the appalling noise. Captain Pelsart kept his head, and so did his mates and the stalwart petty officers. The cannon were jettisoned at once, to lighten the ship in the hope that she might come off, for soundings showed plenty of water under her stern. But the wind and the sea drove her on farther and farther, and she quickly began to break up.

Daylight showed a frightening scene, with a wild sea of breakers in almost all directions and the great southern rollers sweeping up astern. It was cold and raining. The wind and the sea got up, and a boat trying to carry out an anchor was knocked to pieces against the ship's sides. It was useless to think of getting the ship off, but as far as could be seen from the deck, none of the wretched islets and rocks in view would stand above the surface of the sea at high water, or anything like high water. Pelsart had first to find somewhere to land. The big boat was got out and safely launched, and the mate was sent to reconnoiter. He reported an island, which was at least dry, about three miles away, and immediately the orderly abandonment of the ship was begun. The chests of money were brought out, or as many as could be got at, for the water was already rising high in the hold, and the steward brought up casks of bread and other provisions. The sailors broke out barrels of water, which they threw overboard to drift ashore.

At this time, Cornelius and his party of pirates broke into the spirit room and rapidly drank themselves into a state of stupidity, and it was a pity they were not left behind to drown. But they were rounded up and flung helpless into the boat and ferried ashore with the rest of the people—that is, all except Cornelius himself. He was not to be found. One hundred and eighty people were safely rowed ashore before the end of the first day, and a cache of provisions was made. As soon as they awakened from their drunken slumber, Cornelius's pirates fell on this cache and greedily began to devour everything, saying they would die anyway and they might as well die with their bellies full. Captain Pelsart soon put a stop to this sort of thing, but there were open threats of murdering him. The men looked about for Cornelius to lead them, but he was not there.

Bad weather made it impossible to get further stores from the ship, which could not be approached, and a stock-taking showed that the party had only 40 gallons of fresh water. Nor did the most diligent search reveal any fresh water on the island. A quick look at the other cays and islets seemed to show that they were as waterless, and Pelsart decided to go in search of water to the mainland.

Before doing this, he caused a curious document to be drawn up
and signed by all the sailors with him in the boat. This document,
which is still in existence, reads:

Since on all the islands round about our foundered *Batavia* there is
no fresh water to be found, in order to feed and keep the people who
are saved, therefore, the Commodore has earnestly requested and proposed that an expedition should be made to the main Southland to see
whether it is God's gracious will that fresh water shall be found, of
which so much may be taken to the people that they shall be certain
of having enough provision for a considerable time; that then meanwhile someone shall be told off to go to Batavia, in order to let the
Lord General and his Councillors know of our disaster and to ask him
for early assistance. To which we, the undersigned, have all voluntarily
assented, since necessity forces us thereto, and since if we acted otherwise we could not answer for our conduct before God and the high
authorities. Therefore we have unanimously agreed and resolved to
try our utmost to do our duty and to assist our poor brethren in their
great need. In certain knowledge of the truth we have signed this
with our own hand and have all of us sworn to it, on the 8th day of June,
1629.

There follow the signatures of Pelsart himself, Gerrits the second
mate, and seven of the best petty officers and seamen. This was
only a few days after the wreck. It looks as if Pelsart was anxious
to be off to Batavia and was clearing his yardarm in advance. He
must have known that Cornelius was a dangerous character and
that trouble had been brewing in the ship. If he felt he had to sail
the boat to Batavia, which after all was a fine-weather run with a
fair wind, it seems a pity to have taken a good second mate and
several of the most reliable seamen. At any rate, within a day or
two, Pelsart was skimming off before the fresh southeast wind
toward Batavia. He had set up no proper organization on the
island, though he was well aware that there was serious dissension
there, and the unruly gang of Cornelius's comrades was already
making serious trouble. Within three weeks, Captain Pelsart had

arrived off Java. There he did his best to get hold of a ship and go back to rescue the *Batavia's* people and treasure.

The longboat with Captain Pelsart and the seamen aboard was not out of sight before there was more trouble. Cornelius drifted ashore on a spar, having survived eight days aboard the wreck until she finally broke up. After that, he was for two days washing about the reefs on the main-tops'l yard, which had worked adrift. At any rate, that was his story, but the truth was that he had been drunk in the spirit room those eight days, and left the ship only when the spirit room disintegrated. It was a piece of good fortune for him that he found the floating spar and got ashore on that.

Cornelius at once took charge. Calling his cronies together, he explained to them that, despite the loss of the ship, his scheme could still succeed, for the captain was bound to come back in another vessel after the treasure. They would then seize him, and turn pirates, or sail away with the treasure and the women, to live a life of joy in the West Indies. They brought the soldiers, many of whom were French, into the plot, but some of the soldiers would have nothing to do with it. Fortunately for their survival, the party of passengers had split into three groups and were spread among different islets. One group had found a sort of brackish water, which though poor stuff sufficed to keep them alive.

The habit of preparing signed documents must have been deeply ingrained aboard Dutch East Indiamen, or possibly the *Batavia* was exceptional. Cornelius, like his captain, prepared a pompous screed which he required his henchmen to sign or mark. This strange epistle read:

We the undersigned, in order to remove all cause of dispute that is or may come among us, hereby bind ourselves on the faith of our souls and by the most solemn oaths, so help us God, to be faithful to each other in everything, and to hold each other in brotherly love, that we may not in any way hurt one another in body or goods, until we have first given due notice by word of mouth. In witness whereof we have signed this the 12th day of July, 1629, on the island of the ship *Batavia's* grave.

They all signed this, and then Cornelius called a council of all the survivors on the largest of the islands. Among these was a buxom woman named Lucretia van Milen, described as voluptuous and accommodating, whose husband had been lost when the ship stranded. Cornelius announced that he was taking her to wife, and proceeded to distribute the better looking of the other women among his followers. The preacher's daughter was assigned to a ruffianly seaman, and the women who were not allocated specifically were required to give themselves freely to all. Some cases and bales of finery had drifted ashore, and Cornelius, breaking them open, bedecked himself in robes of scarlet and gold which were intended for the Lord General's use on state occasions, and his henchmen were also attired in gorgeous uniforms. The women were required to swear allegiance to the men, on pain of being beheaded at once if they did not, but the preacher's daughter made a break for it and, for the moment, managed to escape.

More pompous documents were drawn up, everyone being required to bind themselves "on their soul's salvation and by the help of God" to accept what was done, and to agree to the appointment of Cornelius as Lord Dictator. Lucretia van Milen was his queen, and after they had signed, more bales of finery were distributed among the women and the other men. In a few moments, the windy low island, with its outcrops of bare coral here and there and its squawking sea birds, presented as astonishing a sight as ever was seen on any island in the Indian or any other ocean, while the crowd of strange Europeans, bearded, dirty, and unkempt, strutted about the place in scarlet robes of court and plumed helmets and gold-striped pants. In the background the bones of the wrecked *Batavia* writhed in the surf. Cornelius was described as Captain General as well as Lord Dictator, and yet another wordy document was drawn up and signed by all—again on the pain of death—swearing "severally and unanimously in the name of God to be faithful and obedient in whatever he shall command us; and whoever shall do aught to the contrary shall be the Devil's own," and so forth. The survivors, who were pretty thin by this time— for they had been subsisting on shellfish and crackers washed down by a mouthful of brackish water—were required also to "cancel and retract all previous public and private promises and oaths, comprising all secret comradeships, tent-mateships, and other alliances of whatsoever name or nature." This was drawn up and signed on August 20.

Meanwhile, food was getting short. There were crackers for only a few more days, and there was no sign of the return of Captain Pelsart. Captain General Cornelius decided to reduce the population. He and his few henchmen had control of all the arms. At the first light of dawn on the morning of August 31, the conspirators rose and began at once to murder every man, woman, and child who was not in their immediate group. With sword, ax, knife, and hatchet they went at their bloody work, but the alarm was soon given by the cries of the dying, and in a few moments the coral beach was a frightful scene. Men, women, and children ran in all directions, some into the sea, where they were taken quickly by sharks or were drowned. The murderers had no mercy.

But a few escaped and made their way to one of the other islets on a beam of timber from the wreck. Here they found some of the soldiers and Judith, the preacher's daughter, with Preacher Bastians himself. This party had found water, but they had no arms. When they heard of the murders, they did their best to arm themselves with sticks and staves with the largest nails they could find hammered into them with rocks. When at last the cries died down from the larger island, Cornelius and his cutthroats were seen making toward the preacher's refuge, in a boat. Their scarlet robes and their fine feathers were now bedraggled, and their faces were the faces of demons. The blood lust was on them and they made toward the beach screaming like demented men, shouting curses and imprecations. But the soldiers and the preacher were not dismayed. Though their arms were only sticks and stones, they rushed into the water and put up so brave a show that, muttering oaths about "putting them where they belonged that night," Cornelius and his party made off, back to their own island. The preacher's party defended themselves with such competence and ferocity that they succeeded in killing several of the Cornelius gang, and wounded others. But they lost some of their own best men.

Cornelius, ever bent on treachery, next sought to undermine resistance by secretly addressing a letter to a group of the French soldiers, offering them a share of the treasure if they would agree to stab the preacher, his daughter, and the leader of the soldiers (whose name was Webbye Hays) in the back. The letter called the soldiers "beloved brethren and friends," and asked particularly that they should deliver alive a party who had escaped from the main island in a small boat. But the soldiers gave the letter to the preacher. On his instructions, they carried on negotiations with Cornelius and induced him to come across to their island again, bringing a bale of clothing which was needed. As soon as Cornelius and his party landed, the soldiers sprang on them and tried to seize them. Four were killed in the ensuing fight, which was short and savage. Cornelius was taken and bound. He was lashed to a mangrove and held for justice, as Preacher Bastians was sure that Captain Pelsart would return.

When he was captured, Cornelius began to whine, promising all sorts of things if only he could have his freedom. But he was kept in bonds. A few of his henchmen had escaped and made their way back to the main island. One of these, by name Loos, was promoted temporarily to command, and the following day Loos led a determined attack on the soldiers' party. These now had a few better arms than sticks and staves, and the attackers were once again beaten off. But the situation was desperate. Lucretia van Milen, the virago whom Cornelius had taken to wife, was shrieking for his release and threatening to murder all the men herself if another attack was not launched immediately, this time with success. It could be only a matter of time before the weaker party was inevitably overpowered. It was then the first week of September, 1629.

Meanwhile, Captain Pelsart was driving south with the good ship *Saardam*, sent by the authorities at Batavia to the rescue. The Abrolhos lay beyond the region of the permanent winds, amid a zone of variable winds and strong currents. The *Saardam* came close twice, only to be blown away again. By mid-September, Pelsart at last was within sight of the reefs again. To his joy he saw smoke rising from one of the islets and gave orders for a boat to be hoisted out at once. While he was making for the land in this boat, a small boat was noticed making frantically toward him, with a few people in it, including one woman, shouting and waving. In this boat were the soldier Hays, Preacher Bastians, and his daughter Judith. Pelsart waited for them, his boat rolling in the big swell and the *Saardam* lying hove-to, just beyond the breakers. The story that Hays and the preacher shouted to him horrified him.

"Make back for the ship at once!" they urged, saying that the main party, led by Loos, would soon be coming out under guise of joyful castaways, but well armed and determined to seize the ship by any means, for she was vital to their survival. Captain Pelsart, accompanied by Hays's boat, returned with all speed to the *Saardam* and got back only just in time. Two large boats, saved from the *Batavia*, were that moment approaching, full of large men in every conceivable exaggeration of ceremonial attire. No arms were in sight, and Loos hailed the captain cheerfully. The murderers' boats were alongside and they made for the gangway.

"Hold now!" barked Pelsart in a cold voice. "Hold now, you scum!"

"What now, my captain? Are you not come to save us all?" whined Loos, looking pathetic. But a well-primed pistol fell with a clatter from beneath his coat.

"Why do you come armed?" shouted the captain.

"You will see, damn you, when we get aboard!" screamed Loos, making a rush for it with his blackguards behind him. But they stopped in their tracks for the *Saardam* rolled toward them and they saw that her decks were full of armed men, covering them. They stopped clambering up the sides. Loos fell back into the boat.

"Now drop those arms into the sea. At once! And, one by one, come aboard here. Or jump into the sea and drown!" There was a ring in Captain Pelsart's voice they had not heard before.

The miscreants had no alternative but to obey. They threw their arms into the sea and came aboard. As each came over the rail, he was seized, bound, and led away forward. Loos began to whine again, that it was all the fault of Cornelius, and they were peaceful men.

"We will see about that," said the Captain.

Cornelius, still bound, was brought aboard later, and for a week the *Saardam* anchored among the islets and the reefs, while her people, under Captain Pelsart's direction, salvaged all they could of the treasure and the Company's goods. They found several chests of money and much finery and valuable stuff. But some of the treasure was still beneath the sea, and it was too dangerous to work in the exposed place where the remains of the *Batavia* were fast sinking in the sand.

As soon as all the treasure and goods which could be saved were aboard, and the surviving people had been rounded up from the various islets and given succor, Captain Pelsart called a council of the ship to decide what would be the best course with the murderers, whether to take them to Batavia for trial or deal with them there and then. The *Saardam* was a small ship and she was now crowded. The treasure she was carrying was considerable, and Cornelius, though in irons, was known as a desperate and most dangerous man. The ship's council made the only possible decision. The criminals would be dealt with at once. Examination had shown that they had murdered at least 125 persons. One man admitted that he alone killed twenty-seven. Lucretia van Milen, swearing that Cornelius had forced her against her will, turned state's evidence. But there was no need for that. The evidence was plain enough. Nonetheless, the accused men were solemnly arraigned and allowed to answer the charges brought against them.

The next morning, the wind blowing up cold from the south and the sea gray and cheerless, Cornelius and the other ringleaders were led out on deck. It took the rack to get a confession from Cornelius. The others confessed. Seven of the ringleaders were strung up to the yardarms without further delay, the worst of them having their right hands chopped off immediately before they swung. Last of all, Cornelius had both hands chopped off at the block. Then he, too, was swung aloft, to kick a while at the sighing wind and then to hang there, a lifeless and useless weight, rolling with the ship's slow motion.

There is a record that considerable treasure remained in the hold of the *Batavia,* for the native divers brought along in the *Saardam* found the water too cold to work, and the largest treasure chests were too heavy to lift. The same record states that Captain Pelsart marked the place where the unlifted chests lay by means of "an anchor with a gun tied to it, and a buoy." This treasure has never been found and no one knows where to look for it now. Though one of the islands of the Abrolhos group bears the name of Pelsart Island, there is no certainty that this was the scene of the *Batavia's* wreck.

Many other vessels were to come to grief on the Abrolhos through the succeeding centuries, and the islands took their toll, right down to recent years. Employees working a guano concession have come upon grim relics from time to time—the skulls of murdered children, some rosary beads, and other things. The Dutch East Indiamen *Zuytdorp* and *Zeewyck* followed the *Batavia* onto the rocks. Later came the iron ship *Ben Levi;* the American barque *Cochituate,* out of Boston; the schooners *Marten* and *Eveline*

Mary; and the steamer *Windsor,* bound for China. These are only a few of the vessels wrecked in that vicinity.

Not far away, the English ship *Triall* was wrecked in 1622, and a boat full of her people rowed and sailed to Batavia. The other hundred survivors were never heard of again. Perhaps some self-appointed Captain General like Jerome Cornelius had set himself up among them, to reign a brief while as dictator before meeting his inevitable end.

CHAPTER XVIII

The Romance of the Cocos-Keelings

"Crabs eat coconuts, fish eat coral, dogs catch fish, men ride on turtle, the shells are dangerous man-traps . . . and the greater part of the sea-fowl roost on branches and many rats make their nests at the tops of high palm trees." So wrote Admiral FitzRoy about the Cocos-Keeling Islands, which lie some 600 miles southwest of Java Head, in the middle of the Indian Ocean. Admiral FitzRoy called at the islands in 1836, when he was in command of H.M.S. *Beagle*, on her famous voyage around the world with Charles Darwin aboard. Darwin himself was much impressed with the beauty of these atoll islands.

"I am glad to have visited these islands," he wrote. "Such formations surely rank high amongst the wonderful objects of the world." Long after the illustrious Charles Darwin, another interesting visitor, as unique in his own way, added his words of praise. This was Captain Joshua Slocum, who, in the last decade of the nineteenth century, was the first man to sail a small vessel singlehanded around the world. Captain Slocum took his tiny *Spray*—which he sailed from the Torres Straits in twenty-three fine sailing days—into the lagoon.

"If there is a paradise on earth, it is Keeling," was the old master mariner's summing up.

259

The Cocos or Keeling Islands—now usually called the Cocos-Keelings—were first seen by Europeans when an East Indiaman commanded by Captain William Keeling passed by in 1609. There are two principal islands lying in a north-south line, 15 miles apart, the southern being really a group of islets formed upon the fringes of an oval coral reef which encircles a lagoon. Nowhere is the land higher than 20 feet and, in great storms, the sea breaks right over most of it. The islets with their rich foliage and high coconut palms fringing the blue-green lagoon are as lovely in their way as the most romantic South Seas island, but they are indeed mere skeletons, on which the broken coral and dust have been driven by the wind and the sea and mashed for countless aeons until sufficient was accumulated to give sustenance to coconut palms and other tropic growth, the seeds of which came scattered on the sea, driven before the unfailing southeast trade wind. The outer edges of these islets are higher than the inner. The lagoon is shallow and liberally filled with branching coral, niggerheads, and minor reefs. The sand of the islets is a brilliant white, and the colors of the lagoon shimmer in a range from the deepest blues to the greenest greens, as multicolored and as striking as the fish which live there, and as attractive as the famous snow-white tern for which the Cocos-Keelings are well known.

There is one charming bird [said Darwin]. It is a snow-white tern which smoothly hovers at the distance of a few feet above one's head, its large black eyes scanning, with quiet curiosity, your expression. Little imagination is required to imagine that so little and delicate a body must be tenanted by some fairy wandering spirit.

The Cocos tern is indeed an established landmark for the islands, for it is found nowhere else and, when ships approach, it comes out to meet them. Slocum was met by one while the *Spray* was still out of sight of land.

The first unmistakable sign of the land was a visit one morning from a white tern that fluttered very knowingly about the vessel, [he wrote]

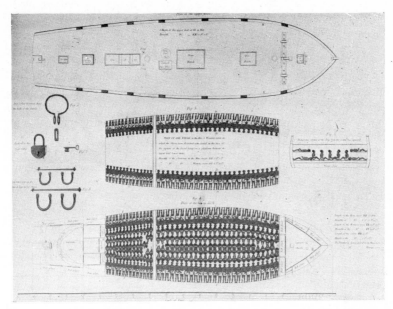

Method of stowing slaves in a West Indies slaver

The Comoro Islands were a favorite resort

Old-time whaling

Yankee clipper. Now the Stars and Stripes are not so often seen in the Indian Ocean.

and then took itself off westward with a business-like air. . . .
The tern is called by the islanders "the pilot of Keeling Cocos."

There is an entrance into the main lagoon which ships can use,
with good anchorage; though, outside, the islands shelve down very
steeply to immense depths. The whole vista is most attractive, and
the big liners of the Orient and P. and O. companies, passing by on
the busy route between London and Sydney, by way of Colombo,
often give their passengers a thrilling glimpse of the lovely place
while they throw overboard casks of mail and provisions for the
men of the cable station there. To anyone coming up from the
sandy shores of West Australia, the blue, green, and golden islets
look like fairyland, a haven in the sea and a retreat from the
modern world.

They were just this when, more than a hundred years ago,
the first Europeans—and apparently the first inhabitants—settled
there. These were an unusual Scotsman named John Clunies-Ross,
who hailed from the Shetland Islands, and a strange Englishman
named Alexander Hare, who might have forestalled Rajah Brooke
in Borneo if he could only have restrained his tremendous lusts.
These pioneers did not arrive together, though they were old ac-
quaintances and had once been partners. The story of their coming
and of their colony is an interesting one.

Clunies-Ross was an old Greenland whaler who had gravitated to
the South Seas and Indian Ocean grounds, and from these, to the
general Eastern trade. As any other Greenland whaler might have
done, he took a great liking to the luscious islands of the East Indies. He lived in upset times, when the stability of Europe seemed
hopelessly menaced. A dictatorial regime had recently threatened
to overwhelm the world and had almost succeeded in doing so.
Disturbing new ideas and revolutionary developments were matters of weekly occurrence, and the outlook for an intelligent family
man was as bad, almost, as it was to be again, a century and a
quarter later.

In these circumstances, Captain Clunies-Ross, like many another man, thought of migrating with his wife and family. But where would he go? The usual places—America, Australia—did not appeal to him. The forthright whaling captain has left a journal of his early days, in which he gives a revealing glimpse of these plans of his for taking his family abroad. He knew the Cocos-Keelings from a visit there in a whaler, and the idea of going there appealed to him. He discarded all America "as being out of sight of the sea, and similarly all other interior positions." The Shetland Islander must have regarded even Manhattan as an inland place. As for the "Eastern Australian Colonies," these "would long retain a disagreeable taint of their origin," for the export of convicts as cheap labor was at its height then. He liked the Falkland Islands, but turned down the idea of going there—he says—because "he did not expect the government would extend its protection to a settlement on them."

He thought, too, of the remote and storm-swept islands of the far southern waters in the Indian Ocean, where his whaling ships had also taken him, and he turned down the project of colonizing the Kerguelens on the score only that he lacked sufficient capital to begin. St. Paul's attracted him more than Kerguelen (as well it might) but although he had been "in its basin in a whale-boat," he did not know enough about it to warrant the experiment of founding a colony there. Then there was Christmas Island, only a few miles from the Cocos-Keelings—as distances are reckoned in the Indian Ocean—but this is a high island, more in the sea route toward the Straits of Sunda by which ships in the days of sail used generally to make for China. Captain Clunies-Ross turned down the idea of settling on Christmas because of his fear that the island would be annexed by the Dutch, who were then well entrenched in the East Indies.

As for the Cocos-Keelings, he was noncommittal. He did not then know, he wrote, what sort of fresh-water supply the atolls could offer, if any. But at the time he had command of an excellent vessel he had built himself on the coast of Borneo, and this was named *Borneo*. He decided that, as soon as the opportunity came, he would sail to the Cocos-Keelings in the *Borneo* and thoroughly examine the group.

Though Captain Clunies-Ross had built the *Borneo*, he had been financed in this by Alexander Hare, who continued to be the principal owner. And so the *Borneo* was more or less under the control of Hare, who, as the owner of a small brig, had been Clunies-Ross's first employer in the East. Alexander Hare had been employed by a Lisbon house in the Indian trade and, later, by the East Indies Company, for whom he became eventually the governor of Banjermassin and controller—more or less—of whatever was then controllable in Borneo. Hare had insatiable passions and, wherever he went, he immediately set up a large harem. Women of any race were welcome, so long as they were young. If possible, he preferred them to be slaves, and most of his harems lived in a state of serfdom. At Calcutta, at Malacca, in Banjermassin, at Batavia, he set up his harems, often keeping as many as a hundred women at a time. He must also have had a flair for profitable trade, to support so large an entourage. Not even he knew the number of his children. As he was at one time a sort of British agent in Java, where the opportunities for making wealth were immense, it is probable that he was an extremely rich man. When control of Java was restored to the Dutch, he began at once to carve out a holding for himself in Borneo, and he was one of the first to see the possibilities there. It was another twenty years before Rajah Brooke was to come on the scene. But Hare could never bring himself to leave his harem, and the colony in Borneo was soon handed over to Clunies-Ross.

Having built the 400-ton *Borneo*, the Shetland Islander departed to find Hare again and see what employment he proposed for the vessel. This was, in the first instance, to remove Hare and harem across the Indian Ocean, for Batavia had become too hot for him. And so, one warm and windy day in 1818, the homemade ship *Borneo*, of 400 tons, John Clunies-Ross master, touched at the

Cape of Good Hope, where he landed Alexander Hare and upwards of one hundred women, who included beauties from Java, Bali, Malaya, China, the Celebes, Siam, Burma, and Banjermassin. Even the Cape had rarely seen the like. Hare would have been content for the *Borneo* to remain at the Cape indefinitely with his harem aboard, for he distrusted his beauties ashore in the settlement. But the ship was freighted for Europe, and thither Captain Ross sailed. Hare told him he intended to make a settlement with his party on the Seychelles or the Andamans, or perhaps on Christmas Island. He made no mention of the Cocos-Keelings.

On his way back from England to the East for another cargo with the *Borneo*, Captain Ross called in at the Cocos-Keelings, and this time thoroughly examined them. He must have come with his mind already made up to settle there, for he had brought seeds and plants. These he left. The *Borneo* anchored inside and remained there several days. The islands would do.

Again the home-built ship loaded in the Eastern roadsteads and sailed the long voyage homeward, across the whole Indian Ocean and around the Cape, up past St. Helena and Ascension, across the line in the steamy doldrums, through the northeast trades, past the Azores, and then with the west winds at last toward the Channel and the white cliffs of England. This time, Captain Ross was a man with a purpose. The turn-round of his teak full-rigger was hastened, and when she left the old country, she had aboard his wife, his mother-in-law, his six children, and a party of eight strapping and lusty young Scots, who included carpenters, crofters, and fishermen. With these were a Portuguese husbandman, a Chinese shipwright, and a Malay plantation worker. The *Borneo* carried building materials, furniture, and household goods for the party.

On this voyage, Captain Ross drove the little ship along, snoring down the trades under a press of sail and racing past the Cape with the strong westerlies of southern latitudes, though he got out of these as soon as he could and stood up into milder weather. The *Borneo* was a stanch ship, and the voyage pleasant. He had often told his family of the great beauties of their new home, and all looked forward to life in their Indian Ocean solitude. At last the happy day came when they approached the islands. There was a great deal of rain about that day, heavy tropic downpours such as they had had in the doldrums. Captain Ross was a little anxious about his reckoning. It was very easy to sail past the islands, even on a clear day, without seeing anything.

Toward midday, after a particularly heavy rain squall, one of the beautiful white terns came and circled the ship, passing so close to the little group standing by the wheel aft that it seemed to recognize Captain Ross and his vessel. The children waved to it, and a brawny Highlander bounded aloft to look out for the land. There it was! A line of coconut palms just emerging from a black cloud of rain! And high above, now the sky was its customary noble blue, was one large and beautiful white cloud. It was a marvelous landfall. The date was November 27, 1827.

As if to make up for its previous bad behavior, now the weather could not be good enough. The sun shone gloriously and the trade wind hummed in the rigging, sending the ship along at the rate of knots. They cleared away both bower anchors and swung out the big boat, towing it in readiness for helping to enter the lagoon. Sail was shortened as the islands were approached. Captain Ross picked out his marks. The ship was on soundings as she came on the transit line joining North and South Keeling. The entrance was between the islets known as Horsburgh and Direction, but there were many dangers in the form of shallows, reefs, and jutting mushrooms of new coral protruding to catch the unwary ship's bottom and rip it as with a saw. The Captain climbed aloft. The courses were hauled up, the ship now running under the fore and main tops'ls and the main t'gall'nt, with the fore-and-afters handy to swing her clear of sudden dangers.

The mate—a Mr. Leisk—went away in the boat to sound ahead, just to make doubly sure, for the *Borneo* had a precious freight. The good ship trod gently in the wake of her longboat, with the calls of the sailors, the conning of the captain, and the answering shouts of the man at the wheel echoing amongst the palms.

She was out of the ocean depths and well into the coral circle. The brilliant colors of the lagoon, transparent to six fathoms down —sky blue, jade green, purples, pale green, and every imaginable shade between all these, with the white crests of breaking water scintillating in the strong sunlight— reflected the somber bulk of the weather-beaten vessel. Here and there breakers indicated the presence of dangerous reefs, but there was always a way between. Noisy birds were squabbling over a rich haul of fish. A sting ray, frightened by the sudden shadow of the ship above him, darted for the shelter of a coral garden. The lazy fin of a shark broke the surface of the lagoon, and ripples like oil followed the unhurried motion of the ominous scavenger as, in clear view, it scoured the waters. Now the *Borneo* was well inside.

"Clew up the fore tops'l! Stand by the main!" was the shout from aloft. The Chinese shipwright was already standing by the windlass for'ard, in readiness to let an anchor go. The bigger children, barefoot and sun-tanned, ran with the men, delighting in helping with the work. The swift water breaking against the curved cutwater quieted now. Captain Ross was approaching his selected anchorage.

"Back the mainyard!"

The singing of blocks, the melodious shouts of the boatswain at the head of the line of men on the tops'l and course braces, were the instant response. With her main tops'l aback and her other sails all clewed up, showing little area, the *Borneo* slowed rapidly, stopped, slowly picked up a little sternway.

"Let go!"

Let go it was. The big bower fell into the lagoon with a tremendous splash, which frightened the fish and the birds for miles. The men immediately ran for the rigging to get a snug stow on all the sails. The boys had the gig cleared away to take the family ashore.

Then, and then only, had Captain Ross time to attend to other matters besides the immediate pilotage, and to look round. And there among the palms upon the loveliest of the islets he saw a wisp of smoke above the fronds. Then, his eyes traveling downward, he made out a rough sort of house, a group of houses, one larger and better built than the rest. Now the noise of his pilotage and his anchoring had all subsided, he thought he could hear, of all things, the lilt of girlish laughter by the beach. He was right. That was just what he did hear. In a moment or two, a boat was approaching him, full of bare-breasted, buxom young women with flowers on their ears. Captain Ross stared amazed, for sitting in the stern sheets, with the tiller in his hands, was a figure which looked like his late, unlamented partner, Alexander Hare. The braw Scots laddies stopped at their work and gazed at the wondrous apparition, open-mouthed. They were not looking at Mr. Hare.

It *was* Hare, right enough, complete with harem, 117 strong. Not all the islands of the Indian Ocean or the South Seas, or all the long coast of Madagascar, Araby the Blest, or romantic Ceylon had ever seen the like.

At last, Captain Ross found his voice.

"For God's sake!" he said, and stamped down below.

Hare swore that stress of weather and the absence of an anchorage at Christmas Island had compelled him to land at Cocos-Keeling. But he did not intend to leave. He called himself "Lord of the Manor, all its Waifs and Strays, &c" and was doing very well from Captain Ross's seeds and plants, which had thrived. The women did the work and Hare, whose own house was magnificently furnished and equipped, lived a better life than King Solomon. Fruit, fish, and fowl abounded, and his beauties tended his every want. But from the first day, some of them showed a keen appreciation of the obvious strength and manly bearing of the *Borneo*'s redheaded Highlanders, and the said Highlanders returned the interest in full measure. Alexander Hare's little paradise was threatened more than he knew, and he would have been well advised to make for Christmas Island.

Captain Ross was too committed to his new settlement to draw back now and, Hare or no Hare, he intended to make the Cocos-Keelings his home. But first, having landed his family, his working party, their building material and goods, he had to sail the *Borneo* to Batavia to discharge her freight and collect more stores. By the time he was back at the islands again, there was already trouble. In addition to his Highlanders, Portuguese, and Chinese shipwright, he had left some good men from the *Borneo's* crew. Now the first thing he saw was Hare, and Hare was shouting about the loss of many of his harem. He was reduced already, he bellowed, to a mere forty wenches. Couldn't Ross call off his men? He had retreated to a small island and put up a stockade, but nothing could keep the Highland lads away. The nights were warm, the water was shallow, and they could wade. So could the women.

In truth, Hare was getting no more than his deserts. Not content with degrading them, as the years passed he had taken to bullying his women more and more and to keeping them in a state as near to abject slavery as he could maintain. They were allowed no property of any kind. Their working hours were from dawn to dusk and they had to husk a hundred coconuts a day, in addition to whatever other tasks he might care to set. Their children were taken from them as soon as they were weaned. The girls were put into a big stockade from which, as they came of age, they were removed one by one to Hare's bed as he wanted them. The boys were put to work at the age of six. Old lecher as Hare was, he had always an eye on the main chance. His idea was to make the colony self-supporting by the sale of coconut oil and copra, which he intended to take to Batavia in a schooner he was going to build, if he ever got round to it.

This was precisely Captain Ross's idea, too, and he was the originator of it. Since he had no legal title to the islands, Ross could not throw Hare out. If he took him away by force, where could he go? Hare was still legally the principal owner of the *Borneo*, which was then being used as storeship and general freighter between the Cocos-Keelings and ports all round the Indian Ocean. He offered Hare transport anywhere he wished to go, even to England. Hare was a wealthy man and could well have set up an elaborate establishment in the United Kingdom, but he was afraid that his harem would be taken from him. So he refused to budge.

His harem was taken from him anyway, despite all his efforts to preserve it. The *Borneo* brought more settlers, under Captain Ross's control, and they all found wives. Hare built a minor fortress and tried to confine the survivors of his harem inside its wooden walls. He imported large quantities of rum and served it freely to the Ross men, in the hope of keeping them from what he termed his "flower garden." The rum only made things worse. But after all, he had many women. He stuck it for eight years. By 1835, Hare had had enough and, with no harem at all, he took passage in a passing trader for a port variously stated to have been Batavia, Singapore, and Malacca. There, an old man, but far from a worn-out one, he set about establishing another harem. But there were new laws against slavery and he found things hard. Within a few years, he was reported to be dead.

Dead or not, he was gone from Cocos-Keeling and he did not return. He had founded better than he knew. His selection of well-built and attractive young women became the mothers of a fine race. Whether fathered by Hare himself or by braw Highlanders, Malays, Chinese shipwrights, Javanese, or Bugis, the children were invariably brown and happy stalwarts, and they thrived. In trying to steal his honest captain's islands, Hare had done for him what he had not planned to do himself. He had provided the new colony with the makings of an excellent population, which was the best asset it could have.

From these beginnings, the new settlement on the Cocos-Keelings prospered greatly. Captain Ross was forty-nine years old when he became the undisputed "king" of his islands, and the dynasty he founded has lasted out the century and still exists. For the following twenty years he guided its destinies through fair fortune and foul. His son, his grandson, and his great-grandson succeeded him in turn and, as good Scots of fine stock could be expected to do, each has guided the little island colony quietly and successfully on its gentle way. Troubles they have had, fierce cyclones which, time and again, destroyed everything; wars and bombardments; a mighty sea fight at the very front door; and a hostile landing. But from its curious beginnings, and under the leadership of the clan of Clunies-Ross, the islands have gone steadily forward.

In World War I, the cruiser *Emden* was battered to a hulk in Cocos waters by H.M.A.S. *Sydney,* which outgunned and outranged her, and some of her metal still lies rusting on the northern island. The wireless station was destroyed and a party from the *Emden* made off with the islands' schooner *Ayesha,* the voyage of which under von Mücke was a minor classic in its way. In World War II, the islands were bombarded again, this time by a Japanese submarine, for they were an important link in Indian Ocean communications and a cable station had been operating there since 1901. Later, the largest of the islets became an air strip, and a contingent of airmen occupied the Cocos-Keelings for several years. From here squadrons of large aircraft scoured the nearer waters of the Indian Ocean on antisubmarine patrol.

The military administrator at this time has left on record a tribute.

It must have taken the Ross family many years of patient endeavour to educate these people up to their present standards [he wrote in his report on the islands]. Among the artisans there are no shoddy workers, but many excellent craftsmen. In the home, the womenfolk are just as capable; on Monday mornings the menfolk go to work in spotless clothes, and the houses are always clean and tidy. . . . They have a keen sense of humour and . . . a solid Scots habit of industry and pride of craftsmanship grafted upon the natural courtesy and charm of manner common to all races of the Malay Archipelago. . . . They are excellent seamen and their standards of boatwork are unsurpassed. Their economic and social structure are . . . the natural development of free men. . . . The village, the craftsmanship, and the appearance of the people are a standing tribute to the work of four generations of the Ross family, whose work for Cocos is a monument of good government.

The only serious crime was pregnancy before marriage. The shade of Alexander Hare still haunts the islands.

It is interesting to recall that the Ross family had the greatest difficulty in inducing the British government to accept any sort of responsibility for their settlement, and the idea of doing so was flatly refused for years. Those who are accustomed to think of the British Commonwealth as formed by a coterie of ferocious island grabbers and land-hungry exploiters eager to seize any continent, island, or tract of land anywhere, will perhaps learn with astonishment that the upshot of Captain Ross's many petitions both to the Admiralty and to the Colonial Office was the curt report that "a settlement on Cocos could not be productive of any advantage," etc. When one day in 1857 H.M.S. *Juno,* with Captain Fremantle in command, touched at the lagoon to proclaim the group part of His Majesty's dominions, it was discovered after the ceremony that she had come to the wrong Cocos. Captain Fremantle should have annexed a group of that same name in the Andamans. It was another twenty years before the Cocos-Keelings could legally fly the British flag, half a century and more after the *Borneo* had first visited them. In the meantime, vast deposits of rich phosphate rock had been discovered on nearby Christmas Island. The Ross dynasty had had concessions there and profited greatly and George, the son of John, left, when he died, upward of a million dollars.

By 1950, so well had the foundations of the Cocos-Keelings been laid, intentionally and unintentionally, that the islands had become seriously overpopulated. By 1949, the population numbered 1,700 persons, which was at least 700 more than the islands could support. But where could the surplus go? For a long time, they did not want to go anywhere. Probably more people would like to immigrate rather than emigrate, and the inhabitants were well content with their balmy atolls. True, the Royal Air Force had done something to unsettle the younger people. While the men of the R.A.F. were there, there were insufficient fresh supplies for everybody. The black market was introduced, and the cinema came. For the first time, the islanders saw beyond their horizon. If much of what they saw was alarming and even frightening, and if all of it was foreign to their way of life, yet they saw that that life was circumscribed, and they became aware that perhaps there were more of them in the Cocos-Keelings than could ever hope to earn a living there.

By that time, the islands were administered from Singapore. The Singapore government began to look round for a suitable place to accept some of the people from the Cocos-Keelings. There were other problems besides the islanders' own wish to remain where they were. Their health was so good that they had little resistance to the multitude of diseases accepted elsewhere in the tropics as more or less inevitable. And because, too, they had been cut off from the rest of the world for so long, they had developed a measure of naïvete which made it difficult to settle them elsewhere.

But the government of Borneo stepped into the breach. A healthy and comparatively isolated spot was found at Tawau in southwest Borneo. Thither, early in 1949, a representative group was cautiously moved. The party of thirty included a headman, boatbuilders, fishermen, plantation workers, and craftsmen. The government of Borneo had arranged a fitting reception and provided houses and employment. The first party, after a few months, reported back favorably, and since then other family groups have followed until by March, 1951, some 500 of the islanders were established at Tawau.

And there, from all accounts, they are proving to be an asset to Borneo; but the luckiest ones still live upon their lovely atoll.

CHAPTER XIX

Shipwrecks and Adventure

"Snug her down, Mr. Second. She'll do well enough on this tack now," Captain Davies had said, or rather, shouted at the top of his voice against the screaming of the wind. Then he had gone below. "Mr. Second" was a youth aged twenty-one who had signed on as second mate, after serving his apprenticeship aboard in the United Kingdom before setting out on that voyage.

The ship was the 2,000-ton full-rigger *Monkbarns*, belonging then to John Stewarts, of London, in the early 1920s. One of the last of her class, she was outward bound from the Bristol Channel toward Australia, with a cargo of railway iron and patent fuel— a heavy, dead, and dangerous cargo for a ship in the Roaring Forties in the middle of winter. Now she was caught off the pitch of the Cape in a black southeaster, which howled and screamed through the rigging as if shrieking with demoniac delight to find a victim. The water smashed aboard the length of her low main deck, making it dangerous for men to work there. But they *had* to work there. It was much more dangerous to be on deck than to fight their way into the high rigging, to do battle with the sodden, gale-stiffened canvas there. She had been caught on the wrong tack when the sudden southeaster screamed upon her, out of the terrifying murk. Captain Davies had to wear her round and put her on the tack that took her away from the land. Now she was standing down toward the Antarctic somewhere. But she had sea room. For the moment, she was safe.

It was while they were wearing the ship round that the great sea had come aboard and knocked the mate into the scuppers, twisting him round a pair of bitts and smashing his right leg. The ship had to run off before the wind, and that was well enough. But she had to be brought up to it again on the other tack, and that was not well. She turned on her heel in a welter of foam with a great wake running back from her as if she were a quadruple-screw steamer, and the height of the sea was frightening. As she brought her shoulder to it again, a giant graybeard fell upon her like a torrent from Niagara Falls, raced along the exposed main deck, and caught the men at the braces. Some leaped for the rigging and clambered up out of the weight of water, for their lives; others jumped for life lines, for the boat skids, for any place which was out of the worst of the water and offered them something to cling to. There they clung with every ounce of their strength.

Among those who could not get out of the way of the sea was the mate. The water picked him up and swept him into the lee scuppers, knocking his head on the steel bulwarks, trying to wash him out through a wash port or over the side. Then a roll of the ship the other way swept him across the deck again. He could not get his feet. When the worst weight of the water had gone and a little group of sailors, led by the bos'n, could get to the mate, they found him unconscious and bleeding heavily. His trousers were torn from one leg, which was a mass of blood and torn tissues. His head looked as if it were stove in, and his face was that of a dead man. The ship still rolled and lurched, now leaping as if she wanted to get out of the furious embrace of the contorted waters, now sinking down as if she were tired of the struggle and wanted nothing better than to drop below the turmoil and be done with it forever. Both rails rolled under, alternately. She still had too great a press of canvas on her, and the rigging roared and shrieked a discordant protest. Like all modern vessels, the *Monkbarns* was very strongly rigged, and her backstays and shrouds were of heavy iron wire set up to steel turnbuckles as wide round as a strong man's arm. She could stand the punishment for a while.

"Short notice, soon past; long notice, long last"—the second mate remembered the old sailor's couplet as he set about the work of shortening her down. There had been no notice of this blow: perhaps it would go quickly. Captain Davies was superintending the work of carrying the badly injured mate below, and the steward was already struggling forward to the galley, which looked like a half-tide rock in the waste of waters swirling and smashing on the main deck. He was going to get the galley fire going again, to get hot water for some surgery on the mate. Captain Davies was the only doctor, and the steward had to act as nurse.

For the next three hours, the second mate had his hands full looking after the ship. Everyone was on deck, of course; all hands were always ready for a call in that kind of weather. In a sailing ship watchkeeping and everything else took second place to the safety of the ship, and everyone knew it. When men's lives were at stake and their safety lay in the strength of their own stout hearts and their own strong arms, they got on with the job in hand. Gales knew no routine. Shortening down the ship *Monkbarns* while she was fighting for her life off the Cape of Good Hope was a dangerous and extremely difficult business. Her three mastheads described agonized circles under the heavy sky, and the footropes on her wet, high yards seemed invitations to death. Far below the sea boiled in insensate fury. The ship bucked and jumped, lurched and stumbled and rolled, as if she were intent on shaking the fighting mariners down from her rigging, for every slightest motion was communicated tenfold up there. The wind tried to hurl the men down from aloft by sheer force, and the sea strove to shake them down.

Nor were they all men. Half a dozen of them were boys, apprentices of the John Stewart Line, serving their time for deck officers' certificates. These were indistinguishable from the rest. As a team, skilled and fearless, all fought for the safety of the ship. Up one mast they went, to fight a sail blown out like the side of a circus tent gone mad in a black squall. That done, down again, and fight along the main deck, taking care not to be knocked down or swept overboard; and work furiously with the clew lines, buntlines, and other gear, to get another sail under control; aloft again, and fight that until it has been defeated and snugged along the yard, held prisoner by the gaskets. From mast to mast and on to the jib boom they worked, paying no attention to the hours. Still the wind screamed and the waters leaped, but as the sail came off her, the motion of the full-rigged ship lessened a little, at first almost imperceptibly.

After four hours, the second mate had time to come aft and check that all was well with the man at the wheel. The helmsman then had little to do. Under short canvas, brought up on the port tack with her yards braced sharp up, the sails reduced to the three lower topsails and a few storm fore-and-afters, the ship was steering herself. She was practically hove-to. It was coming on to nightfall, and a darkening gloom swept rapidly over the face of the waters, adding to their height, strengthening the scream of the wind. Short notice, soon past? Not this time! Not off the horrible Cape of Good Hope.

The lee skylight above the captain's saloon was open to bring air to the man down there. Even above the roaring of the wind the second mate could hear, sometimes, the scream of the poor wretch as the captain dealt with him. The mate would live, he heard; but his right leg had a compound fracture and there were other serious injuries. The sea had twisted him like a cane. Captain Davies had to straighten the leg and set it, then dress and deal with all the other wounds. Captain Davies had no surgical experience. The ship had only the commonest medicine chest as prescribed for long-voyage sailing vessels. The captain had a little blue book called the *Ship Master's Medical Guide*, and that was all. But he had been master in sail for many years and had dealt with many crises. He had set bones before, but not compound fractures. Only the previous voyage, he had had to put six stitches in his own face, before a mirror, when a slip in the empty 'tween decks had sent him crashing down the hold, and the mate, who hated the sight of blood, was fumbling the job. "Here, give me the needle!" he'd said, then had taken it and got on with the stitching.

He had his hands full with that compound fracture now, and that injured skull. Hour after hour, the second mate walked the poop, now clinging for a few moments to the weather mizzen rigging under the shelter of a brief weather cloth, now struggling aft to look for the hundredth time into the binnacle, to see whether there was any change in the direction of the wind. It was a black night, and the ship's own automatic coming up (for the sails were trimmed so that she could take care of herself) would tell him of wind changes he could not see.

Now and again came the muffled screams of the tortured mate. No anesthetics were kept aboard, and no one could have administered them, if there had been any. The second mate saw some apprentices carry along a handy billy, a small tackle kept about the decks for the lighter lifting jobs. He heard the rattle of blocks when the tackle was set up in the saloon below. That would be to haul the mate's fractured bones back into alignment. The carpenter was helping.

Toward midnight, the second mate heard the measured steps of the Captain ascending to the poop. The screams had died down, then. There had never been many. Down in the saloon everything was quiet.

"I think he'll do," was all the Captain said, as he took over the weather side of the poop. "Any easement in the wind, Mister?"

Before the words were out of his mouth, a squall greater than any which had previously beset the ship screamed upon her like a solid, living thing making an attack, unprovoked, violent, insupportable. For the moment the very sea was driven flat by the fury of the wind. Over, over, over went the ship, until her main yardarm was in the water. Captain, second mate, helmsman, everyone on deck, held on for their lives. Would she never come up? Was *this* what happened to missing ships? Then the wind eased a little, and the sea leaped, and the ship labored as if she had had more than she could stand, as if she were not going to come up again. At that precise instant, they heard a mightier roar even than the tumult of the wind and the shrieking of the rigging. They heard the dreadful roar of the cargo of steel rails breaking adrift below and shifting bodily to leeward, to pin the ship's lee side down in the sea. This, indeed, was the end.

And yet the very fury of that last squall seemed to take, as it passed, the worst sting from the gale, and there were no more squalls of such ferocity. The sea, after a wild dance, began to ease a little. The ship went over no farther. Her decks were now heeled at a drunken angle and it was quite impossible, while the storm lasted, to walk. All that anyone could do was to hang on. But there were no more ominous sounds from down below. The hatches stood. The *Monkbarns* did not roll over or founder.

So the dawn found them, haggard with the loss of sleep, a group of oilskinned men clinging to the ship as she lay wallowing at a crazy angle. But their ship still had fight in her and so had the crew. There was a way into the hold through a booby hatch. The ship was rolling with a frightening lurch in the dreadful troughs, her lower yardarms dipping in the sea to leeward at every roll. She was far from the tracks of shipping, save for other sailing ships like herself, and they were rare. If she was going to be saved, her people must save her. Led by the captain himself with the second mate after him, all hands descended into the hold, their purpose to fight that railway iron and those hundreds of tons of patent fuel back to windward, to restow the shifted cargo properly, and then to get sail on the ship again and stand onward for her destined port.

It took them three days to get her up again—three days during which they could not sleep save now and again to drop in the dirty coal and shut their eyes for perhaps five minutes. Nor could they eat a bite, except hard ship's biscuits and cold bully beef. Nor could they know that, despite all their utmost efforts, they would survive at last. At first, for every shovelful of coal pitched back to windward, two others rolled alee. The railway iron, down in the dangerous black cavern of the unlighted hold, was deadly. They had three hurricane lamps. They dared not open any hatch, for the sea would break in. It took four hours to move one piece of iron, and this was a painful and extremely dangerous business of much labor with tackles and toms. But they were good men, well used to working together. They were not appalled. They knew what was to be done and they got on with it. Captain Davies, the second mate, the apprentices, the cook, the carpenter, the bos'n, the able seamen shoveled and strained in the hold for three ghastly days, and the only man out of the hold in that time was the steward, who came up at intervals to see to the injured mate.

A week afterward, the *Monkbarns* was on an even keel again, racing before the west winds on the long run toward Australia, and, at a casual glance, there was no sign of the ordeal she had survived. Her rust-streaked gray sides and her general look of weatherbeaten grace were normal there. As she raced on, still under shortened sail, it is doubtful whether any of her people even gave a thought to the narrowness of their recent escape. The sailing-ship man learned to accept such things as part of his life. The mate, lashed up in his bunk with handy billies and tommed off with boards against the ship's heavy rolling, was making progress. The cargo did not shift again. The west winds were fair winds and they could blow, for they would bring the ship to her destination.

When at last she came in from sea, no one put out flags. Cargo shifted, in a black southeaster? Mate badly injured? Touch and go? Yet another sailing ship had been brought in from sea by the superhuman efforts of a devoted band of shipmates, assembled casually at the shipping office in England, working together like a band of brothers month in, month out, outward around Good Hope and homeward around the Horn, then to be dispersed just as casually at the shipping office once again—aye, aye, all this was normal, more or less routine in the Indian Ocean in the days of sail. Yet they knew they were lucky to be alive.

The mate made a good recovery, and the surgeons in Australia marveled at the skill of the old sea captain. He had done things with skin and bone that they would scarcely dare to do, with all the resources of great hospitals beside them. He had done them bravely, and he had done them well, as things had to be done aboard ship in the days of sail. In the four and a half centuries since Europeans had first stormed around the Cape of Good Hope, many, many a brave ship fought for her life down there, and many lost the fight. The *Monkbarns* was a lucky ship to come through.

Consider, for example, the case of the beautiful big five-masted barque *København,* the pride of the Danish merchant marine. The *København* was one of the most magnificent big sailing ships ever launched. No expense was spared on her. She was built by the famous Scottish firm of Ramage and Ferguson, at Leith, in 1921, as a school ship for the Danish East Asiatic Company, which prided itself upon its ships, its establishments, and its men. The *København* registered almost 4,000 tons. She had an auxiliary engine, and was equipped with wireless and every safety device she could have. She was exceptionally stoutly built. She was well manned with a full crew of good Danish sailors, in addition to her cadets. The cadets were drawn from among the best families in Denmark. Her officers were the best in Scandinavia.

Yet, somewhere in the zone of the wild west winds of the far southern Indian Ocean, the *København* was overwhelmed. She sailed from Buenos Aires bound in ballast toward Australia on December 14, 1928, with a crew of sixty, all told, including forty-five cadets. A week later she exchanged greetings by radio with a company's ship. After that, nothing whatever has been heard or seen of her or of anyone aboard. She was in ballast and should not have foundered quickly, even if she struck an iceberg. She had radio and should have been able to send out a distress call. She had plenty of boats. If she had foundered, some of them should have got away. If she had run up on one of the bleak islands of the Roaring Forties, at least some wreckage would have remained there and some of her people would have survived. Most such islands were given castaway depots with food and clothing. Many shipwrecked parties had survived on such places, even before the depots were put there. A Blue Funnel ship spent months searching among the islands, and found nothing. Ships nosed into the Antarctic pack, thinking perhaps the big five-master, partially dismasted and not under control, might have drifted down there, as other ships had done. But nothing, nothing, nothing—nothing ever has been found.

The general opinion among sailing-ship men is that the *København* probably sailed headlong into some great iceberg or field of ice and was crushed like a big tin can and that she sailed right under before the wireless operator had time to switch on his set. The boats and all else would have been secured for the run in the west winds, and so nothing would float off and nobody would survive. That may have happened. Many ships have collided with ice, which reaches north of 40 south in the summer months. But it is more probable that the *København* was blown over in a squall and capsized. The big, square-rigged ship in ballast was vulnerable that way. High out of the water, with her enormous spread of canvas and her tremendously heavy masts and yards, some sudden squall catching the too strongly rigged ship might have been too much for her. The old wooden ships had hempen rigging, which could be cut away and parted easily. The great steel carriers of the last days of ocean sail were the most heavily rigged vessels that ever went to sea.

Many a ship went missing, like the *København*, on that wild run. They had to go into the Roaring Forties to take advantage of the west winds; once there, they took their chances. Each voyage was an adventure and a trial, and the way of the deep-sea sailing ship was of necessity hard. There were great compensations. That master of ships and of writing, Captain Joseph Conrad, has written of his experiences when driving the little barque *Otago* (which he commanded) down there in the farther reaches of the Indian Ocean.

I well remember [he said] a three days' run got out of a little barque of 400 tons somewhere between St. Paul and Amsterdam, and Cape Otway, on the Australian coast. It was a long, hard gale, grey clouds and green sea, heavy weather undoubtedly, but still what a sailor would call manageable. Under two lower tops'ls and a reefed fores'l the barque seemed to race with a long, steady sea that did not becalm her in the troughs. The solemn thundering combers caught her up from astern, passed her with a fierce boiling up of foam level with the bulwarks, swept on ahead with a swish and a roar: and the little vessel, dipping her jib boom into the tumbling froth, would go on running in a smooth, glassy hollow, a deep valley between two ridges of sea, hiding the horizon ahead and astern. There was such fascination in her pluck, nimbleness, the continual exhibition of unfailing seaworthiness, in the semblance of courage and endurance, that I could not give up the delight of watching her run through the three unforgettable days of that gale which my mate also delighted to extol as "a famous shove." *

The little *Otago* was a graceful barque, built of iron, a worthy successor of the noble race of tea clippers which had sailed so beautifully and so briefly across the Indian Ocean, outward and homeward bound from China. These, too, had stormed before the wild west winds and benefited from many a "famous shove," but their races home with cargoes of a new season's tea were flying-fish voyages, for the greater part—down through the China Sea, through the Straits of Sunda, across the whole broad stretch of the Indian Ocean toward the Cape of Good Hope with, for much of the way, the southeast trade a fresh and favoring wind; then around the Cape with the Agulhas current and whatever winds might offer, close in by the land; and after that, the south winds to drive the little ships, under a spread of lovely sail, onward to the trade winds,

* Joseph Conrad, *The Mirror of the Sea*, J. M. Dent & Sons, Ltd., London.

across the line, through the northeast trades, and home. To them, the whole width of the Indian Ocean was only a lap on their great voyages.

In this grand fleet, the art of wooden shipbuilding and the art of sailing ships found, in some ways, their ultimate expression. Some of those clipper ships were perfect of their kind. They sat upon the water with the grace of ocean birds and they raced through the sea with a breath of air. In port, they looked as if a push with a child's hand would send them moving. At sea their towers of white canvas, symmetrical and lovely, were spread from a tracery of masts and yards which represented the ultimate in seafaring man's skill to harness the wind. Their names were as lovely as the ships themselves—*Titania, Ariel, Sir Lancelot, Lord of the Isles, Crest of the Wave, Spirit of the Age, Flying Cloud.* The Americans led the way with their great clipper ships, but the Scots shipbuilders were not far behind. The tradition of barrel-hulled, easy-going wanderers died hard in England, lulled by two centuries of monopolistic trading. But when the owners, the builders, and the seamen of the United Kingdom began at last to look to their laurels, there were some magnificent exhibitions of sailing and of seamanship such as the world had not seen before and may never see again.

Many of the tea-clipper races were classics. Most of the true clippers were ships of less than a thousand tons. To get such ships, under sail alone, from the anchorage off Foochow or wherever else they loaded, down through the reef-strewn China Sea and through the maze of the East Indian archipelago, across the whole width of the Indian Ocean, around the Cape and home, making the best of every puff of air and driving the ship to the utmost of her endurance in every gale, with never a letup, never a respite, never a moment off, was a trial of endurance for ship and men. Those clipper masters were great sailors. They had good ships, and they knew how to get the best out of them.

With the opening of the Suez Canal in 1869 and the steady improvement of steamships which followed it, the tea races were ended and the clipper ships were doomed. They survived a while in the Australian trade, taking out immigrants, bringing home gold, passengers, and wool. Some of the most famous clippers made their name in this trade—the *Cutty Sark* and the gracious *Thermopylae*, the American-built *James Baines* and *Lightning*, and the *Champion of the Seas* (which once made a noon-to-noon run of 465 miles across the Indian Ocean when bound from Liverpool toward Melbourne, in 1854). The *Champion of the Seas* was built by the famous builder Donald Mackay in New England, for the Liverpool Black Ball Line's Australian trade. The following extract from the Melbourne *Argus* gives the brief story of her wonderful run.

Dec. 26th, 1854—Arrived *Champion of the Seas*, 2,722 tons, A. Newlands, Commander. Liverpool, Oct. 11th, Melbourne Dec. 24th. 45 in Cabin, 735 in Intermediate and Steerage. 4 Deaths.

The *Champion of the Seas* is not only the largest sailing vessel that has ever entered the Heads, but she is without doubt the noblest. . . . Her model is faultless, her appointments all that could be desired, and the fittings for the accommodation of passengers more elegant, convenient, lofty, and airy than those of any other in the Australian line. Of her sailing qualities there can be no question. She has made the run in 72 days and a few hours, having been under canvas 67 days. In 24 consecutive hours she ran the astonishing distance of 465 miles, a run never yet equalled, so far as we believe, by any other sailing vessel in the world, and her average run during the passage was 199 miles the day.

The great run was actually made not in 24 hours, but in 23 hours and 17 minutes, which was the elapsed time between the *Champion*'s noon on December 11 and her noon on December 12. It is undoubtedly the greatest achievement of any kind of sailing ship of which any record has been discovered. The *Sovereign of the Seas*, the *James Baines*, the *Great Republic*, the *Donald Mackay*, and the *Lightning* made runs across the Indian Ocean covering more than 400 miles in a noon-to-noon day. The *Thermopylae*, which was perhaps the queen of all the clippers, ran from London to Melbourne in 1868 and again in 1871 in 60 days—a wonderful record for a 14,000-mile passage. The *Cutty Sark*, her great rival, never did better outward than 64 days, and that was from the Lizard to landfall on Cape Otway. The best of the American-built clipper runs from the United Kingdom to Australia was that of the *James Baines*—63 days from Liverpool to Melbourne, in 1854.

Some of the ships of the Honourable East India Company made tolerable passages to India in the very last days of the Company's long reign. In the 1830s the *Earl of Balcarres* was only 79 days from London to Bombay, which was not bad going. The competition of American ships had to be met then. The *George of Salem,* which sailed so consistently and well in the trade between Salem and India that she was known throughout the Indian Ocean as the Salem Frigate, was steadily making outward passages of less than 100 days, from the east coast of the United States, by the early 1820s.

Not all the great immigrant clippers which raced outward toward Australian or New Zealand ports in the colorful gold-rush days reached their destinations. There were some dreadful wrecks, none worse than those which occurred at the very end of the voyage, such as that of the *Duncan Dunbar* on Sydney Heads, with the loss of every person aboard except one. The clipper *Strathmore* went up on the Crozet Islands, with heavy loss of life, and the survivors were eight months on the island. It was easy, and often fatal, for a ship running in the almost constant westerly gales down there to be a little out in her latitude, and there was a dreadful affinity between the errant clippers and those desolate subantarctic islands. Sometimes captains tried deliberately to pass close by some of the higher islands, in order to check their longitude before running for the coast of Australia. In the days before radio, the only way to get a ready check on longitude or chronometers (which to a sailing ship were the same thing) was by sighting land. But the difficulty was that in trying to sight an island the ship might get unwarrantably close and then a sudden gale, pitch-black and screaming, would throw her up onto it before she could get out of its way.

The little barque *Meridian*, for example, did just that. Though she was not of more than 600 tons, she had more than a hundred persons aboard, and her 84 passengers included 40 children. In the middle of a black and gale-filled night, she ran into the cliffs of Amsterdam Island. She hit the island with such a shock that the masts fell out of her, forming a bridge from her decks to the cliff top, but the crew did not know that until the morning. Meanwhile, breakers swept over her, taking the master and several seamen to their deaths. The women and children spent a dreadful night in the midst of the raging waters, waiting for the daylight and fearing that it would never come for them. But with the dawn, they saw the rough bridge the falling masts had made. The mate took charge and, under his leadership, the crew got every child and every woman somehow up the tangled mess of the rigging and onto the cliff top. Some of the cargo washed ashore and this provided clothing and some shelter. But Amsterdam Island was a bleak, cold hole for the 40 children. Rain stormed upon them almost constantly. The cliff top was rugged, and much of it was covered with slippery moss. There was no warmth. The sailors contrived a sort of shelter in a bit of a lee behind an outcrop of rocks, and here the shipwrecked passengers and the ship's company settled in as well as they could. They had food for perhaps ten days. There was plenty of fresh water.

But they were luckier than they knew. When they had been marooned only four days, a sail broke the horizon and they saw a vessel making for the island. The sailors said she was a Yankee whaler, by the look of her. She nearly made the island and then a black squall of rain came down, forerunner of yet another gale. When the rain passed, the whaler had gone. After three days the weather cleared again. Again the sails of the sturdy little whaler broke the horizon. This time she made it. A boat put out from her when she was as close in as she dared come, but the breakers running at the cliff base were so great and so constant that the whaler's people shouted that they could never make a landing safely there. The shipwrecked people would have to trek across the island to the lee side.

The island was only a few miles across, but it took three days to get the women and children over that short distance. The sailors carried the little children. While they were on the way, another gale blew up and the whaler was driven off once more. But she came back a third time. By then the castaways were in a dreadful state. Their food was gone, and many had to be assisted into the boats. Nevertheless, every man, woman, and child was safely taken off.

The whaler was the little Yankee *Monmouth,* Captain Ludlow. She took the castaways at once to Mauritius, which was a warm and pleasant spot after miserable Amsterdam.

There was also the odd case of the government's transport *Megaera,* outward bound with troops for Australia in 1871. Nobody worried much about the state of ships which were provided as troop transports in those days, and the *Megaera* was falling to pieces. She was so leaky and generally decrepit that, by the time she had run her easting down as far as St. Paul Island, her captain thought the best thing to do with her was to drive her up ashore while she was still, more or less, in one piece. So he sailed her right for the best place he could see on the rocky beach. She had more than 650 persons aboard, and it was the middle of winter. However, conditions aboard had been so crowded and generally intolerable that even some sailcloth tents on St. Paul's were an improvement, and the voluntary castaways were able to land most of their necessities, including coal to keep a fire going. A proper military routine was established, and the castaways lived more or less happily until, three months later, they were taken off by a passing Dutch vessel. It speaks well for their discipline that not a life was lost and the spirit of the makeshift establishment remained good from beginning to end.

A chronicle of the wrecks and disasters in the southern waters of the Indian Ocean alone would more than fill a large book. One of the most tragic things that occurred down there, to my knowledge, was the loss of the boat from the Swedish barque *Staut* in the last days of sail. The *Staut* was a pretty barque, of about 1,000 tons, making the familiar voyage from Norway to Melbourne with tongue-and-groove planks. Early one evening, while snugging her down (for it looked like being a dirty night) a boy fell from the main upper tops'l yard into the sea. A lifeboat was manned immediately and the ship hove to, for the boy was seen to grasp a lifebuoy flung over for him. The boat went back and the barque waited. But a black squall came down, and when it had passed there was no sign of the boat. It was near nightfall then. The *Staut* waited through the night, making flares. In the morning there was still no boat. There never was a sign of that boat again, nor of the boy or any of the people who formed the boat's crew.

The boy who fell overboard was the captain's younger son, and the second mate who went back in charge of the boat was his only other son. The *Staut* beat about the vicinity for a fortnight, despite the ferocity of the gales, but she had to turn away at last and head for Melbourne.

The tragedies were not confined to the days of sail. Several large passenger steamers have gone missing in the Indian Ocean. There is, for example, the mystery of the fine steamer *Waratah*, which was the latest in passenger vessels for the Australian trade when she was built, in 1908. On her second voyage, the *Waratah*, with a large passenger list, sailed from Melbourne for the United Kingdom via the Cape of Good Hope, and on July 26, 1909, left Durban for Cape Town, in continuation of the voyage. All had gone well. She was a good ship, well built, competently manned. Yet from that day onward no sign of the *Waratah* has ever been found, and nothing was ever heard from anyone on board. She simply disappeared from the face of the waters.

A few years later, the fine passenger vessel *Koombana,* which was in the West Australian coastal trade, left Port Hedland bound for Broome and never arrived, nor was anything ever heard of her or any of the 200 persons who sailed with her. Yet the *Koombana* was a first-class vessel and the run was short and without dangers other than the familiar perils of pilotage (if she had driven ashore, she would have remained there to be seen). The most intensive search discovered nothing whatever, and the *Koombana* has been missing since March, 1912. The area where she went is notorious for severe cyclonic storms, which often lead to the loss of pearling luggers; but the *Koombana* was no pearling lugger and she should have survived a blow.

When the Hain Line's steamer *Trevessa* foundered in the Indian Ocean, homeward bound with a heavy cargo in 1923, her people were more fortunate. They took to the boats and rowed and sailed almost 2,000 miles, one boat to the island of Rodriguez, the other to Mauritius. It would have been a shorter run to the coast of Australia, but the southeast trade wind made it easier to make for the islands to leeward. At the time, the voyage of the *Trevessa's* boats was considered second only to the great boat passage made by Captain Bligh after the mutiny in the *Bounty.*

Since that day, in the Indian Ocean and elsewhere, such passages in open boats, after sinkings of merchant ships by submarine and raider in World War II, were to become tragically commonplace. Several groups of Europeans, escaping before the rapid Japanese advance into Malaya and the Dutch East Indies, sailed incredibly broken-down and unsuitable craft across the Bay of Bengal and even, in one instance at least, down to Australia. I saw a sort of half-caste junk at Fremantle, just after the war, which had sailed from Singapore, but I sought in vain for her story. Such adventures then had become too familiar to be noted. "Story?" I was told. "The story is they were damned lucky to get away with it. Who were they? Some bunch of landsmen who didn't know any better. Where are they now? God knows."

CHAPTER XX

The Two World Wars

In the first fifty years of the twentieth century, the Indian Ocean was to know the havoc of two world wars. In the first, there was little action either in the waters of the ocean or on the adjacent coasts. The campaign in the German territories of East Africa was a minor affair, and the fighting in Mesopotamia and Arabia went toward the Mediterranean. In the ocean itself there were the isolated activities of a couple of German raiding cruisers and one armed merchantman, which did not last long. But World War II was a very different matter.

Two ships stand out from World War I (1914–1918) in Indian Ocean waters, both German. They are the light cruisers *Emden* and *Königsberg*. The *Emden*, under the command of Captain von Muller, was a cruiser of 3,600 tons, which at the outbreak of war was in Chinese waters, based on the then German-held port of Tsingtau. Before Britain came into the war, the *Emden* got out from Tsingtau and cleared the coast, with a number of other German ships. She was detached to damage Allied shipping in the Indian Ocean, acting independently. So she made a wide circling course by way of the southern Korean coast, passing south of Japan and near the Marianne Islands, southward past Pelew and Yap, and then, seeking unfrequented routes, through the Dutch East Indies to the west of Halmahera, through the Moluccas, round Timor. After that, streaking at full speed by day and blacked out by night, she navigated through dangerous waters toward the Straits of Lombok (between Lombok and Bali), and by the coast of Java and Sumatra into the Bay of Bengal.

Here the *Emden* cruised off Rangoon, off Penang, off Madras. She went into the Arabian Sea and took heavy toll of shipping on the Aden-Colombo and Aden-Bombay routes, while she dodged backward and forward, hiding a while now in the Maldives, now in the Laccadives, now pouncing out once more to sink a brace of ships before dashing down to the Chagos Archipelago or Diego Garcia, to coal from some captured collier full of the best Welsh coal. One of her nightmares was this need for coal. She required prodigious quantities if her engines were to do their best, and her greatest speed was only 24 knots. She had the luck to capture collier after collier, always treating the crews as well as possible and carrying out her unpleasant duty of first stealing their cargoes and then sinking them, as pleasantly as she could. Captain von Muller showed concern for his involuntary prisoners, always sparing a ship—frequently a good ship—to take them into neutral ports when he had collected an embarrassing number.

The *Emden* cruised a second time off Ceylon and dashed a second time into the Bay of Bengal, to shell oil installations at Madras and bring the shock of war into the Indian dominions. But the end was inevitable. After a few months, she was caught off the Cocos-Keeling islands, where the Australian cruiser *Sydney* put an end to her career. She had sunk more than twenty merchant ships, many of them large and valuable, and she had seriously dislocated Allied shipping on some of the most important routes in the Indian Ocean.

Some curious incidents stand out from her brief and effective career. At Diego Garcia the inhabitants had not heard of the outbreak of war, and von Muller did not enlighten them. At that time the island was dependent for its communications on a small sailing ship which went to Mauritius four times a year, and the little vessel had not come in. So the citizens of Diego Garcia made their enemies

welcome and did all they could to help them. One day the *Emden*
sighted a strange vessel which at first seemed like a haystack adrift
at sea. This proved to be the *Ponrabbel,* a river dredger going out
to Tasmania. This was the second attempt to get a dredger to
Tasmania. The first had sunk in bad weather. The crew of the
second had drawn all their wages in advance and, when they saw
the *Emden,* they packed their bags and waited cheerfully to be
taken off, for they knew then that they had come as far as they
were going. Their wages were earned. They had heard of the
Emden's good reputation for releasing merchant crews. They would
have been most indignant if von Muller had not sunk the poor
Ponrabbel and allowed them to take the vessel on to Tasmania.

When the *Emden* sent a boarding party to Mr. Holt's new liner
Troilus, then on her maiden voyage and a very fine vessel laden
with a valuable cargo, Captain Lauterbach, a former master in
German passenger vessels, was in charge of the boarders. Rushing
up the gangway armed to the teeth, he was astonished to be greeted
in a cheerful, very English voice.

"How do you do, Captain Lauterbach. Imagine meeting you
here!"

A pretty English girl stood at the head of the gangway, smiling.
She had been a passenger in his ship before war was declared. It
took Lauterbach a moment or two to remember her, but though
the *Troilus* had to be sunk, he saw that she and all the other passengers received every consideration. Indeed, the raiders of World
War I were vastly different from those of World War II. There
were no exchanges of pleasantries after 1939.

When the *Emden* was finally cornered off Cocos-Keeling, while
her landing party was ashore destroying the cable and wireless
installations, she put up a brave fight. She was hopelessly outgunned. Against her ten 4.1-inch guns, the Australian cruiser *Sydney* had eight 6-inch guns. The *Emden* then was foul and in need
of maintenance. But she fought while she had a gun to fire and

Running across the Indian Ocean

"She nearly went right over"

The missing *København*

The German raider *Emden* (*Courtesy Office of Naval Records and History*)

LCI (*Courtesy Office of Naval Records and History*)

long after she had been driven ashore, a burning and battered hulk, the imperial flag still flew.

Her record was continued by her landing party, which seized the schooner *Ayesha* in the lagoon and got away under cover of darkness. First, the *Ayesha* made for the coast of Sumatra. Thence she headed for the Red Sea, her people intending to go as far as they could and then land and trek through Arabia to the Turkish lines, and thence return to Germany. It was a brave idea, though it seemed a forlorn hope. Big troop convoys, well protected, were steaming across the Indian Ocean from Australia toward Egypt, to build up the force there which was to land in Gallipoli. In the whole of the ocean, every hand was against the *Ayesha* and her people. Without the *Emden* to hunt, there were plenty of ships to track the schooner down. It is doubtful if her people would ever have escaped, had they not been helped by the German steamer *Choising*, a collier, which followed the *Ayesha* from the Sumatran coast and joined forces. Eventually the whole party transferred to the collier, sinking the *Ayesha*. They got through the Straits of Bab-el-Mandeb and landed on the coast of the Yemen, not far from Hodeida. Their journey across the deserts of Arabia is a classic in its way, but eventually the survivors safely reached Stamboul. Sailors everywhere admired them for their courage, loyalty, and endurance.

Another German raider which did far too well in the Indian Ocean was the famous *Wolf*, a former Hansa Line steamer which, given a heavy armament and made into an auxiliary cruiser, had run the British blockade in the early winter of 1916 and made at once for the Indian Ocean. Here she laid several mine fields, off Colombo, off Bombay, and in the Gulf of Aden. She captured a merchantman named the *Turritella*, which was converted into a mine layer, but she had not long been sent about her dangerous ways before she was, in turn, captured by a British armed merchantman. When this capture revealed the presence of the *Wolf* in the Indian Ocean, the *Wolf* made for the Pacific, where she operated for a while. But the Pacific is a large ocean and the hunting was better in the Indian. After a while, the *Wolf* returned to the Indian Ocean by way of the East Indian archipelago, laying a mine field in the approaches to Singapore on her way. The Japanese passenger steamer *Hitachi Maru*, the old barque *Beluga*, the American schooner *John H. Kirby*, and the Spanish steamer *Igotz Mendi* were in turn captured, and all but the Spaniard were sunk. Several hundred prisoners were transferred to the *Igotz Mendi*.

By that time, the *Wolf* was out of ammunition and in urgent need of overhaul. She had been at sea for more than fifteen months. She rounded the Cape, in company with her Spanish prize, and safely returned to Germany. Her cruise lacked the spectacular dash of the *Emden* and she had taken only fourteen ships. But she had dislocated shipping seriously, her mine fields sank at least one large liner and took a long time to clear up, and she had more than three-score Allied war vessels searching for her over at least a year, without once picking her up.

The third raider was the *Königsberg*, another light cruiser, similar to the *Emden*. The *Königsberg* was built in 1907. She was a cruiser of 3,350 tons, armed with ten 4.1-inch guns, and her exploits in the Indian Ocean were confined to the coast of East Africa. She was sighted by H.M.S. *Hyacinth* on July 31, 1914, within a few days of the outbreak of war, and her whereabouts were then well known. She was the only German cruiser on the coast. Yet she successfully sank several steamers, bombarded the old cruiser *Pegasus* and sank her off the island of Zanzibar, and finally, when she was unserviceable and trapped in the delta of the Rufiji River from which escape was impossible, she kept a considerable fleet of ships engaged for months in the effort to destroy her.

Yet the *Königsberg* could have done better. When she was off Zanzibar, she seemed in a great hurry to get away, though the place, with a loaded collier anchored off, and an important cable and wireless station ashore awaiting destruction, was practically an undefended gift. The smoke of a steamer coming up from the south frightened the *Königsberg* away, and she made off for her hiding place in the Rufiji at such speed that she did serious damage to her engines. In the Rufiji there were no repair facilities. It was September 20, 1914, when the *Königsberg* entered the Rufiji for the last time.

Meantime, British cruisers were dashing about the Indian Ocean looking for her, while a party of her artificers were struggling through the jungle toward the foundry facilities of Dar-es Salaam, to have the vital parts of her engines repaired. Intelligence on both sides seems to have been affected by the lassitude of the steamy East African heat. Twice the British came upon evidence that the *Königsberg* was at Salale in the Rufiji—once when a German signalman was picked up from an island off the coast of German East Africa (later Tanganyika) with a diary in his possession in which he had noted, in plain language, the cruiser's movements; and the second time, when a receipt for coal delivered to the *Königsberg* was taken from the steamer *Präsident*, with the date and place carefully and correctly recorded. Yet the British cruisers still continued to dash about the ocean, and H.M.S. *Chatham* got herself badly damaged on the reef off Mombasa in the process.

Apparently it was not believed that a vessel of the size of the *Königsberg* could enter the Rufiji or find a useful berth there. It was not until the end of October that the German was tracked to her lair, where she had then been for six weeks. Then began an expensive, lengthy, and almost entirely futile blockade, for the British cruisers could not go into the river (they drew too much) and the *Königsberg* could not get out. In the end, the only result was that a useless hulk was sunk in the Rufiji mud, at great expense of men and time and ammunition, and in the meantime the German's guns had been saved, with most of her crew, to carry on the war elsewhere. The story of the trek of those guns through the Tanganyika bush is as stirring, in its way, as that of the trek of the *Emden* survivors through Arabia to Stamboul.

Two monitors had to be towed from Malta to shell the *Königsberg*. A fleet collier was sunk to bottle her up, but she was already well bottled up herself and, in any event, the collier was sunk in the wrong entrance. The Rufiji had many ways in and several ways out, and they could not all be made ineffective simultaneously. For that matter, it took the river a very few days to cut a new channel past the sunken *Newbridge*—a channel which is used by the big Arab dhows to this day.

Captain Looff, in the *Königsberg*, expected the *Chatham* to come up the river, but she was never within range. The Germans, with characteristic thoroughness, had the whole delta ranged and covered by a system of lookouts with telephones. Had the *Chatham* entered, she would have had a hot welcome. A seaplane was brought up from the Cape to spot and generally assist the blockade, but it was a primitive machine and it did not last long.

Meanwhile, the German Navy was trying to get a relief ship into the Rufiji with spares for the *Königsberg*'s engines, and nearly succeeded in this, despite the blockade. It was intended that the *Königsberg* should fight her way out again as soon as she could. But, though the relief ship landed some material for her in the delta of the Rufiji, she was sunk before her mission was completed. The *Königsberg* remained immobile. Finally, on a steamy day in July, 1915, the monitors *Severn* and *Mersey* were able to enter the river and to do the *Königsberg* such damage that she could no longer fight, and her crew completed her destruction. But the two monitors narrowly escaped.

So at last the gray hulk of what had been a fast light cruiser sank into the Rufiji's dark embrace, like a big hippo sliding into the muddy stream. Years afterward, the hulk of the *Königsberg* still showed above the Rufiji mud. When I was there in a dhow in 1939, much of the vessel was still visible, lying on her side.

The raiders of World War II were of different stuff. Not only the odd merchant raider but submarines and aircraft invaded the Indian Ocean and, for a time, surface fleets of Japanese war vessels prowled the Bay of Bengal. The Germans made effective use of fast merchantmen disguised and heavily armed, to raid shipping in the South Atlantic and the Indian Ocean. Some of these vessels could make 20 knots and were more heavily armed than many British light cruisers. They carried at least five 5.9-inch guns, as a general rule, as well as torpedo tubes, mines, and frequently also, motor torpedo boats and aircraft. One use of the aircraft was to destroy ships' radio installations by pulling away their aerials, by means of a trailing plummet on a long wire.

Some of these raiders made remarkable voyages and some, unfortunately, were distinguished for the extreme brutality of their attacks on isolated merchantmen. The objective was to sink without leaving a trace. The raider *Komet,* under the command of Rear Admiral Eyssen, made an extraordinary passage from Germany to the Far East by way of the Northeast Passage around the top of the world, taking only twenty-three days to steam from the Barents Sea to the Bering Sea, a passage which included navigating in ice 750 miles through. The *Komet* later returned to Germany through the Indian Ocean and around the Cape of Good Hope.

Another fine feat of seamanship was the rescue of the crew of Raider 16, which was sunk by H.M.S. *Devonshire* in the South Atlantic in November, 1941. The 300 survivors in boats and rafts were far too many to be picked up by the submarine which found them. So they were taken in tow across the South Atlantic, until a rendezvous could be kept with a German supply ship off the coast of South America. They were transferred to the supply ship, which was herself sunk a week or two later, off the Cape of Good Hope. Again the survivors had to take to boats and rafts. Again long-range U-boats came to the rescue. Two of these vessels, which were actually on the scene of the sinking, took the boats and rafts in tow. After some days, they were able to join forces with two other U-boats. Each U-boat now took 100 survivors, and the four set out to return to France. The large number of survivors could not be carried below decks in the submarines, big as they were. So 50 men lived below and the other 50 in the open, on deck, where they made their temporary homes in rafts, in order that, if the U-boats had to crash-dive, the rafts would float off and the men still have a chance. In this way the whole party reached the neighborhood of the Azores Islands, where four Italian U-boats arrived to carry 50 survivors apiece. The eight submarines then ran the gantlet to the Biscayan coast, which the whole party reached in safety.

A German raider known to the British Navy simply as Raider "E" made a successful cruise in the Indian Ocean during 1942, sinking the tankers *Olivia* and *Herborg,* the cargo steamers *Madrono* and *Indus,* and capturing the *Nankin,* which was taken to a port in Japan. Raider "E" also reached Japan, as did the German steamer *Tannenfels* and several other vessels, including a few long-range, cargo-carrying submarines.

When the *Olivia* was sunk, almost in the center of the Indian Ocean, four Europeans and eight Chinese got away in a boat from the blazing tanker. A month later, the surviving three Europeans and one Chinese safely reached the coast of Madagascar.

The outstanding success of the German raiders was the sinking of the Australian cruiser *Sydney,* a vessel built to replace the destroyer of the *Emden.* The new *Sydney* was sunk with heavy loss of life by the German raider *Kormoran,* in the Indian Ocean, not far (as distances are reckoned there) from the *Emden*'s graveyard. The *Kormoran* was also sunk, but she had earned her keep.

Encouraged by the German success, the Japanese also sent some raiding merchantmen into the Indian Ocean, but they were not very successful. There were, apparently, never more than three of them. Though they were even more elaborately equipped than the Germans and carried aircraft and midget submarines, they sank few ships. When one of the raiders was sunk by an Indian warship, the others were soon withdrawn. The Japanese raiders, like the Germans, played an important part in refueling and re-victualing U-boats, which carried on far too successful campaigns against Allied shipping off the Cape of Good Hope, in the Mozambique Channel, and off Madagascar. The sea routes of the Indian Ocean were of vast importance at that time. Allied merchantmen were making prodigious efforts to keep the maximum flow of supplies reaching Russia through the Persian Gulf ports, and the supply of oil from the Gulf was also vital. A great base for future attacks had to be built up in India. Food had to be brought from Australia and East Africa. There were plenty of targets for the wandering U-boats. Submarines were operating in the Indian Ocean until March, 1945, but as the Allied strength slowly mounted there, the same tactics of air-sea cooperation which had won the day in the North Atlantic made it perilous for U-boats to operate.

But in the meantime, the Japanese had come very near to over-throwing British sea power in the Indian Ocean. The initial impetus of their early victories had brought them right into the Bay of Bengal, and all India and Ceylon lay before them, more or less for the taking. Their swift capture of Hong Kong, Singapore, Java, Sumatra, the Philippines, all Indonesia, and most of Burma; their victories in the Java Sea; and the sinking of the battleship *Prince of Wales* and the battle cruiser *Repulse* put them in a highly advantageous position. They occupied the Andaman and Nicobar Islands as advanced air bases. Their fighter aircraft were superior to any which could be used against them, in the early days, and their torpedo bombers pressed home their attacks with gallantry and skill. Their carrier force was the best then in the Indian Ocean.

Yet the Japanese did not succeed in destroying British naval power in the Indian Ocean and, indeed, they made only one really determined effort to do so, in strength. This failed, though it came near to success. The British Navy had to withdraw from Trincomalee and base itself hurriedly, and without adequate repair or maintenance facilities, at Kilindini on Mombasa harbor, in East

Africa. The demands on the navy were world-wide, infinite, and enormous. There never were enough ships. By the beginning of April, 1942, the strength of the navy in the Indian Ocean was low, far lower than it should have been. The old battleship *Warspite* and the four elderly battleships *Revenge, Ramillies, Resolution,* and *Royal Sovereign* were the backbone of the force, with three aircraft carriers, one of which was old and all of which still carried the biplanes with which the Fleet Air Arm had had to begin the war. Only two of the available cruisers, the *Dorsetshire* and the *Cornwall,* carried 8-inch guns.

Air reconnaissance was dependent on the use of slow, twin-engined flying boats which, if they ever saw a hostile force, would be doing very well to get off an alarm report before being shot down by its fighters. There was little cloud cover in the Bay of Bengal during the northeast monsoon, and these flying boats were practically sitting ducks. Yet they regularly flew their long patrols, keeping ceaseless watch, and when at last a large Japanese battle force was approaching to attack Colombo and Trincomalee, one of the big boats just succeeded in getting off a report before being shot down. Another, taking up the patrol, adopted wave-hopping tactics, and was able to do some useful shadowing by flying practically at wave-top height.

The Japanese force consisted of four large battleships, a fleet of carriers equipped with modern and most effective aircraft, as well as cruisers and destroyers. The objective of this fleet was to find the British ships in port and destroy them there, preferably by air attack; but when the first wave of aircraft flew over Colombo on the morning of Easter Sunday, 1942, the fleet had gone. Admiral Sir James Somerville had taken his ships to sea, to give battle when he could. But he was without his more powerful vessels, and the cruisers *Dorsetshire* and *Cornwall* were sunk by dive-bombers while they were on the way to join him. The elderly carrier *Hermes* soon followed them to the bottom. The situation of the British fleet was fairly desperate, for there were plenty of Japanese submarines at sea, as well as the large force of surface vessels, which was then between Admiral Somerville and his base. However, the Japanese fleet, after making an attack on the naval base at Trincomalee, retired across the Bay of Bengal again, destroying an unfortunate convoy which got in its path. British strength afterward was built up slowly. But it was a good thing for the Allies, firstly, that the main sea routes now lay in the western waters of the Indian Ocean and, secondly, that the Japanese, for some reason, did not venture into that ocean in strength again. They lost thereby their chance of gaining overwhelming mastery there—a chance which had been within their grasp, but did not come their way again.

In the meantime, an Allied landing operation was made for the occupation of the island of Madagascar, to make certain that its many roadsteads and harbors could not be used as bases of supply for enemy submarines, as once they had given succor to the sailing pirates. Madagascar was French, and the French at home were prisoners of the Nazis. So Madagascar was occupied and the flank of the route around the Cape of Good Hope was secured. The Japanese, too, were suffering severe losses of their merchant ships in their own waters, as American submarines bravely pressed home the attack. They set up a great program of wooden shipbuilding, using the woods of the Andamans and Malaya to build small diesel vessels and a fleet of junks. But the Fleet Air Arm, at last armed with effective modern aircraft, so harassed the program that it was never able to get properly under way and when, in early September, 1945, Singapore was occupied at the Japanese surrender, the port and the ways were full of these small wooden ships which had not been to sea.

This is not the place for the story of the campaign in Burma. That has in part been told in such works as the Report to the Combined Chiefs of Staff, by Vice-Admiral the Earl Mountbatten of Burma, Supreme Allied Commander in South-East Asia from 1943 to 1945. In part, it remains to be told. During the campaign, mainly toward its close, the Arabian Sea and the Bay of Bengal floated some curious vessels. None was more strange than the fleets of landing craft sent from Britain to operate on the beaches of Malaya and, if need be, as far off as Japan. These craft included the British-built LCT's whose purpose was to land tanks and mechanized transport, and the American-built LCI(L), whose business was to land assault troops and, that done, to build up beachheads and bridgeheads.

The LCT's—landing-craft tanks—were queer little flat-bottomed, ramp-bowed, steel boxes, with a couple of diesel engines, a few small cannon, a dumpy but distinctive funnel, and a slight tendency to break up in the sea. They were designed to form a bridge across the Channel when the great day came for the invasion of Europe. They were not intended to be ocean-going vessels, and they were not intended to enjoy a long life. They were built by bridge builders, metalworkers, canners—any riverside plant which could assemble a few persons who knew anything at all about working in metal. They were extraordinarily successful. When it was first proposed to take them as far as the Arakan coast and to Malaya, a scheme was worked out for towing them in merchant-navy convoys, one on the quarter of each ship. But the first lot sank, for they were towed under. The second lot, though filled with empty oil drums to give them buoyancy, fared little better. So the rest had to go under their own power. A few broke up at sea, but the majority arrived. By early 1945, they were beginning to assemble by the hundred at hide-outs along the coast of India, principally at Mandapam. They arrived in time to have some share in the campaign on the Arakan coast, to help in the unopposed landing at Rangoon, and to do great service in the rehabilitation of Singapore and Malaya and the East generally. They went to Batavia and to Bangkok, to Saigon and Palembang, to the Andamans and the Nicobars. They lowered their stub-nosed ramps on a thousand tropic beaches; and when their military usefulness was at an end, enterprising Chinese got hold of them and made fortunes carrying logs and rubber and the products of the East to Singapore.

But it was the LCI(L) which were, in some ways, the most interesting vessels. LCI(L) means Landing Craft Infantry, Large; and they were small, narrow-gutted vessels which were more or less prefabricated on the eastern seaboard of the United States of America and hurriedly welded together at Newark, New Jersey, and Quincy, Massachusetts, for service in the Mediterranean campaign. There were no marine engines to spare for them, so they were given eight bus engines in two "quads," with a sort of gearbox to drive variable-pitch propellers. These were electrically operated and had to be put into negative pitch to give the ships stern power. LCI(L) were constructed of the thinnest metal, and no escort was wasted on the first 150 when, in the winter of 1943, they set out from Norfolk, Virginia, to cross to the Mediterranean. No one then dreamt that such apparently fragile and almost wholly make-shift ships would ever operate in Eastern waters, and many senior officers doubted, even, that they would reach their first destination. The official estimate of losses on the transatlantic passage was 40 per cent. Any U-boat, singlehanded, could have come up among them, sat on the surface, and sunk them by the score, for their only armament was a few Oerlikon cannon each. But they reached the Mediterranean, and they were of importance in the landings on the beaches of Sicily. Before that, they had proved their worth in North Africa and at Pantelleria. They went on to the landings in Italy, to Salerno, Anzio, the campaign in the Adriatic. They were fast and they had tremendous endurance. They could carry about 200 troops, very uncomfortably, for at first they had only rough wooden benches for the unfortunate soldiers to sit upon. Later, they were given pipe cots, and that was better. From Anzio many returned to Britain for the assault on Normandy, and hundreds of LCI(L), both in the British and the United States navies, did excellently there on D-day. After the beachhead was thoroughly established, many were withdrawn to go to Burma.

I had had a squadron of these vessels since the winter of 1943. After Normandy, my survivors were withdrawn to Oban, on the west coast of Scotland. From there we hastened to Bombay, with stops at Plymouth, Malta, the Bitter Lakes, and Aden, on the way. We went in groups of 24 ships, and my lot made the passage together in thirty-five days, which I thought good going for such makeshift vessels, which were never intended to survive more than, perhaps, three landings, or to last out the European campaign. They did well, indeed, and they continued to do well in Eastern waters—on the Arakan coast, at Rangoon, later in Malayan waters. Unlike the LCT, the LCI(L) were very livable little vessels, and they played a useful part in rehabilitating many odd holes and corners, and some big ports, in the fascinating East. In the end, being lend-lease vessels on loan to the British Navy from the government of the United States, they were handed back at Subic Bay in the Philippines, but before that they had seen service on the coasts of Java, along the Mekong River in French Indo-China, in the Gulf of Siam, far up the rivers of hot Sumatra, round the islands of the Riouw Archipelago, and many other places. It is unlikely that a fleet of more curious vessels was ever seen in the waters of the East, and I felt as I handed them over that they had, perhaps, added their mite to the maritime history of the Indian Ocean. The little that they were able to do was inevitably overlooked when so many greater things were done by better known vessels. But I knew that they had earned their keep.

While Malaya and all Indonesia were still in Japanese hands, some Indian sailing vessels were used for carrying cloak-and-dagger men across to be landed surreptitiously upon remote beaches. Here they melted away, to be swallowed up in the great jungle, from which sometimes they emerged again, but more often not. Others crossed by submarine and landed from rubber canoes. Many were dropped by aircraft. They were an extraordinary collection of men, incredibly courageous. For them no flags flew and no martial bands ever played. They went quietly about their dangerous work, against terrible odds.

Just as courageous were the midget submarines which penetrated the mine fields, passed boom defenses, and cut their way through nets, to damage and sink enemy ships of war right in the innermost strongholds of their own bases.

In the end, a tremendous fleet of assorted vessels, of every conceivable shape, size, and purpose, was assembled in the Indian Ocean, mainly in the ports of India. So-called fleet "trains," floating breweries, ships which could dock big landing craft in their holds, ships which could carry a flotilla of landing craft and all their crews, ships full of fierce commandos complete with assault landing vessels, ships with operations rooms and the ultimate in communications where admirals and their staffs could keep some sort of control over the mighty and heterogeneous fleets under their command, aircraft-carrying ships of all kinds, destroyers as big as small cruisers, and submarines not much smaller—these were only a few of the types assembled. The major ports were so full with these ships and the great armada of merchant vessels bringing stores for them, and troops, and ammunition, that my landing craft were forbidden to go to such places as Colombo or Trincomalee and were got rid of as soon as possible from all other places, except our own hot roadstead at Mandapam.

From the first part of 1944, the East Indies fleet had been able to go much as it willed. It could seek out the enemy in his strongest bases; send powerful air strikes against his ports, his shipping, his oil installations; and maintain its own ports and bases secure against attack. A great military, air, and naval force was ready to continue the campaign on beach after beach, from Malaya onward to Japan. But the Japanese had spent their force. They were rapidly being overwhelmed in the Pacific and throughout the Eastern seas. Four years after their sudden show of strength had astonished the Western world and their virile marines and hard-fighting soldiers had swung from victory to victory, down the China Sea and over the Java Sea, the Arafura Sea, the Timor Sea, part of the Indian Ocean, and a considerable area of the west and southwest Pacific, they were utterly beaten. The Japanese resources were strained past the breaking point. Defeat on their own homeland stared them in the face, and they surrendered.

The great armada, the largest assemblage of ships the East had seen, was slowly dispersed. Here and there the wreck of an LCT, mined in the Rangoon River or bombed on the beach off Akyab or Kyaukpyu, the twisted hulk of an LCI (L) which had been beached too well and swung broadside in the surf, may remain as mute and rusting reminders of a blaze of destructive warfare which came all too close to changing the balance of power over the length and breadth of the Indian Ocean and, as it was, left much of ruin in its wake.

CHAPTER XXI

Until Today

The opening of the Suez Canal in 1869, the steady improvement in mechanically propelled vessels, and finally, the coming of the air age, have vitally affected the commerce and the shipping of the Indian Ocean. There had been many attempts to construct a canal between the Nile and the northern waters of the Red Sea, some of them successful, before the French consular officer Ferdinand de Lesseps first began to play with the idea when an enforced period of quarantine at Alexandria caused him to look into the problem. The great Portuguese Affonso d'Albuquerque had thought of diverting the waters of the Nile to the Red Sea somewhere near Suakin, but his intention was not to bring prosperity to Egypt but ruin.

Thousands of years earlier, there had been a navigable ditch along which shallow-draft vessels could be hauled to the Red Sea when the Nile was in flood. The ruins of the temple of Der-el-Bahri, near Karnak, on the Nile, contain representations indicating the existence of a sort of Suez Canal about the year 1500 B.C. The historian Herodotus speaks of another canal, which he alleges cost 120,000 men their lives in its excavation. When Vasco da Gama found the way to India around the Cape of Good Hope, the merchants of Venice and Genoa thought seriously of resurrecting one of these ancient waterways. Later, the French adopted the idea, and early in the nineteenth century Napoleon Bonaparte

307

caused an extensive survey to be made of the project. But his
engineers told him that there was a difference of almost 30 feet
between the levels of the Gulf of Suez at the northern end of the
Red Sea and the Mediterranean. It was one thing to restore a
ditch and widen it, but quite another to excavate an expensive
canal with a system of locks. Napoleon dropped the idea.

De Lesseps was not an engineer, but he refused to believe that
there was any appreciable difference between the levels of the two
seas. Nor was there any. De Lesseps went ahead, but it took him
twenty years even to make a beginning on his plans, and another
fifteen years after that before the canal was finished. The Isthmus
of Suez lent itself admirably to the project, with its depressions
and its lakes, but even so, construction proved costly and difficult.
Sand blew in constantly, and the cuts through the lakes silted up.
Dredging was expensive, and at first the canal did not pay its way.
But slowly, as steamships became more efficient and trade grew,
the canal began to pay. Its length is about 100 miles, and its width
is sufficient to allow two ships to pass, though there are still halting
places where ships can be secured to allow others to pass.

The large-scale exploitation of Persian and Arabian oil is the
greatest single factor in the canal's recent greatly increased use.
In 1950, for example, of a total of nearly 82 million tons of shipping
using the canal, oil-tank steamers and motor ships represented
almost 64 per cent. The transit figures are staggering. In the same
year of 1950, 11,751 ships passed through, carrying nearly 73
million tons of cargo and nearly three-quarters of a million
passengers, including troops. Britain led the list with 4,098 ships
passing through. Norway was second with 1,602 (including a high
proportion of oil tankers) and the United States third, with 1,020.

On the mole at the Mediterranean end of the canal stands a
bronze statue of Ferdinand de Lesseps. It should stand at the Red
Sea end, or, preferably, there might be statues at both ends. With
the opening of the Suez Canal, a steamer could be designed to
carry a reasonable amount of cargo, and the advantages of its

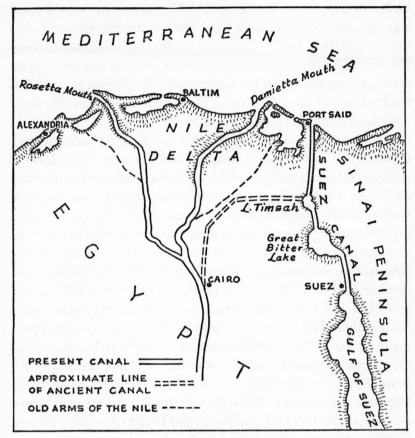

The Suez Canal

shorter length of passage from Europe to almost any port of importance in the Indian Ocean trade, as compared with the route around the Cape of Good Hope, were enormous. Previously, steamers in that trade had to allow more space for coal as bunkers than they could carry freight. Such enterprising spirits as James McGregor, of Glasgow, and Alfred Holt, of Liverpool, saw the opportunity. McGregor was a partner in the famous sailing-ship firm of Allan Gow and Company. Holt was a Liverpool engineer who began his shipowning activities in the West Indies trade but soon looked to the other side of the world. The same year that the canal was opened, McGregor built the 1,600-ton steamer *Glengyle,* at a cost of $100,000, for the China tea trade. She was a success from the start. The best of the clippers could not race the tremendous distance from the China tea-loading ports to London in much less than a hundred days. The *Glengyle* did the passage in fifty days. Soon Holt ships were bettering that.

The clippers were finished, though the Eastern trade boomed. Cheaper and more reliable means of transport soon made Eastern products more generally available than they had ever been before, and such things as tea and spices slowly made their way into working-class homes. Industrial expansion in Europe caused a rapidly growing demand for raw materials of all kinds. The great increase in the tea trade was fostered by the vast scale of the then new Indian tea industry. Before long, instead of sending a few ships of less than 2,000 tons through the canal to India, Malaya, and China, McGregor's Glen Line was maintaining a schedule of fortnightly sailings by vessels up to 5,000 tons, which were bringing the ports of China within less than six weeks of London. Other great lines advanced similarly—the Blue Funnel, the *Shires,* the *Bens;* Stricks to the Persian Gulf; the famous B.I., Harrison's, Ellerman's, the *Clans* to India, East Africa, Burma; the well-known Peninsular and Oriental, and the Orient Line to Australia. French, German, Austrian, Dutch, and Italian lines prospered similarly, but the Stars and Stripes of the American merchant service was not seen in the Indian Ocean then as much as it had been in the days of the great Yankee pioneers, in the era of sail. The advantages of the European shipbuilders were too great. American expansion was inward, for the continent itself held limitless possibilities and there was not the same need to develop external trade.

Today, great Glen and Blue Funnel cargo liners race at 18 knots with cargoes of 14,000 to 15,000 tons on a tight schedule between the ports of North Europe and the emporiums of the East. They have special deep tanks for the carriage of vegetable oils and latex in bulk, and they carry the latest navigational aids—radar, direction-finding, echo-sounding, gyrocompasses, and the like. So also with the other lines. Instead of the wallowing old wagons of the Honourable East India Company, magnificent 20,000-ton and 30,000-ton liners of the P. and O. and Orient companies, and of other lines, steam at 20 knots and more between the ports of Britain, India, and Australia. The new vessels of these companies, built to replace losses by bombs and torpedoes in the recent war, cost up to $20,000,000—ships such as the P. and O. Line's *Himalaya* and *Chusan*, and the Orient Line's *Oronsay*, which sailed on her maiden voyage from London to Sydney in May, 1951. The *Oronsay*, a vessel of 28,000 tons, able to steam at better than 25 knots, is fitted throughout with the ultimate in luxury accommodation. Air conditioning makes the passage of the Red Sea as pleasant as a balmy run in the western Mediterranean. Cinemas, cafés, swimming pools, enormous sports decks, libraries, taverns, ornate public rooms, and cabins which are the last word in comfort, make the long passage across the Indian Ocean a happy interlude—or would, perhaps, if the modern amenities did not include a too-efficient radio system in touch with the broadcasting stations of the world.

The tankers taking the oil from the Persian Gulf are now frequently vessels of almost 30,000 tons. Any one of them is of greater tonnage than the whole of the Honourable Company's annual fleet. The pilgrim trade from India and from Indonesia to the Red Sea is organized and is carried entirely by large vessels, almost all of which are registered in Europe. The resurgence of the new India, the birth of the new dominion of Pakistan, and the rebirth of Indonesia, together with the developments along the East African coast and the rapid postwar development of Australia, have led to considerable increases in shipping and trade, and a number of Indian and Pakistani shipping lines have been formed to share in it. All round the Indian Ocean there is, at the moment, prosperity abounding, yet there is still plenty of room for development. A few of the ancient ports have foundered. Hormuz, in the Gulf, no longer is of importance. Muscat has fared little better. But their places have been taken by a score of new places and rejuvenated older ones.

Such a horde of deeply laden ships now voyages to Ceylon and to Australia that the ports are no longer able to cope with them. To avoid having to wait days and even weeks for a berth in the congested ports, ships like the *Oronsay* and the *Himalaya* make their passages outward and homeward with less than half their cargo capacities occupied, at a time when all the ports they serve are in urgent need of the goods that they can carry. Their mail and passenger schedules can be kept in no other way. To that extent, these great ships are largely wasted.

It is perhaps a question just how long this state of affairs will be allowed to continue. A civilization which cannot handle the ships it builds or properly employ them is imperiling its chances of survival, in the Indian Ocean or anywhere else. Ships into which such colossal amounts of wealth are poured, which are fitted with every conceivable luxury that can possibly be taken to sea and several that would be better left ashore, can be justified only by their effective use to the maximum degree. They can scarcely continue to serve ports which cannot handle their cargoes. It was real wealth which went into those ships, and their lives are limited. Real work must pay for them in the end.

The geography of the Indian Ocean makes its fringes of value to great air lines. Apart from necessary transports which flew between Ceylon and West Australia in time of war, there has not been a great deal of transoceanic flying. The ways around are better than the ways across. The Pacific and the Atlantic must be crossed, but the Indian Ocean offers land routes to most of its important air lines. Recently, the Australians have been interested in a transoceanic route between Australia and India, and to South Africa, and in June, 1951, the air strip at the Cocos-Keelings was being restored to act as a stopping place for aircraft on a projected service to Africa.

The pioneer flights followed the fringing routes—across Iraq and down one or other coast of the Persian Gulf, across India, down the length of the Malay Archipelago and the Indonesian islands. Transoceanic flights were left to the days of multi-engined flying boats of long range, such as the wartime Catalinas, the big four-engined Sunderlands, and the other Short Brothers' boats. Catalinas and Short flying boats did yeoman service on real oceanic flights, especially during the war years, and the American four-engined Liberator and twin-engined Douglas DC 3 made countless flights across the Bay of Bengal and over the ocean itself. Liberators flew for a time between Ceylon and West Australia, and several went missing on this route. When a heavy aircraft goes missing on an ocean flight or a land passage, there is not much need to speculate where it may be—splattered in pieces over a mountainside, or a shambled twist of fragile metal at the bottom of the sea.

The longest sea hop on the normal air route between Europe and Australia is the few hundred miles across the Timor Sea. By the route the aircraft take, it would almost be possible for a man to walk to Australia if he had an aluminum canoe to ferry him over a few short stretches.

It has always seemed to me that the airplane is a frantic form of transport, perhaps suited to our age—costly, complicated, involved, apparently fast and sleek, but in fact dependent upon a host of ancillary services and the efforts of thousands who might be more productively employed. Nor is the airplane really mobile. Without the vast chain of radio aids to navigation, a costly array of enormous flying fields, a great gasoline industry, an unfailing supply of skilled and reliable maintenance men, the best airplane is nothing but a shapely piece of wasted metal.

In my mind's eye, flying over the Indian Ocean—as once I had to do during the war—I see something of the great array of the illustrious past across those blue and sunlit waters. I see the curious ships of Egypt putting out for the land of Punt. I see the Chinese junks; the Arab, the Indian, the Persian dhows in their thousands; the *proas* of the East and the sewn boats of Shihr and Lamu. I see all these with their peaked and handsome lateen sails full of the life-giving wind, and the hulls of the good vessels graceful as they skim upon the sea, an element to which they belong and which they serve as well as the men who built and man them. I see the caravel of Bartolomeo Dias dart suddenly by the Cape of Good Hope and head west again, after a few days, with the glorious news that the way to the East is now open. I see the *navs* of Vasco da Gama follow, and Almeida, d'Albuquerque, and their illustrious countrymen; and long after them, the Hollanders and the English, with the good ship *Edward Bonaventure* touching at Zanzibar; and then, the long, lumbering procession of the stately East Indiamen, Dutch and English, which had the Indian Ocean largely to themselves for almost two hundred years.

These sail into the mists, and the ships of Salem and old New England come, in quest of trade, carrying the bold new flag which is so strangely like the ensign of the British East Indiamen. Then the clippers race in beauty over the wide, deep sea, and the trade wind and monsoon sing gently in their riggings. It is a swan song, for already the belch of smoke shows upon the western horizon and, far away, a score of thousands of lean brown hands are scraping at the sands of Suez.

The vision fades. Far below me, a great steamer, a 20,000-tonner with an enormous, bolt-upright, and curiously ugly stack, is belting at the gentle mounds of rippling water at her heedless bows. The year now is 1951, and the radio at my side is telling, in a toneless and affected voice, of warfare in Korea; dock strikes in Australia, New Zealand, London; a festival in Britain; an immense rearmament drive in the United States.

Ten thousand miles away by Sagres Point, the sun sinks into the Atlantic sea, and there the shade of the great Prince Henry may wonder, too, at the shape of the tremendous developments his vision was to lead to, when, knowing there must be a route south and eastward to the Indian Ocean, he sent brave Portuguese sailors to blaze the European way.

BIBLIOGRAPHY

The following books and periodicals have been consulted in preparing the text.

HISTORY

BAKER, J. N. L.: *A History of Geographical Discovery and Exploration*, George G. Harrap & Co., Ltd., London, 1931.

BALLARD, ADMIRAL: *Rulers of the Indian Ocean*, London and Boston, 1928.

BARBOSA, DUARTE: *Beginning of the Sixteenth Century*, Hakluyt Society, London, 1866.

Barlow's Journal, transcribed by Basil Lubbock, London, 1934.

BEAZLEY, C. R.: *The Dawn of Modern Geography*, 3 vols., London, 1897–1906.

BURTON, H. E.: *The Discovery of the Ancient World*, Cambridge, 1932.

CABLE, BOYD: *A Hundred Year History of the P. and O.*, London, 1937.

Cambridge Ancient History, Vols. I–IV.

CHATTERTON, E. KEBLE: *Old East Indiamen*, London, 1934.

COLOMB, CAPTAIN R. N.: *Slave Catching in the Indian Ocean*, London, 1873.

COTTON, SIR EVAN: *East Indiamen*, London, 1949.

COUPLAND, R.: *East Africa and Its Invaders*, Oxford, 1938.

ELDRIDGE, F. B.: *The Background of Eastern Sea Power*, Georgian House, Melbourne, 1945.

EVANS, A. J. (Ed.): *The Penguin Herodotus*, Penguin Books, Ltd., London, 1941.

317

FAYLE, C. ERNEST: *A Short History of the World's Shipping Industry,* George Allen & Unwin, London, 1933.

GALVAO, ANTONIO: *The Discoveries of the World,* Hakluyt Society, London, 1862.

GOSSE, PHILIP: *The History of Piracy,* London, 1932.

HART, HENRY H.: *Sea Road to the Indies,* New York, 1950.

HICKEY, WILLIAM: *Memoirs,* reprinted, London, 1949.

HORNELL, JAMES: *Water Transport,* Cambridge University Press, London, 1946.

HOURANI, GEORGE FADLO: *Arab Seafaring in the Indian Ocean,* Princeton University Press, 1951.

HOWE, SONIA E.: *In Quest of Spices,* London, 1947.

INGRAMS, W. H., and L. W. Hollingsworth: *School History of Zanzibar,* 1926.

INGRAMS, W. H.: *Zanzibar,* London, 1931.

JOHNSON, C.: *A General History of the Pyrates,* London, 1724.

JONES, H. L. (Trans.): *The Geography of Strabo,* London, 1917.

Journals of the Polynesian Society, Royal Geographical Society, Royal Central Asian Society.

LEY, C. D. (Ed.): *Portuguese Voyages,* London and New York, 1947.

LUBBOCK, BASIL: *The Blackwall Frigates,* Glasgow, 1924.

PRESTAGE, EDGAR: *The Portuguese Pioneers,* A. & C. Black, Ltd., London, 1933.

RAWLINSON, H. G.: *Times to the Fall of Rome,* Cambridge, 1926.

ROGERS, STANLEY: *The Indian Ocean,* London, 1932.

SANSEAU, ELAINE: *Indies Adventure,* London and New York, 1936.

SYKES, SIR PERCY: *A History of Exploration,* Routledge and Keegan Paul, Ltd., London, 1950.

The American Neptune, a quarterly journal of Maritime History, The American Neptune, Inc., Salem, Mass.

The Mariner's Mirror, the quarterly journal of the British Society for Nautical Research, Cambridge University Press, London.

The Periplus of the Erythraean Sea, translated from the Greek and annotated by Wilfred H. Schoff, M. A., Longmans, Green, & Co., Inc., New York, 1912.

Three Voyages of Vasco da Gama, and His Viceroyalty, Hakluyt Society, London, 1869.

VINCENT, W.: *The Voyage of Nearchus from the Indus to the Euphrates,* London, 1797.

WILSON, SIR ARNOLD: *The Persian Gulf,* Oxford University Press, New York, 1928.

YULE, HENRY: *The Travels of Marco Polo,* London, 1931.

SHIPS AND SHIPPING

BULLEN, FRANK: *The Cruise of the Cachalot,* London, 1905.

Disastrous Voyage of the Vessel Batavia, being the Log and Records of Frances Pelsart, Amsterdam, 1647.

GOLDSMITH, FRANK H.: *Treasure Lies Buried,* Perth (W.A.), 1946.

MORISON, S. E.: *The Maritime History of Massachusetts,* Boston, 1941.

PINKERTON, JOHN: *Voyages and Travels,* London, 1814.

SPRY, W. J., R.N.: *Cruise of H.M.S. Challenger,* London, 1895.

VAIDYA, K. B.: *The Sailing Vessel Traffic on the West Coast of India,* Bombay, 1945.

VILLIERS, ALAN: *The Sons of Sindbad,* London and New York, 1940.

TOPOGRAPHY, ETC.

CROSSLAND, C.: *Desert and Water Gardens of the Red Sea,* Cambridge, 1913.

FINDLAY, A. G.: *Indian Ocean and Bay of Bengal Directory,* London, 1882.

HORSBURGH, CAPTAIN JAMES: *Indian Directory,* London, 1809.

Africa Pilot, Part III, Admiralty, London.*

Bay of Bengal Pilot, Admiralty, London.*

Eastern Archipelago Pilot, Parts II, III, IV, Admiralty, London.*

Ocean Passages for the World, Admiralty, London.*

Persian Gulf Pilot, Admiralty, London.*

Red Sea and Gulf of Aden Pilot, Admiralty, London.*

South Indian Ocean Pilot, Admiralty, London.*

West Coast of India Pilot, Admiralty, London.*

GENERAL

HUGHES, JOHN SCOTT: *Kings of the Cocos,* London, 1950.

Life and Letters of Charles Darwin, London, 1887.

* The Admiralty volumes are of various dates.

Slocum, Captain Joshua: *Sailing Alone around the World,* London, 1949.

Wood-Jones, F.: *Coral and Atolls,* London, 1910.

Abstract of Evidence . . . On the Part of the Petitioners for the Abolition of the Slave Trade, London, 1841.

Slave Trade, Instructions for Officers, Etc., Admiralty, London, 1892.

Origins and Purpose, His Majesty's Stationery Office, London, 1949.

Various Colonial Reports, His Majesty's Stationery Office, London.

Various Handbooks prepared under the direction of the Historical Section of the Foreign Office, His Majesty's Stationery Office, London.

WAR

Mountbatten of Burma, Vice-Admiral the Earl: *Report to the Combined Chiefs of Staff by the Supreme Commander, South-East Asia, 1943–1945,* His Majesty's Stationery Office, London, 1951.

Chatterton, E. Keble: *The Königsberg Adventure,* London, 1932.

Franz Josef, Prince of Hohenzollern: *My Experiences in S.M.S. Emden,* London.

Looff, Vice-Admiral Maz: *Kreuzerfart mit S.M.S. Königsberg,* Berlin, 1929.

The Campaign in Burma, His Majesty's Stationery Office, London, 1947.

INDEX

321

MEDITERRANEAN SEA
Alexandria
Cairo
Suez
Tigris
Euphrates
Basra
Kuwait
Persian G.
Hormuz
Indus
ASIA
BAHREIN
G. of Oman
Kosair
Red Sea
Nile R.
Sur
Cape Hadd
Jidda
Pt. Sudan
Suakin
Kuria Muria I.
ARABIAN SEA
Bombay
Goa
Aden
SOCOTRA
Madras
PERIM
G. of Aden
Cannanore
Calicut
LACCADIVE IS.
Cochin
Palk Str.
Jaffna
AFRICA
Djibouti
Berbera
C. Guardafui
VASCO da GAMA
Colombo
CEYLON
Obbia
Itala
Mogadishu
Merka
Brava
Kismayu
MALDIVE IS.
EQUATOR
SOUTHERN LIMIT OF
Malindi
PEMBA I.
SEYCHELLES
CHAGOS ARCH.
Loanda
ZANZIBAR
Dar es Salaam
AMIRANTES
C. Delgada
COMORO IS.
Rovuma
Diego Suarez
Mozambique
Mozambique Channel
INDIAN OCEAN
Zambesi R.
Quelimane
Gt. Fish Bay
Beira
MADAGASCAR
Tamatave
MAURITIUS
RODRIGUEZ
REUNION
Walvis Bay
Limpopo
Inhambane
Lourenco Marques
St. Helena Bay
Durban
VASCO da GAMA
SAILING ROUTE FROM AUSTRALIA
Cape Town
E. London
Algoa Bay
Cape of Good Hope
DUTCH ROUTE FROM EUROPE
AMSTERDAM
ST. PAUL
SAILING ROUTE TO BOMBAY
SAILING ROUTES TO CHINA AND JAPAN
PRINCE EDWARD IS.
CROZET IS.
KERGUELEN IS.
HEARD IS